EFFECTIVE CURRICULUM FOR TEACHING L2 WRITING

Effective Curriculum for Teaching L2 Writing sets out a clear, practical, and efficient big picture for curricular thinking about L2 writing pedagogy. Its main purpose is to help pre-service and practicing teachers design courses for teaching academic writing and to do this as efficiently and effectively as possible. Uniquely connecting curriculum, writing instruction, and language building, the text offers a step-by-step guide to curriculum design for teaching second language writing, with practical examples and illustrations. The central premise is that writing and language instruction need to be integrated, based on a clear understanding of the writing needs of academic writers, and that principled and language-focused curricula are necessary to guide this endeavor.

- Part 1 examines curricular foundations in general and focuses on what is socially valued in L2 writing and pedagogy at school and at the college and university level. The findings of relevant empirical studies are reviewed throughout Part I. Two chapters survey the guidelines and learning goals for L2 writing on the Common Core State Standards required at school and in higher education.
- Part 2 is concerned with the nitty-gritty—the daily realities of curricular design and classroom instruction.
- Part 3 takes a close look at the key pedagogical ingredients of teaching academic L2 writing: vocabulary and collocations, grammar for academic writing, and down-to-earth techniques for helping L2 writers to organize discourse and ideas.
- The Appendix provides an extensive checklist for developing curricula for a course or several courses in language teaching. It can be useful in its entirety or in pieces and portions, as needed.

Bringing together the what and the how-to of developing course curricula with research-based principles of effective teaching in L2 writing courses, what sets this book apart is its overarching focus on language pedagogy and language building. To enhance its usefulness as a course text, each chapter includes an outline of the main points covered; boxed highlights and illustrative examples; practice activities and tasks; practical techniques and suggestions for curriculum design and teaching; summary points; and suggested further readings.

Eli Hinkel is Professor, Linguistics and MA-TESL Programs, Seattle Pacific University, USA.

ESL & Applied Linguistics Professional Series
Eli Hinkel, Series Editor

Hinkel • *Effective Curriculum for Teaching L2 Writing: Principles and Techniques*

Farrell • *Promoting Teacher Reflection in Second-Language Education: A Framework for TESOL Professionals*

Nunan/Richards • *Language Learning Beyond the Classroom*

Christison/Murray • *What English Language Teachers Need to Know Volume III: Designing Curriculum*

Turner • *Using Statistics in Small-scale Language Education Research: Focus on Non-parametric Data*

Hong/Pawan • *The Pedagogy and Practice of Western-trained Chinese English Language Teachers: Foreign Education, Chinese Meanings*

Lantolf/Poehner • *Sociocultural Theory and the Pedagogical Imperative in L2 Education: Vygotskian Praxis and the Research/Practice Divide*

Brown • *Pronunciation and Phonetics: A Practical Guide for English Language Teachers*

Birch • *English Grammar Pedagogy: A Global Perspective*

Liu • *Describing and Explaining Grammar and Vocabulary in ELT: Key Theories and Effective Practices*

deOliviera/Silva, Eds. • *L2 Writing in Secondary Classrooms: Student Experiences, Academic Issues, and Teacher Education*

Andrade/Evans • *Principles and Practices for Response in Second Language Writing: Developing Self-Regulated Learners*

Sayer • *Ambiguities and Tensions in English Language Teaching: Portraits of EFL Teachers as Legitimate Speakers*

Alsagoff/McKay/Hu/Renandya, Eds. • *Principles and Practices of Teaching English as an International Language*

Kumaravadivelu • *Language Teacher Education for A Global Society: A Modular Model for Knowing, Analyzing, Recognizing, Doing, and Seeing*

Vandergrift/Goh • *Teaching and Learning Second Language Listening: Metacognition in Action*

LoCastro • *Pragmatics for Language Educators: A Sociolinguistic Perspective*

Nelson • *Intelligibility in World Englishes: Theory and Practice*

Nation/Macalister, Eds. • *Case Studies in Language Curriculum Design: Concepts and Approaches in Action Around the World*

Johnson/Golumbek, Eds. • *Research on Second Language Teacher Education: A Sociocultural Perspective on Professional Development*

Hinkel, Ed. • *Handbook of Research in Second Language Teaching and Learning, Volume II*

Nassaji /Fotos • *Teaching Grammar in Second Language Classrooms: Integrating Form-Focused Instruction in Communicative Context*

Murray/Christison • *What English Language Teachers Need to Know Volume I: Understanding Learning*

Murray/Christison • *What English Language Teachers Need to Know Volume II: Facilitating Learning*

Wong/Waring • *Conversation Analysis and Second Language Pedagogy: A Guide for ESL/EFL Teachers*

Nunan/Choi, Eds. • *Language and Culture: Reflective Narratives and the Emergence of Identity*

Braine • *Nonnative Speaker English Teachers: Research, Pedagogy, and Professional Growth*

Burns • *Doing Action Research in English Language Teaching: A Guide for Practitioners*

Nation/Macalister • *Language Curriculum Design*

Birch • *The English Language Teacher and Global Civil Society*

Johnson • *Second Language Teacher Education: A Sociocultural Perspective*

Nation • *Teaching ESL/EFL Reading and Writing*

Nation/Newton • *Teaching ESL/EFL Listening and Speaking*

Kachru/Smith • *Cultures, Contexts, and World Englishes*

McKay/Bokhosrt-Heng • *International English in its Sociolinguistic Contexts: Towards a Socially Sensitive EIL Pedagogy*

Christison/Murray, Eds. • *Leadership in English Language Education: Theoretical Foundations and Practical Skills for Changing Times*

McCafferty/Stam, Eds. • *Gesture: Second Language Acquisition and Classroom Research*

Liu • *Idioms: Description, Comprehension, Acquisition, and Pedagogy*

Chapelle/Enright/Jamieson, Eds. • *Building a Validity Argument for the Test of English as a Foreign Language™*

Kondo-Brown/Brown, Eds. • *Teaching Chinese, Japanese, and Korean Heritage Language Students Curriculum Needs, Materials, and Assessments*

Youmans • *Chicano-Anglo Conversations: Truth, Honesty, and Politeness*

Birch • *English L2 Reading: Getting to the Bottom, Second Edition*

Luk/Lin • *Classroom Interactions as Cross-cultural Encounters: Native Speakers in EFL Lessons*

Levy/Stockwell • *CALL Dimensions: Issues and Options in Computer Assisted Language Learning*

Nero, Ed. • *Dialects, Englishes, Creoles, and Education*

Basturkmen • *Ideas and Options in English for Specific Purposes*

Kumaravadivelu • *Understanding Language Teaching: From Method to Postmethod*

McKay • *Researching Second Language Classrooms*

Egbert/Petrie, Eds. • *CALL Research Perspectives*

Canagarajah, Ed. • *Reclaiming the Local in Language Policy and Practice*

Adamson • *Language Minority Students in American Schools: An Education in English*

Fotos/Browne, Eds. • *New Perspectives on CALL for Second Language Classrooms*

Hinkel • *Teaching Academic ESL Writing: Practical Techniques in Vocabulary and Grammar*

Hinkel/Fotos, Eds. • *New Perspectives on Grammar Teaching in Second Language Classrooms*

Hinkel • *Second Language Writers' Text: Linguistic and Rhetorical Features*

Visit **www.routledge.com/education** for additional information on titles in the ESL & Applied Linguistics Professional Series.

EFFECTIVE CURRICULUM FOR TEACHING L2 WRITING

Principles and Techniques

Eli Hinkel

First published 2015
by Routledge
711 Third Avenue, New York, NY 10017

and by Routledge
2 Park Square, Milton Park, Abingdon, Oxon, OX14 4RN

Routledge is an imprint of the Taylor & Francis Group, an informa business

© 2015 Taylor & Francis

The right of Eli Hinkel to be identified as author of this work has been asserted by her in accordance with sections 77 and 78 of the Copyright, Designs and Patents Act 1988.

All rights reserved. No part of this book may be reprinted or reproduced or utilised in any form or by any electronic, mechanical, or other means, now known or hereafter invented, including photocopying and recording, or in any information storage or retrieval system, without permission in writing from the publishers.

Trademark notice: Product or corporate names may be trademarks or registered trademarks, and are used only for identification and explanation without intent to infringe.

Library of Congress Cataloging-in-Publication Data
Hinkel, Eli.
  Effective curriculum for teaching L2 writing : principles and techniques / by Eli Hinkel.
    pages cm. — (ESL & applied linguistics professional series)
  Includes bibliographical references and index.
  1. English language—Study and teaching—Foreign speakers.
  2. English language—Composition and exercises. I. Title.
  PE1128.A2H56 2015
  428.0071—dc23
  2014029191

ISBN: 978-0-415-88998-8 (hbk)
ISBN: 978-0-415-88999-5 (pbk)
ISBN: 978-0-203-83015-4 (ebk)

Typeset in Bembo
by Apex CoVantage, LLC

Printed and bound in the United States of America by
Edwards Brothers Malloy on sustainably sourced paper

CONTENTS

Preface	*ix*
Acknowledgments	*xi*

PART I
Curriculum Foundations for L2 Writing and Language   1

1	Introduction: Effective Teaching and the Curriculum	3
2	What's Valued in School Writing and Language?	18
3	What's Valued in College and University Academic Writing?	49
4	Second Language Writing and Language Learning	77

PART II
Curriculum Design for L2 Writing and Language Building   113

5	How to Design Effective Curricula for Language and Writing Courses	115
6	Choosing Teaching Materials and Adapting Textbooks	160

PART III
Language-Focused Curriculum Elements 183

7   Language Focus: Teaching Academic Vocabulary, Collocations, and Pre-Fabs   185

8   Language Focus: Teaching Academic Grammar for Writing   216

9   Language Focus: From Text to Discourse   258

Appendix: Curriculum-Development Checklists   *293*
Index   *299*

PREFACE

The main purpose of this book is to help teachers design courses for teaching academic writing and to do it as efficiently and effectively as possible. It seeks to provide pre-service and practicing teachers a perspective on curricular thinking in L2 writing pedagogy. There are plenty of books and textbooks for teaching L2 academic writing to students and books for teachers on how to teach it.

However, given the sheer number of publications on, about, and for L2 writing pedagogy, navigating the vast body of theoretical and empirical knowledge, suggestions for teaching, and classroom activities is not exactly quick and easy work. After all, given that information abounds, it seems important and highly necessary to see a bigger picture of teaching L2 academic writing. *Effective Curriculum for Teaching L2 Writing* sets out to be a clear, practical, and efficient bigger picture for curricular thinking in L2 writing pedagogy.

The book is divided into two parts: Part I examines curricular foundations in general and focuses on what is socially valued in L2 writing and pedagogy at school and, in addition, at the college and university level. Part II is concerned with the nitty-gritty—the daily realities of curricular design and classroom instruction. Part III takes a close look at the key pedagogical ingredients of teaching academic L2 writing: vocabulary and collocations, grammar for academic writing, and the down-to-earth techniques for helping L2 writers to organize discourse and ideas.

The Book Structure

Part I includes four chapters. Chapter 1 takes a brief look of the components of a curriculum and the foundations of curriculum design. Chapters 2 and 3 review the attributes of school and academic writing that are valued in society. These chapters survey the guidelines and learning goals for L2 writing on the Common Core State Standards required at school and in higher education. Chapter 4 addresses studies of L2 writing and their recommendations for teaching the elements of language and skills that students must learn in order to be able to produce passable academic writing. The findings of empirical studies are reviewed throughout Part I as they analyze a broad range of language and discourse features that present a detailed and thorough picture of the requirements of student writing (i.e., what is valued in society), and the investigations of L2 academic writing (i.e., the studies of the learners).

Part II—chapters 5 and 6—focuses on how to develop a curriculum and the specifics of curricular thinking, as well as the details of instruction (e.g., choosing textbooks and adapting and creating teaching materials). The purpose of Part II is to help teachers to become more effective and efficient, based on current research in L2 instruction.

Part III consists of 3 chapters. Chapters 7 and 8 address a few shortcuts for principled instruction and techniques in L2 writing: academic grammar and academic vocabulary and collocations. Chapter 7 also includes useful and practical techniques for teaching L2 writers to edit their text. Clear and simple teaching techniques for organizing ideas in academic L2 prose are the topic of chapter 9.

The Appendix provides an extensive checklist for developing curricula for a course or several courses in language teaching. It can be useful in its entirety or in pieces and portions, as needed.

ACKNOWLEDGMENTS

My eternal, undying, and never-ending gratitude to Naomi Silverman, the Big Cheese at Routledge, for her support, kindness, friendship of many years, and infinite—immeasurable—patience. I have it on good authority that Naomi's patience is beyond compare.

For their support, diligent reading, cleaning, editing, and locating hundreds of typos, oversights, goofs, flubs, and screw-ups, my deepest appreciation and sympathy go to Bruce Rogers, the Ohio State University, and Rodney Hill. Thank you more than I can say. Thank you to Anne Hepfer, Seattle University, for helping me refine my ideas and for enduring friendship and thoughtfulness.

Through the decades, I have learned from thousands of my students, L1 and L2 alike. It has been my honor to work with them and serve them the best way that I knew how. My thanks to them for trying out various techniques, materials, activities, exercises, short-cuts, tasks, and topics.

PART I
Curriculum Foundations for L2 Writing and Language

1
INTRODUCTION

Effective Teaching and the Curriculum

This chapter discusses:

- A curriculum for teaching
- Curriculum design and access to education
- The essentials of a curriculum design
- Contemporary views on curriculum and teaching effectiveness
- Building an effective curriculum for teaching L2 writing

Introduction

The intense debates about teacher effectiveness and the characteristics that make for good teaching are not likely to be resolved in the near future. It may be that all the claims about the component elements of excellent teaching are correct and valid, and that the key question concerns their proper mix at the appropriate time.

As in all other human endeavors, though, in second language (L2) teaching one needs to keep an eye on the big picture while being mindful of the incremental tasks that comprise the daily pursuits of virtually all teachers. That is, in the space of a day, a week, or a school term, teachers have to be able to move from point A to point B relatively effectively and efficiently, while keeping their wits about them in the long run. Like all other human beings who work for a living, teachers need to see that what they do day in and day out actually makes at least some positive difference in their students' learning and skills (see Darling-Hammond, 2010, for a discussion on teacher efficacy).

To achieve progress, improvement, growth, advancement—a positive difference—in student L2 abilities, teachers have to keep what they do in perspective. That is, they need to see connections among the students they teach, the material that they teach, and the goals with which they teach this material to these students. In the debates on teacher effectiveness and the characteristics of excellent teaching, as well as those on student learning, a broad view of the connections among the learners, the learning, and the purposes of teaching has been often referred to as "a curricular perspective" or "curricular thinking" (e.g., Byrnes, 1998; Darling-Hammond, 2005, 2006; Grandin, Einbeck, & von Reinhart, 1992).

In today's global and migratory society, which is especially relevant in L2 teaching, the types of learners, contexts, objectives, contents, sociocultural frameworks, and available resources for learning are enormously diverse. Thus, for teachers, it is more important than ever to analyze, identify, appraise, evaluate, select, and structure the contents of teaching, the attendant concepts and materials, and the suitable teaching methods and techniques. Accomplishing these complex intellectual tasks and teaching effectively requires curricular thinking. Effective teaching cannot—and does not—take place without a curriculum that has a clear view of the inter-relationships between the learners, the multi-layered objectives of teaching, the societal goals of education, and the subject matter contents.

A Curriculum for Teaching

In L2 teaching, as with other subjects, such as math or social studies, a curriculum is often seen as something very vague. Although most L2 teachers have course plans, syllabi, or required topic areas to cover in their classes, the concept of a curriculum is not something that many people spend a great deal of time thinking about. However, it is the curriculum that practically always determines whether instruction, the content, or the implementation of the teaching activities result in effective teaching and lead to productive student learning.

Speaking generally, most people who teach have very different ideas of what a curriculum is, where it comes from, or how it comes into being. Some might say that a curriculum is the material that a course or a program of study is expected to cover in a certain amount of time.

Others might claim that a curriculum refers to a specific subject matter or set of skills that students need to acquire. That is, it is what students should know, or be able to describe or do to meet the expectations of the society in the form of, say, school administrators, parents, or testing agencies.

The methods for instruction, teaching techniques, classroom activities, the subject matter, the content areas, course syllabi, and guidelines for material sequencing do in fact refer to various concepts that are intrinsic to a curriculum. However, these elements of instruction and education are only loosely associated with what a curriculum is, how it is developed, and what its educational objective can be.

A dictionary definition of the term "curriculum" is, in fact, also rather vague: "an aggregate of all the courses of study offered by a school, college, or university," or "a group of related courses, often in a special field of study: the engineering curriculum" (Webster, 1996, p. 492). However, in his well-known and thorough book, *Analyzing the Curriculum*, George Posner provides the definitions of at least six concepts that, taken together, typically refer to academic curriculum. Each of these "has different consequences in terms of accountability" because "no definition of curriculum is ethically or politically neutral" (Posner, 2004, p. 12).

COMMON COMPONENTS OF ACADEMIC CURRICULUM

- Scope and Sequence of language skill development. THIS IS THE FOUNDATIONAL AND MOST ESSENTIAL GUIDE OF A CURRICULUM FOR INSTRUCTION AND ASSESSMENT.

  Curricular objectives to determine the scope and the goal of teaching and learning (or learning outcomes) expected at each of the sequential levels of language proficiency or school grades.

  Objectives are typically organized in sequence, according to a common language skill/dimension (i.e., scope; e.g., listening, speaking, reading, or writing) or sub-skill (e.g., note-taking).

- A Course Plan (also called *syllabus*): A COURSE OUTLINE ENCOMPASSES THE GOALS AND THE MEANS FOR ACHIEVING THEM (i.e., the *what* and the *how* of the course). These elements also include the rationale, topics to be addressed, teaching materials, assignments, and assessment/evaluation criteria.

  COMPONENTS OF A COURSE PLAN can include:

  Language/content coverage to meet the curricular objectives: An organized set of subject matter topics that are to be covered.

  Standards, which can be internally or externally determined: The types of knowledge and skills required of students for successful completion. Standards, however, do not delineate teaching methods, techniques, or activities. Standards, for example, can help distinguish between what represents beginning, intermediate, or advanced language skills. Standards may be an incremental step toward achieving curricular objectives.

  Instructional materials: Textbooks, workbooks, study guides, teaching manuals, lab and supplementary materials, and assessment instruments or tests that are used to guide instruction and evaluation.

- Overall Course of Study: A set or series of courses that a student is required to complete to achieve their language learning objectives. WELL-DESIGNED CURRICULUM ENTAILS COORDINATING INSTRUCTION WITHIN AND ACROSS LANGUAGE LEARNING LEVELS (e.g., coordinated teaching within beginning level skills, such as reading and writing, as well as coordinated teaching across beginning and intermediate reading levels).

> Course of Study can apply to, for example, a specific level of language proficiency (e.g., beginning level courses—listening, speaking, reading, and writing) in some cases. This concept can also refer to the entire instructional sequence and language learning process (e.g., beginning, intermediate, and advanced levels that encompass all required language skills).
>
> Based on Posner (2004)

Curriculum Design and Access to Education

The quandary of what a curriculum is or how it impacts the effectiveness of teaching is certainly not new. To begin with, a curriculum at any level of education and at any period in history has always been a social, cultural, ideological, economic, and political endeavor. Today, it seems largely axiomatic that social values, cultural norms and expectations, and the state of a national economy in any country determine what is valued or devalued in education. As with most other social, cultural, and economic phenomena, the political aspects of human functioning and matters of ideology play an integral role.

Much of our current and predominant view of the values and objectives in education is rooted in the humanistic social outlook that took hold in the 1930s and 1940s. On the heels of the Great Depression, during World War II, and in response to rigid secondary and university curricula, American educators and social economists actively sought to liberalize access to higher education. In the early 1930s, a consortium of government and funding agencies commissioned a landmark Eight-Year Study of curriculum effectiveness and learning outcomes in terms of high school to university transition for middle-class students and without the gate-keeping function of entrance exams. Ralph Tyler, a professor from the University of Chicago, spearheaded a national study of 30 high schools and 300 colleges and universities to identify the characteristics of effective curricula that could provide such students access to university education. To this day, the landmark Eight-Year Study is considered to be the most comprehensive and reliable investigation of the role of the curriculum in the democratization of education and curricular development.

In the late 1940s, nearly a decade after the study was completed, Tyler published a small, 83-page book, titled *Basic Principles of Curriculum and Instruction* (Tyler, 1949). Since its original publication, the book has undergone 38 new editions, countless attempts of a reformulation of its principles, and scores of re-interpretations. Nonetheless, Tyler's principles have continued to dominate much of the educational thought in curriculum design and development possibly because these frameworks fundamentally reflect the social assumptions and cultural values that lie at the core of Western schooling and education (Posner, 2004).

The Tyler approach to curriculum planning centers on four rationales germane to the perspectives on education in his time. However, Tyler's first "fundamental question" (1949, p. 3) has had an encompassing and profound influence on education and curricular schools of thought because it clearly formulates an approach to uncovering the crucial elements in all types of schooling. To develop a curriculum that enables teachers to teach effectively, one must first ask (ibid.):

> The Essential Question and Foundation of Curriculum Development:
>
> What educational purposes should the school seek to attain?

The Essentials of a Curriculum Design

The key to building a productive curriculum is first to identify the objectives of teaching. Once these objectives are established, they can become instrumental in selecting suitable teaching materials, content and topic areas, teaching techniques, and classroom activities, as well as a means for evaluation and assessment.

As previously noted, the objectives of education are almost always rooted in the social, cultural, economic, and political values in any human society. Thus, the educational purposes have to be aligned with the values held in the society, as well as in the social and local contexts in the school or even in a student cohort. Identifying the purposes of teaching and the desired outcomes of learning is unavoidably subjective, value laden, and context specific.

According to Tyler (1949), a systematic examination of educational objectives needs to account for at least three integral elements:

> - Methodical studies of the learners
> - Studies of contemporary life in society
> - Analyses of the subject matter by specialists and their recommendations

Studies of the learners can differ greatly across geographic, political, and economic contexts. For example, a curriculum design can consider students' demographic characteristics, such as their native language, age, gender, parents' education, individual learning goals, educational and personal interests, attitudes and beliefs, as well as cognitive abilities and skill levels. While not all these factors necessarily come to bear on developing a curriculum for any particular group of learners, nor are they always clearly discernable, these considerations can reflect more important or less prominent variables that can—and often do—affect a curricular plan.

Along these lines, the social factors that impact educational objectives can be widely divergent in terms of commonly held social, cultural, civic, and moral

8 Curriculum Foundations

values, as well as economic, racial, linguistic, and literacy stratification, and a degree of control exerted by national or local administrative and political agencies.

> To put it plainly, the social and cultural values determine what is valued as knowledge in society, and what types of knowledge and skills are valued.

For example, in a country where the knowledge of mathematics is believed to be more prestigious or advantageous than language aptitude, a national curriculum prescribed by, say, the ministry of education is likely to focus on mathematics. Thus, a curriculum design has to align its objectives with the societal goals and values, which in turn support education (e.g., see Ryle, 1949; Stenhouse, 1975). Dewey's work in the 1920s and 1930s similarly postulated that social and educational objectives are closely related: the values of schooling reflect those of the society, and the societal values are congruent with the social situation in a specific country.

In curriculum building, the choices of specific contents, teaching methods, and instructional activities require decisions that must be based on solid knowledge of the subject matter. For example, if an English language program for L2 learners has an objective to help learners to expand their vocabulary range, then choices must be made in regard to what vocabulary to teach and how best to teach it. Of course, even in such narrow and very specific cases, the choices of the what and the how of vocabulary teaching are subjective and not devoid of value judgments. Nonetheless, today, much research-based and empirical evidence pertaining to the types of knowledge that are socially and pragmatically valued has become available. So, for the experts in, for example, the contents and effective techniques for vocabulary teaching, it is possible to arrive at responsible, research-based curricular decisions that are most suitable for meeting particular educational objectives. As Posner (2004, p. 17) comments, "after all, who is better equipped to make these decisions than the people with the most knowledge relevant to the decisions?"

Talking Shop

Given how many different ideas can be found about what curriculum is and what it is for, what has been your experience with curriculum development? In what ways do you think societal values are reflected in curricular elements? Discuss this important point with your colleagues. As is usually the case with curricular thinking, discussing views, perspectives, and experiences is important throughout the process.

Contemporary Views on Curriculum and Teaching Effectiveness

Given that all curriculum design and contents are strongly dependent on social and cultural values, it is not particularly surprising that the 20th century has seen a range of philosophical and theoretical perspectives emerge and wane. All these have reflected specific coherent assumptions about the nature of learning, socially valued objectives of learning, the types of content considered to be important for life in society, and the extent of the connections between schooling and society. It goes without saying, however, that curriculum designs of any kind have been subject to much criticism and controversy possibly because any theory or position in the field of education (or language study, for that matter) can and does eventually become an object of criticism and controversy (see, for example, Stenhouse, 1975; Taba, 1962, 1966).

Nonetheless, it can be useful to identify four or five philosophical perspectives that have had an important influence on the current schools of thought. Among them, for example, the experiential school, strongly associated with the work of Dewey, has had an enduring impact on how education and its purposes are envisioned in the United States. The experiential perspective views education as the totality of the experience that influences the development of a human being, and hence, this framework assumes a very broad understanding of the curriculum, including a student's learning both at school and outside of it. The traditionalist curriculum, on the other hand, promotes student enculturation in the societal values and the shared body of knowledge that is considered requisite for any member of the society. Some very well known traditionalist works, such as those by Allan Bloom and William Bennett, have emphasized the transmittal of foundational cultural knowledge and the sociopolitical knowledge shared by the members of the community.

In addition to these two well-known perspectives on the purposes of curriculum and instruction, two widely adopted models of curriculum have endured the test of time. However, their essential assumptions are somewhat contradictory in regard to educational objectives and contents of teaching. The predominant behavioral model assumes that the main objective of teaching is to change learners and thus prepare them for the life outside the school: (a) change students (b) in desired directions, and (c) not in undesired directions (Mager, 1975). Mager (1962) has a highly influential description of the steps involved in developing specific and well-defined learning objectives that take the form of observable knowledge and skills that are attained as outcomes of instruction and curriculum planning.

As a follow-up to Tyler's (1949) book, Benjamin Bloom's (1956) *Taxonomy of Educational Objectives* became a hallmark of learning gains that are envisioned as a behavioral matrix of cognitive maturation and change. According to Bloom's taxonomy, as an outcome of learning, students should be expected to, for example, know (e.g., recall and systematize) content particulars, such as facts, methods, and processes, as well as comprehend and interpret the material, apply abstract concepts to new situations, analyze the constituent elements of ideas and concepts, and synthesize information obtained from a variety sources. Clearly, regardless of the criticisms these descriptions of learner abilities have seen over the years, much of what is referred to as learning outcomes[1] today is derived from these elements of educational objectives, and particularly so in teaching, assessment, and testing.

Constructivist (cognitive, mental, and experiential learning) perspectives on curriculum represent a modern-day version of Socratic education and Plato's philosophical precepts of innate knowledge. That is, people are born with knowledge and ideas, and the teacher's job is to help students "recall" these (see, for example, Posner, 2004, for a discussion). Early education rooted in constructivist ideals strives to develop a child's intelligence, creativity, introspection, and self-initiated learning. The work of Jean Piaget has been pivotal in the constructivist view of teaching and curriculum. Piaget's understanding of learning postulates that children's thinking and minds are distinct from those of adults. Hence, a central concept of a curriculum is the timing of teaching when learners are cognitively ready and when abstract learning can take place. One of the key discussions in the constructivist school of thought is the connections between knowledge and performance, where knowledge is not always accurately reflected in performance, and vice versa (Bereiter & Scardamalia, 1992, 1996). In contemporary terms, constructivist views on learning and human development have given rise to a broad range of curriculum frameworks and such notions as multiple intelligences, the thinking- or meaning-centered learning, scaffolding instruction, and classroom community learning.

The purposes of curriculum and instructional content have been the subject of a persistent debate between the proponents of the behavioral and constructivist perspectives. Although both recognize that the purpose of teaching is to promote learning, what represents the desired educational objectives, productive curriculum designs, and positive learning outcomes is at the core of the differences between behaviorists and constructivists. The former contend that the purpose of learning is to produce a change in learner behavior, while the latter believe that education should focus on meaning-making, individual cognitive progress, child development, and knowledge construction.

The constructivist perspective supports curriculum development (but not necessarily curriculum design) inasmuch as it is supported by the theory of learning. In practical terms, constructivism is not a theory of teaching, and it can only inform and guide instruction. Thus, applying learning theory to the practical matters of teaching is up to the individual teacher, and this task can be both difficult and somewhat vague. However, in light of the numerous changes that have recently been taking place in teacher education since about early 2000s, constructivist views have found somewhat limited utilization in contemporary teacher education.

> ### 💬 Talking Shop
>
> What do you think the reasons are for the decline of constructivist theories in teacher education today? In your view, what are the important considerations in the modern-day teacher education? What are your beliefs and personal philosophies about the essential components of teachers' professional preparation?
>
> These are critical to think about and write down for future reference. You can also post them on a listserv or in a blog to see what sorts of responses you may get. Discuss your ideas with a colleague: your views can be valuable to help others sharpen their thinking. Exploring the possibilities is the basis of all curricular thinking.

In recent years, a large number of publications have addressed the role of the teacher's professional knowledge, professional development, and teacher effectiveness in student learning. To date, many empirical studies of teacher attributes, professional expertise, and the teacher knowledge-base have arrived at a conclusion that seems intuitively obvious: teachers' professional qualifications, experience, and effectiveness are of crucial importance to the extent of classroom learning. Practically all experts on teaching and teaching effectiveness have also noted that teachers' education and subject matter knowledge (e.g., advanced academic degrees in the discipline taught) have a great deal of positive impact on student progress and achievement, particularly at the secondary level or higher.

Among other influential publications, the work of Darling-Hammond has advocated the democratization of education to make it accessible to all types of learners. She points out that teacher education cannot be limited to the study of pedagogy alone (Darling-Hammond, 1996, 2005). According to this expert on teaching and teacher education, three general areas of knowledge and skills impact the teaching effectiveness (Darling-Hammond, 2006, p. 83):

- Knowledge of learners: how they learn and develop
- Social purposes, needs, and expectations of education, as reflected in curriculum goals and content—the subject matter and skills to be taught to achieve these purposes
- The content and learners to be taught, as informed by assessment and supported by productive classroom environments

Darling-Hammond (2005, 2006) and Darling-Hammond and Bransford (2005) emphasize that these facets of knowledge are important for teaching as a profession and teachers as professionals: teachers must be prepared to make instructional and curricular decisions in the best interests of their students and, for

12 Curriculum Foundations

this purpose, rely on the best available knowledge. These authors conclude that education of students must serve the purposes of democracy by means of allowing all learners access to political, civic, and economic life in the society (see also Darling-Hammond and Bransford [2005] and Darling-Hammond, et al. [2005] for an extensive discussion of the importance of curricular decisions to student learning and social opportunities).

One observation seems to be important to make at this juncture. The basic elements of curriculum design outlined by Tyler (1949) more than half a century ago necessitate three foundational inquiries. These do not appear to have changed greatly:

(a) Studies of the learners
(b) Studies of contemporary life in society
(c) Analyses of the subject matter and recommendations by specialists

Action Point

What do you think the foundations of a curriculum should be? Create a set of the three (or four or five) essential and foundational elements for building a curriculum. What do they need to be and what factors should they take into account? How can these foundational elements be made flexible and dynamic to change with the times, places, learners, and teaching content?

TABLE 1.1 A (Very) Brief Summary of the Curricular Perspectives

Curricular School of Thought	Main Tenets
Traditional (late 19th century–early 20th century)	• Mastery of basic literacy and numeracy • Knowledge of basic and essential facts, formulas, and terms, which all reasonably well educated people should know, transmitted from teachers to students (e.g., nutrition, human physiology, or climate) • Cultural and civic common values that lead to literate citizenship
Experiential (late 19th century–mid-20th century)	• Functional learning aligned with and derived from students' experiences and interests • Development and growth of individual experience; realistic learning derived from the individual experience • A careful balance among intellectual, vocational/social, and personal learning

Constructivist (late 19th century–most of the 20th century)	• Learning in the classroom to construct knowledge, based on students' own understanding and thinking, with the teacher as a facilitator • Real-world problem-solving and decision-making in purposeful projects/activities, evaluated in terms of self-analysis and self-direction further learning • Negotiated (rather than teacher-imposed) learning objectives, combined with learner-centered responsibility for learning
Post-modern (also called Research-based, Core Knowledge-based, or Standards-based) (early 1990–21st century)	• Equity in learning and access to quality education • Understanding, mastery, and genuine application of essential modern-day skills (e.g., technology, critical thinking, information evaluation and analysis) • Curriculum-embedded assessments of learning • Professionalization of teachers and excellent teacher education

Building an Effective Curriculum for Teaching Language (and Writing)

Today, many, if not most L2 writing teachers, are familiar with the complex issues and dilemmas that accompany practically every conversation on the teaching of academic L2 to learners of from all walks of life. To say it simply, teachers of these students at any level of schooling and education need to make curricular and practical decisions about the contents of their classes efficiently and in a principled way in order to enable these learners to effectively go from point A to point B.

To this end, the book's chapters follow a clear, well-grounded and thoroughly validated path to curricular thinking and effective instruction. With a slight variation in the order of the curriculum design elements, the framework of the curriculum is structured along the three essential and foundational areas of curriculum design, as outlined by Tyler in 1949:

- The features of school and academic writing that are valued in society
- The specifics of curricular thinking and effective teaching of curricular elements, based on current research in L2 instruction
- Recommendations on the teaching of language-focused instruction in the components of L2 writing

In general terms, a curriculum is a methodical organization of interdependent world-views, processes, components, and building blocks. From a lesson to a unit to a course, the foundational premise remains throughout the curriculum design: what students need to know and should be able to do as an outcome (result) of teaching and learning. The day-to-day elements and building blocks of instruction at all levels of the system reflect the overall curricular thinking on teaching and learning needs of students. For instance, it is not possible to produce reasonable quality writing without reasonable proficiency in language, and it is not possible to attain a reasonable degree of language proficiency without foundational language skills, which enable communication.

When teachers envision lessons and make lesson plans, they work to contribute to the course outcomes through learning and quality and language gains. The effectiveness of teaching and learning is ultimately determined by the effectiveness of each lesson plan, instructional material, teaching technique, or pedagogical decision that takes place each day. For instance, lesson plan adjustments, modifications, and alterations are an indelible part of teaching, and instructional flexibility is also a part of the curricular thinking. What is effective and what is not, and what needs to be evaluated and refined is in the eyes of both the teacher and the learners.

Taken together, lesson plans become a course design that more or less effectively leads to achieving the objectives of learning language and L2 writing. In L2 teaching, the design, structure, and effectiveness of a course that can have its own curriculum or be a part of a larger picture of the entire program of teaching and learning. For this reason, the planning of a curriculum, a course, or a lesson begins with identifying the major and incremental learning and teaching objectives at each component of instruction (more on this in chapters 5 and 6).

Action Point

Some say that making a lesson plan is similar to preparing to cook a nice meal with an appetizer, a main entrée, and a dessert, and that planning a curriculum can be compared to designing a nutritional diet program. What do you think the specific correlations might be between preparing a meal and nutritional program design or a lesson plan and course design? Do you agree or disagree with this analogy? Why or why not? How can an excellent cook make a difference in the quality the final product?

From your perspective as a student, make a list of your expectations of a lesson and another list of your expectations of a course. What makes for a good and nutritional lesson (or a meal)? What are the components and outcomes of an excellent course (or a nutritional program)? What are the connections between them? Discuss your views with your colleagues and see what their experiences and opinions are.

Language lesson, course, and curriculum planning and design are cyclical, iterative (repeated), and systematic processes of evaluation and refinement. A lesson plan implemented in the classroom has the purpose of contributing to the curriculum goals and learning objectives. The evaluation of lesson effectiveness affords an opportunity for a refinement of both the lesson and curriculum plan.

> One of the fundamental aspects of all language teaching is that when something is taught, it does not mean that it is learned.

Language learning is a goal-oriented and deliberate activity, and it has the purpose of providing learners with the language skills that they seek to attain.

- Language learning is a highly complex and recursive process.
- Language teaching and learning can be made effective and efficient by the implementation of a goal-oriented and well-planned curriculum.
- The curriculum goals can be more or less effectively achieved within a purpose-oriented lesson and unit that support the overall curriculum design.
- Language learning can take place anywhere and in any context.

The curriculum framework provides guiding principles for effective and efficient language instruction within a social, educational, political, and economic context. Tyler (1949) establishes a solid foundation for the research and analysis of the context in which language teaching and learning may take place taking into account the incremental and ultimate needs and goals of learners: what should be taught, why, how, and in what sequence (more on instructional sequencing in chapter 6).

Chapter Summary

Although most L2 teachers have course plans, syllabi, or required topic areas to cover in their classes, the concept of a curriculum is not something that many people spend a great deal of time thinking about. However, it is the curriculum that practically always determines whether instruction, the content, or the implementation of the teaching activities result in effective teaching and lead to productive student learning. A curriculum provides the big picture and the roadmap for what teachers need to do and what students need to learn.

Historically and philosophically, there are a number of approaches to curriculum development, including constructivist and behavioral approaches. One thing is certain, however: effective teaching cannot—and does not—take place without a curriculum that has a clear of view the inter-relationships between the learners, the multi-layered objectives of teaching, the societal goals of education, and the subject matter contents.

Note

1 For a definition of learning outcomes, see chapter 5.

Further Reading on L2 Curriculum Development for Writing

Brown, J. D. (1995). *The elements of language curriculum: A systematic approach to program development.* Boston: Heinle & Heinle.
Leki, I. (2001). "A narrow thinking system": Nonnative-English-speaking students in group projects across the curriculum. *TESOL Quarterly, 35,* 39–67.
Met, M. (1998). Curriculum decision-making in content-based teaching. In F. Genesee & J. Cenoz (Eds.), *Beyond bilingualism: Multilingualism and multilingual education* (pp. 35–63). Clevedon: Multilingual Matters.
Nation, I. S. P., & Macalister, J. (2010). *Language curriculum design.* New York: Routledge.
Squires, D. A. (2009). *Curriculum alignment: Research-based strategies for increasing student achievement.* Thousand Oaks, CA: Corwin Press.
Taba, H. (1962). *Curriculum development: Theory and practice.* New York: Harcourt, Brace, and World.
Tyler, R. W. (1949). *Basic principles of curriculum and instruction.* Chicago: The University of Chicago Press.

References

Bereiter, C., & Scardamalia, M. (1992). Cognition and curriculum. In P. Jackson (Ed.), *Handbook of research on curriculum* (pp. 517–543). New York: Macmillan.
Bereiter, C., & Scardamalia, M. (1996). Rethinking learning. In D. Olson & N. Torrance (Eds.), *The handbook of education and human development: New models of learning, teaching and schooling* (pp. 485–513). Cambridge, MA: Basil Blackwell.
Bloom, B. (Ed.). (1956). *Taxonomy of educational objectives. Handbook 1: Cognitive domain.* New York: David McKay.
Byrnes, H. (1998). Constructing curricula in collegiate foreign language departments. In H. Byrnes (Ed.), *Learning foreign and second languages: Perspectives in research and scholarship* (pp. 262–295). New York: MLA.
Darling-Hammond, L. (1996). The quiet revolution: Rethinking teacher development. *Educational Leadership, 53*(6), 4–10.
Darling-Hammond, L. (2005). *Professional development schools: Schools for developing a profession* (2nd ed.). New York: Teachers College Press.
Darling-Hammond, L. (2006). *Powerful teacher education.* San Francisco: Jossey-Bass.
Darling-Hammond, L. (2010). *The flat world and education: How America's commitment to equity will determine our future.* New York: Teacher's College Press.
Darling-Hammond, L., Banks, J., Zumwalt, K., Gomez, L., Gamoran Sherin, M., Griesdorn, J., et al. (2005). Educational goals and purposes: Developing a curricular vision for teaching. In L. Darling-Hammond & J. Bransford (Eds.), *Preparing teachers for a changing world: What teachers should learn and be able to do* (pp. 169–200). San Francisco: Jossey Bass/Wiley.
Darling-Hammond, L., & Bransford, J. (Eds.). (2005). *Preparing teachers for a changing world: What teachers should know and be able to do.* San Francisco, CA: Jossey-Bass.
Grandin, J. M., Einbeck, K., & vonReinhart, W. (1992). The changing goals of language instruction. In H. Byrnes (Ed.), *Languages for a multicultural world in transition* (pp. 123–163). Lincolnwood, IL: National Textbook.
Mager, R. (1962). *Preparing instructional objectives.* San Francisco: Fearon.
Mager, R. (1975). *Preparing instructional objectives* (2nd ed.). Belmont, CA: Pitman Learning.

Posner, G. (2004). *Analyzing the curriculum* (3rd ed.). New York: McGraw-Hill.
Ryle, G. (1949). *The concept of mind.* Chicago: The University of Chicago Press.
Stenhouse, L. (1975). *An introduction to curriculum research and development.* London: Heinemann.
Taba, H. (1962). *Curriculum development: Theory and practice.* New York: Harcourt, Brace, and World.
Taba, H. (1966). *Teaching strategies and cognitive functioning in elementary school children.* San Francisco: San Francisco State College.
Tyler, R. W. (1949). *Basic principles of curriculum and instruction.* Chicago: The University of Chicago Press.
Webster's Encyclopedic Unabridged Dictionary of the English Language. (1996). New York: Gramercy.

2
WHAT'S VALUED IN SCHOOL WRITING AND LANGUAGE?

This chapter discusses:

- Writing skills valued in schooling and in the Common Core
- Grade-level Anchor Standards and writing benchmarks
- Past surveys of school writing
- Language skills valued in schooling and in the Common Core
- Grade-level Anchor Standards and language benchmarks
- Common Core Standards for English Language Learners

Introduction

The Common Core State Standards (CCSS) are a set of educational and learning goals mandated in the United States for all school-age learners. The primary focus of the Standards is what K–12 students should know in English Language Arts (ELA) and mathematics at the end of each grade. The Standards are sponsored by the National Governors Association and the Council of Chief State School Officers with the objective of establishing consistent educational standards across the participating states.

The Common Core Standards represent the greatest philosophical and practical shift in schooling and education in the country in the past century. In many ways, the impact of the Standards on the population of the United States cannot be overestimated.

The goal of this chapter is take a close look at the writing and language skills expected of all students and English Language Learners (ELLs) in the CCSS. In addition, the relevant features of writing and language valued in the National

Assessment of Educational Progress (NAEP) assessments are also briefly noted, as they pertain to the design of CCSS. Taken together, the language and writing learning goals explicitly required in CCSS can form a coherent picture of what is valued in schooling and society.

The Common Core State Standards, publicly released in 2010, have been developed from the foundation of NAEP data, with additional research support by other assessment and testing organizations, such as ACT.[1] A supporting ACT (2010) study of 256,765 test takers in various states determined that:

- 31% of all students perform at a level sufficient to "understand complex text"
- 35% of all students have a knowledge of "language varieties" and the "ability to use language skillfully"
- 24% are able to work with science materials at the level of "college and career readiness"

(ACT, 2010, pp. 2 & 5)

The ACT study demonstrates unambiguously that all students, regardless of their first language, need to learn a great deal.

A newer report, NCES (2013) on Reading, points to similar test results for English Language Learners, specifically (inclusion rate of 90% to 92%, depending on the grade level):

- 71% scored below basic at the 4th and 8th grade levels
- 7% scored at or above proficient in the 4th grade
- 3% scored at or above proficient in the 8th grade

Similar results are also found in other national tests. This is not to say that L1 students do spectacularly well at school, but ELLs tend to lag far behind them.

According to ACT's (2013) *The Condition of College and Career Readiness* report, 70% of ELLs in Grades 4–12 are "far off track" (p. 11) in their reading skills—that is, far below the levels that predict these learners' likely graduation from college and their being career-ready. The report also finds that only 2% of "far off track" ELLs are likely to catch up to their grade-level reading when they finish their schooling. Needless to say, students who do not have sufficient language proficiency to read probably do not have the language tools to write well.

A crucial difference between CCSS and other previously established learning standards is that considerations of language learning and usage are addressed for various—at least three—applications:

- Language builds a foundation for learning the content in all school subjects (e.g., history, math, science, social studies, reading, and writing). It may be impossible to undertake learning these school subjects without a substantial

language foundation because "they are inseparable from such contexts" (NGA & CCSSO, 2010a, p. 28; 2010b).
- The development of academic speaking and writing language skills represent specific standards to be achieved in schooling, within the content of ELA and in other school subjects.
- A knowledge of language in and of itself represents an objective of school learning, with a strong focus on academic grammar and punctuation conventions and ongoing building of extensive vocabulary.

Language development and usage are interdependent in the context of schooling, but the Common Core State Standards do not provide clarification or guidance in regard to their curricular and instructional implementations.

> According to the Common Core State Standards, in ELA, language instruction is to be approached in terms of the traditional four skills—that is, listening, speaking, reading, and writing—all of which find applications in the teaching of school subjects and curricula.

For example, language knowledge and conventional usage are described as follows:

> The Language standards include the essential "rules" of standard written and spoken English, but they also approach language as a matter of craft and informed choice among alternatives. The vocabulary standards focus on understanding words and phrases, their relationships, and their nuances and on acquiring new vocabulary, particularly general academic and domain-specific words and phrases.
>
> (CCSS, 2010, p. 8)

As is clearly stated in the Common Core Standards, "the essential 'rules' of standard written and spoken English" are mandatory of all learners at school. In many schools, however, the teaching of "rules" of standard English has been on the wane and all but disappeared since the early 1980s (Bex & Watts, 1999; Chastain, 1990; Hairston, 1982, 1986).

> **Talking Shop**
>
> In 1990, Linda Christensen published her much-lauded opinion on teaching standard English, "Teaching Standard English: Whose Standard?" Christensen's purpose was to provide a personal perspective and a critique of the practice of conforming to standard English when teaching writing at school. Christensen argued that when more attention is paid to form than to content, students' words and thoughts become devalued. She advocated the need to teach students "to hold their own voices sacred," (p. 36) and suggested instructional strategies that encourage personal experiences and linguistic equality.
>
> The Common Core Standards clearly adopt an opposing position that puts much emphasis on the rules of standard English. What are your views on this issue? In your opinion, what type of writing instruction is valuable to school learners of various kinds? What are the pros and cons of each of these positions?

Writing Skills Valued in Schooling and on the Common Core

According to the CCSS (2010, p. 3), the Standards emphasize "required achievements . . . without prescribing how these are to be attained." The document explicitly states that "the Standards do not mandate such things as a particular writing process or the full range of metacognitive strategies that students may need to monitor and direct their thinking and learning." That is, teachers "are thus free to provide students with whatever tools and knowledge their professional judgment and experience identify as most helpful for meeting the goals set out in the Standards." To be specific, the Standards represent a very broad set of teaching and learning objectives for K–12 schooling. They briefly outline what students need to know and should be able to do upon the completion of their education.

The guidance regarding ELLs, specifically, consists of a two-page addendum titled *Application of Common Core State Standards for English Language Learners*. When it comes to these learners, the Standards are vague: "It is . . . beyond the scope of the Standards to define the full range of supports appropriate for English language learners and for students with special needs. At the same time, all students must have the opportunity to learn and meet the same high standards. . . . "

22 Curriculum Foundations

The document states that to achieve the high academic standards, it is essential that ELLs have access to:

- Literacy-rich school environments where students are immersed in a variety of language experiences
- Instruction to develop foundational skills in English and enable ELLs to participate fully in grade-level coursework, postsecondary education or the workplace
- Learning content in a second language (through specific pedagogical techniques and additional resources)
- Ongoing assessment and feedback to guide learning

That is, achieving the Common Core Standards of language use at each grade level is expected of all school-age learners, including ELLs.

> **Talking Shop**
>
> According to Chrys Dougherty's (2014) report, published by ACT, the rate of ELLs who are "far off track" in the their school subjects is markedly uneven:
> Mathematics—57%, Reading—70%, and Science—52%
> What do you think the reasons might be that the proportion of ELLs who are "far off track" is the lowest in science, followed by mathematics?
> One of the most significant and overarching claims advanced explicitly by the Common Core Standards is that, without a solid foundation in language, it may be difficult—if not impossible—to learn math and science at school. Do you think that the Dougherty report disproves or supports one of the main premises of the Standards?

Grade-Level Writing Types and Learning Goals

In addition to the foundations for the Common Core Standards in writing and the attendant language skills, the NAEP (2011) framework also serves as the basis for the distribution rates of writing across of the purposes of writing (Table 2.1) in various school grades. The NAEP framework, adopted in the Standards, promotes three types of texts and writing skills: **to persuade, to explain**, and **to convey real or imagined experience**.

The NAEP evidence collected for the development of the Standards pointed to the need for shifts in the rate of the text types to account for the demands of college and career readiness. Based on the NAEP framework, the Standards

TABLE 2.1 Distribution of Writing Types in Benchmark Grades in NAEP and CCSS

Grade	To Persuade	To Explain	To Convey Experience
4	30%	35%	35%
8	35%	35%	30%
12	40%	40%	20%

align closely with the NAEP's distribution of writing in various grades. Table 2.1 clearly outlines the types of writing expected in three benchmark grades.

Note the shifts in the proportions of expected writing types. Although high school writing is designated in all three forms, the predominant focus of writing throughout Grades 9–12 is on academic argumentation and informative/explanatory texts. This structure of the Standards is derived from and consistent with the 2011 NAEP framework.

In various opinion pieces, blogs, and editorials, the CCSS are often called lofty, unrealistic, and vague. These adjectives apply to quite a few portions of the document. The stated reason for the Standards' imprecise wording is that the CCSS specify the ultimate **learning goals**, rather than the *what*s and the *how-to*s of daily instruction:

> "Educational standards are the learning goals for what students should know and be able to do at each grade level." (NGA & CCSSO, 2010b)

Outside the concrete world, where objectives and achievements are measured in terms of various sorts of numbers (e.g., sales, profits, number of drinks consumed per day, or pounds lost per month), in the Standards, learning goals in reading, writing, or language attainment are typically stated in abstract terms.

Thus, to design a language learning curriculum, the first order of business is to identify, as clearly as possible, what the CCSS say about school writing and language learning at school. As is stated repeatedly throughout the CCSS documents, the goal of school curricula lies in the alignment of what is taught and learned with readiness for college education and career.

Anchor Standards for Writing

The following summary of the CCSS (2010, p. 18) overall objectives applies to student writing across curriculum in Grades K–5 in the "College and Career Readiness Anchor Standards for Writing":

> To build a foundation for college and career readiness, students need to learn to use writing as a way of offering and supporting opinions, demonstrating

understanding of the subjects they are studying, and conveying real and imagined experiences and events. They learn to appreciate that a key purpose of writing is to communicate clearly to an external, sometimes unfamiliar audience, and they begin to adapt the form and content of their writing to accomplish a particular task and purpose. They develop the capacity to build knowledge on a subject through research projects and to respond analytically to literary and informational sources. To meet these goals, students must devote significant time and effort to writing, producing numerous pieces over short and extended time frames throughout the year.

For Grades 6–12, learning goals are similarly stated explicitly for Anchor Standards for Writing in later years of education CCSS (2010, p. 41):

> For students, writing is a key means of asserting and defending claims, showing what they know about a subject, and conveying what they have experienced, imagined, thought, and felt. To be college- and career-ready writers, students must take task, purpose, and audience into careful consideration, choosing words, information, structures, and formats deliberately. They need to know how to combine elements of different kinds of writing—for example, to use narrative strategies within argument and explanation within narrative—to produce complex and nuanced writing. They need to be able to use technology strategically when creating, refining, and collaborating on writing. They have to become adept at gathering information, evaluating sources, and citing material accurately, reporting findings from their research and analysis of sources in a clear and cogent manner. They must have the flexibility, concentration, and fluency to produce high-quality first-draft text under a tight deadline as well as the capacity to revisit and make improvements to a piece of writing over multiple drafts when circumstances encourage or require it.

The overall objectives of writing instruction seem to be "asserting and defending claims," structuring ideas, providing any type of acceptable evidence, using technology, and meeting deadlines.

The College and Career Anchor Standards for Writing "define what students should understand and be able to do . . . by the end of each grade" (p. 63). Together with the CCSS, the Anchor Standards define the skills and understandings that "all students must demonstrate." The gist of the Anchor Standards for Writing is presented in Table 2.2.

TABLE 2.2 Writing Anchor Standards in the Common Core

[For teaching principles and techniques, see chapters 8 and 9.]

Text Types and Purposes

What's Valued: Argumentation, Information/Explanation, and Some Narrative

"Write arguments to support claims in an analysis of substantive topics or texts using valid reasoning and relevant and sufficient evidence."

"Write informative/explanatory texts to examine and convey complex ideas and information clearly and accurately through the effective selection, organization, and analysis of content."

"Write narratives to develop real or imagined experiences or events using effective technique, well-chosen details, and well-structured event sequences."

Production and Distribution of Writing

What's Valued: Clarity, Organization, Editing, Technology, and Collaboration

"Produce clear and coherent writing in which the development, organization, and style are appropriate to task, purpose, and audience."

"Develop and strengthen writing as needed by planning, revising, editing, rewriting, or trying a new approach."

"Use technology, including the Internet, to produce and publish writing and to interact and collaborate with others."

Research to Build and Present Knowledge

What's Valued: Research, Evidence, and More Evidence

"Conduct short as well as more sustained research projects based on focused questions, demonstrating understanding of the subject under investigation."

"Gather relevant information from multiple print and digital sources, assess the credibility and accuracy of each source, and integrate the information while avoiding plagiarism."

"Draw evidence from literary or informational texts to support analysis, reflection, and research."

The Writing Standards strongly emphasize that students need to learn to write based on the evidence and information that they find in a range of sources.

> The Standards mark a crucial difference between the Writing learning goals and the current predominant practice of writing from and about experience.

Writing from research, readings, and text are central to the Writing Standards, thus the importance of the component academic writing skills of summarizing, evaluating, analyzing, and synthesizing information. These component writing skills are currently neglected in school teaching, and they also require intensive and extensive instruction (Addison & McGee, 2010; Graff & Birkenstein-Graff, 2009; Sullivan & Tinberg, 2006; Sullivan, Tinberg, & Blau, 2010).

> In the teaching of school and college writing, the focus on evidence, research, and working with multiple sources represents a tectonic plate shift in curricula and instructional philosophies and practices.

The Writing Standards, which strongly move away from experience and personal writing at school, demand explicit and intensive teaching. It is another, but closely related issue, whether many teachers of school writing currently have the professional knowledge and skills to teach evidence- and text-based writing (Jago, 2011; Kendal, 2011; Zwiers, O'Hara, & Pritchard, 2014).

In regard to the Standard that requires the use of technology for production and distribution of student writing, the Council of the Great City Schools conducted a survey of 67 school districts in late 2013. The survey found that only 29.7% reported being prepared to integrate technology in the classroom (Palacios, Casserly, & Corcoran, 2013).

In California, for example, the policy analysis document (McLaughlin, Glaab, & Carrasco, 2014, p. 9) stated, "Concerns about teachers' technological literacy arose across the state. Many teachers are not comfortable with technology, and are unprepared" to meet the demands of the Standards. According to the analysis, "Worries about technology shortfalls . . . remain. Many of this year's technology fixes were pieced together, and do not represent long term solutions. For instance, some schools borrowed computers from nearby schools" for administering student tests.

> The Standards' requirements for teaching with technology may be difficult to meet in terms of both teacher preparation and the needed equipment.

Talking Shop

In her book, *Teaching Adolescent Writers*, Kelly Gallagher (2006, p. 3) says, "Simply put, there is a literacy stampede approaching, and it is bearing down right on top of you. What should you do?"

What do you think Gallagher means by "a literacy stampede"? How is it "bearing down right on top" of a school teacher? If you were that school teacher, faced with a literacy "stampede," what would you do?

Grade 5 and Grades 11–12[2] Writing Benchmarks

The Standards are organized along the grade-level continuum of learning for the duration of 13 years, from Kindergarten through Grade 12. The benchmarks for assessment and testing are mandated for every grade and every year of schooling, with pivotal points established for Grade 5 and Grades 11–12.

For this reason, the brief overview of grade-level expectations below focuses on these two pivotal benchmarks that address the Standards for a culmination of several years of schooling each.

In Grade 5, all ELA students, including ELLs, are expected to achieve the Standards of Writing and Literacy (CCSS, ELA, W.5.1–9). The gist of Grade 5 Standards is presented in Table 2.3.

TABLE 2.3 Summary of the Writing and Literacy Standards, Grade 5

Text Types and Purposes

Write opinion pieces, narratives, and informative/explanatory texts, supporting the ideas by means of logically ordered reasons, facts, and details; convey ideas and information clearly.

Introduction and Organization

Introduce a topic or text clearly, provide a focus, and create a logical organizational structure in which ideas are logically grouped to support the writer's purpose.

Evidence and Support

Develop the topic with facts, definitions, concrete details, quotations, or other information and examples related to the topic.

Text Linking and Cohesion

Link main points and reasons using words, phrases, and clauses (e.g., consequently, specifically); link ideas within and across categories of information.

Conclusion

Provide a topic-related concluding statement.

Text Formatting

Use formatting (e.g., headings), illustrations, and multimedia when useful to aid comprehension.

Academic Vocabulary and Sentence Transitions

Use precise language and domain-specific vocabulary to inform about or explain the topic; use a variety of transitional words, phrases, and clauses to manage the sequence of events; use concrete words and phrases and sensory details to convey experiences and events precisely.

Text Clarity

Produce clear and coherent writing in which the development and organization are appropriate to task, purpose, and audience.

(*Continued*)

TABLE 2.3 (Continued)

Editing, Revision, and Technology

With guidance and support from peers and adults, develop and strengthen writing as needed by planning, revising, editing, rewriting, or trying a new approach; use technology, including the Internet, to produce and publish writing as well as to interact and collaborate with others; demonstrate sufficient command of keyboarding skills to type a minimum of two pages in a single sitting.

Research and Writing from Sources

Research to Build and Present Knowledge:
- Conduct short research projects that use several sources to build knowledge through investigation of different aspects of a topic.
- Recall relevant information from experiences or gather relevant information from print and digital sources; summarize or paraphrase information in notes and finished work, and provide a list of sources.
- Draw evidence from literary or informational texts to support analysis, reflection, and research.

> **Talking Shop**
>
> The Grade 5 Writing Standards are comprehensive, and they cover a lot of ground, from formatting to formal academic prose and organization to doing and writing up research. Given that there's a lot for teachers to teach and students to learn, it is important to determine curricular and instructional priorities.
>
> How would you prioritize the Standards? How would you prioritize instructional time? How would you go about organizing your teaching in some sort of principled order? Discuss your views with your colleagues.

In Grades 11–12, the Standards represent anchor benchmarks, which, taken together, represent and define college and career readiness. The CCSS (2010, p. 35) guidelines state that college-level standards are "broad," but career-based expectations provide "additional specificity" (CCSS, ELA, W.11–12.1–9).

A synthesis of Grades 11–12 Standards (the 20% of writing associated with the production of narratives is omitted) is provided in Table 2.4.

TABLE 2.4 Summary of the Writing and Literacy Standards, Grades 11–12

Text Types and Purposes
Write arguments and informative/explanatory texts to support claims in an analysis of substantive topics or texts. Examine and convey complex ideas and information clearly and accurately, using valid reasoning and relevant and sufficient evidence and through the effective selection, organization, and analysis of content.

Introduction, Organization, and Coherence
Introduce precise, knowledgeable claim(s) and topics; establish their significance; distinguish them from alternate or opposing claims. Organize logical sequences of claim(s), counterclaims, reasons, evidence, complex ideas, and information so that each new element builds on the preceding one to create a unified whole. Include formatting (e.g., headings), graphics (e.g., figures, tables), and multimedia when useful to aid comprehension.

Evidence, Support, and Evaluating Sources
Develop claim(s), counterclaims, and topics fairly and thoroughly by supplying and selecting the most relevant evidence, significant and relevant facts, extended definitions, concrete details, quotations, or other information and examples while pointing out the strengths and limitations of both in a manner that anticipates the audience's knowledge level, concerns, values, and possible biases.

Academic Grammar, Cohesion, and Clarity
Use words, phrases, clauses, appropriate and varied transitions, as well as varied syntax to link the major sections of the text, create cohesion, and clarify the relationships between claim(s) and reasons, between reasons and evidence, and between claim(s) and counterclaims, and among complex ideas and concepts.

Academic Vocabulary and Metaphors
Use precise language, domain-specific vocabulary, and techniques such as metaphor, simile, and analogy to manage the complexity of the topic.

Establish and maintain a formal style and objective tone while attending to the norms and conventions of the discipline in which they are writing.

Conclusion
Provide a concluding statement or section that follows from and supports the argument/information or explanation presented (e.g., articulating implications or the significance of the topic).

Editing, Revision, and Technology
Develop and strengthen writing as needed by planning, revising, editing, rewriting, or trying a new approach, focusing on addressing what is most significant for a specific purpose and audience. Use technology, including the Internet, to produce, publish, and update individual or shared writing products in response to ongoing feedback, including new arguments or information.

Research and Writing from Sources
Research to Build and Present Knowledge:
- Conduct short as well as more sustained research projects to answer a question (including a self-generated question) or solve a problem; narrow or broaden the inquiry when appropriate; synthesize multiple sources on the subject.
- Gather relevant information from multiple authoritative print and digital sources; assess the strengths and limitations of each source; integrate information into the text selectively to maintain the flow of ideas and avoid plagiarism.
- Draw evidence from literary or informational texts to support analysis, reflection, and research.

To summarize, the characteristics of school writing valued in society and in the Common Core Standards strongly resemble those in traditional formal academic prose. These, together with the emphasis on the traditional organization of ideas, have been a mainstay of educational norms and on-the-job writing for at least the past century (and probably much longer—more on this in chapters 7–9).

> To meet the Standards, curriculum and instruction need to address the required skills for writing logical arguments; making substantiated, documented, and supported claims; and providing relevant evidence.

The writing activities and practice are expected to consist of both short and extended writing tasks.

The Standards emphasize that the content of writing focuses on the analyses and presentations of findings and carrying out research projects. Personal narratives are not mentioned in the Standards, and narrative writing has a much smaller value compared to persuasive, supported, and evidence-based informational texts.

> Based on the Standards, writing assignments and projects address the development of formal academic writing skills, including summarizing, evidence and support, and research.

These component writing skills, such as summarizing and citing evidence, support, and research, have the goal of preparing students for key writing assessments on the Standards' variables and in benchmark grades.

> In the early grades, curriculum and instruction are to focus on writing progressively complex paragraphs, formal essays, and research assignments.

Past Surveys of School Writing

For a bit of a perspective, it may be interesting to take a look at what is known about school writing. In the early 1980s, Arthur Applebee (1981, 1983) undertook and published his now-famous surveys of the types of writing usually found in secondary school education. There were many other similar surveys reported at that time (e.g., Knoblauch & Brannon, 1984; Slater, 1982; Stewart & Leaman, 1983), but Applebee's work has become a classic.

Applebee summarized the kinds of writing being done as: short answers to questions; informational writing (e.g., summarizing, reporting, and analyzing); and a small amount of personal writing, such as journals, letters, or stories. According to Applebee, 44% of class time in all school subjects was devoted to writing, but it mostly consisted of short answers to questions. Testing of the subject-area knowledge and content represented 46% of in-class writing.

Other instructional foci associated with writing were reported as follows (in declining order) (Applebee, 1981):

- to test writing clarity and expression—61%
- to practice writing mechanics—47%
- to force thinking—44%
- to teach proper essay form—28%
- to work with out-of-class material, such as readings—5%

It seems that little has changed in what is valued in school writing since the early 1980s. The Common Core Standards also place a great deal of import on writing clarity, precision and accuracy in vocabulary and grammar, and traditional and highly structured organization of ideas (that is, "proper essay form").

Action Point

On surveys of school writing, various personnel such as teachers, administrators, or curriculum developers, are asked sets of relatively simple questions:

1. How often and how much do students write? How long are typical short or long writing tasks, papers, and assignments?
2. What are the reasons or purposes for teaching writing?
3. How is writing taught and when, and what are teaching practices?
4. What types of writing are taught, when, and for what reasons?
5. What typical writing activities take place in class? Which ones are most frequent? Which are most successful?

You probably already know many answers to some of these questions, based on your own experiences in school. You might also have access to actual school teachers or administrators who wouldn't mind answering a couple of quick questions. Also, you can always survey colleagues to find out what their experiences are.

With the results of your open-ended and highly un-scientific survey questions in hand, construct a summary of school writing activities (incorporating answers to the questions above) and found in Applebee (1981).

Language Skills Valued in Schooling and in the Common Core

The Common Core Standards provide few—if any—indications of how the stated learning goals can be achieved. For example, a directive such as to provide "opportunities for classroom" instruction to "develop concepts and academic language" does not seem very clear. To date, much in the Standards has been received "with well-justified confusion or trepidation" (Kinsella, 2012, p. 19). Considerable and expert leadership in curricular and instructional design is urgently needed to achieve the stated content learning and language goals. So far, a relatively large number of consultants and specialists have begun to fill the void, and it is a government-size void of simply knowing what to do next and how to do it. This book describes in detail specific principles and techniques for designing L2 writing curriculum or smaller tasks, and it presents many strategies and tactics for teaching academic language and writing skills, including improving vocabulary, applying grammar, and organizing ideas.

> **Talking Shop**
>
> The Times Union/Siena Research Institute poll of New York State residents revealed that 82% agreed that the implementation of the Common Core Standards had been rushed, while 14% disagreed. Almost half of those polled opposed the way that the Common Core had been implemented. According to the U.S. Department of Education, the state received $700 million in grants to implement the reforms. The Common Core State Standards, released in June 2010, provided a period of four years for states to prepare.
>
> In your opinion, how much time and funding should be allotted for state education systems to be ready for a major shift in schooling and teacher preparation? What is reasonable, sufficient, or insufficient in such cases?

Grade-Level Language Skills and Learning Goals

In CCSS, Anchor Standards for Language similarly "define what students should understand and be able to do . . . by the end of each grade" (p. 51) and the skill level that "all students must demonstrate."

The Standards place an almost exclusive importance on the conventions of standard English and a large vocabulary base:

> ". . . Conventions, knowledge of language, and vocabulary extend across reading, writing, speaking, and listening. Many of the conventions-related standards are as appropriate to formal spoken English as they are to formal written English. Language choice is a matter of craft for both writers and speakers. New words and phrases are acquired not only through reading and being read to but also through direct vocabulary instruction and (particularly in the earliest grades) through purposeful classroom discussions around rich content."
>
> (CCSS, Appendix A, p. 28)

In fact, to a great extent, the CCSS documents defend their rigid adherence to conventionalized, formal, and standard uses of English: "Students must have a strong command of the grammar and usage of spoken and written standard English to succeed academically and professionally," and "Furthermore, in the twenty-first century, students must be able to communicate effectively in a wide range of print and digital texts, each of which may require different grammatical and usage choices to be effective" (p. 29).

Although language standards focus on the essential rules of standard and formal written and spoken English, by and large, language is seen as a matter of craft and informed linguistic choices. Realistically speaking, however, students are typically more interested in finishing their tasks and assignments on time and with a modicum of effort (Kinsella, 2012) than undertaking to use nuance or embracing the notion that "language choice is a matter of craft."

Vocabulary learning, with its own set of standards, centers on understanding words and phrases, their relationships, figurative language (metaphors), and nuances of meaning, as well as learning new vocabulary, particularly general academic and domain-specific words and phrases.

Anchor Standards for Language

The overall goal of Language Anchor Standards is stated clearly (p. 25):

> To build a foundation for college and career readiness in language, students must gain control over many conventions of standard English grammar, usage, and mechanics as well as learn other ways to use language to convey meaning effectively. They must also be able to determine or clarify the meaning of grade-appropriate words encountered through listening, reading, and media use; come to appreciate that words have nonliteral meanings, shades of meaning, and relationships to other words; and expand their vocabulary in the course of studying content. The inclusion of Language standards in their own strand should not be taken as an indication that skills related to conventions, effective language use, and vocabulary are unimportant to reading, writing, speaking, and listening; indeed, they are inseparable from such contexts.

Anchor Standards for Language (see Table 2.5) includes six College and Career Readiness standards, organized into three areas:

- Conventions of standard English
- Knowledge of language
- Vocabulary acquisition and use

As with all other Anchor Standards, the College and Career Readiness benchmarks represent the basis for all grade-level standards. These benchmarks place a

TABLE 2.5 Language Anchor Standards in the Common Core

[For teaching principles and techniques, see chapters 7 and 8.]

Conventions of Standard English

What's Valued: Conventions of Standard English Grammar and Punctuation

Demonstrate command of the conventions of standard English grammar and usage when writing or speaking.

Demonstrate command of the conventions of standard English capitalization, punctuation, and spelling when writing.

Knowledge of Language

What's Valued: Understanding and Using Context-Appropriate Language

Apply knowledge of language to understand how language functions in different contexts, to make effective choices for meaning or style, and to comprehend more fully when reading or listening.

Vocabulary Acquisition and Use

What's Valued: Extensive Academic and Domain-Specific Vocabulary, and Metaphors

Determine or clarify the meaning of unknown and multiple-meaning words and phrases by using context clues, analyzing meaningful word parts, and consulting general and specialized reference materials, as appropriate.

Demonstrate understanding of figurative language, word relationships, and nuances in word meanings.

Acquire and use accurately a range of general academic and domain-specific words and phrases sufficient for reading, writing, speaking, and listening at the college and career readiness level; demonstrate independence in gathering vocabulary knowledge when encountering an unknown term important to comprehension or expression.

---

great deal of importance on the development and use of general academic and domain-specific vocabulary.

Describing academic language, its uses, and its functions is an old undertaking in pedagogy and linguistics. The Common Core Standards, and particularly the Language Anchor Standards, constitute one more attempt to determine what the component parts of academic language are and what level of academic language proficiency can be expected of high school graduates.

For ELLs, the demands outlined in the Anchor Standards for Language are formidable, as they concern general and discipline-specific academic language uses. The degree of language functionality expected in the Standards entails sophisticated applications, such as advanced grammar uses, making effective and well-suited vocabulary choices, and developing an appropriate linguistic style. Obtaining advanced language proficiency requires curricula and pedagogy that establish meaningful and carefully designed progressions that can enable learners to build language knowledge and skills.

ELLs come from a wide variety of ethnic, linguistic, economic, cultural, social, and educational backgrounds. At present, however, teachers of ELLs do not have a great deal of appropriate training required to meet learners' language needs and to promote the growth of foundational academic knowledge. According to Samson and Collins (2012, p. 12), for example, "teachers must have strong knowledge of . . . language development, and particularly academic language used in instruction."

For instance, according to a report by the National Council on Teacher Quality, more than 75% of elementary teacher-preparation programs do not provide relevant or sufficient training for working specifically with ELLs (Greenberg, McKee, & Walsh, 2013). The report also points out that, among the states with large numbers of ELL populations, only 35% of California's teacher education programs devote sufficient amount of training to ELL literacy instruction and only 15% of New York State's teacher preparation programs provide the education needed to meet the Anchor Standards for Language in the case of ELLs.

Grade 5 and Grades 11–12 Language Benchmarks

What is unusual about the Language Anchor Standards for Grade 5 is that they require specific knowledge of language and about language as a subject, in addition to the requirements for language usage as a skill. The Standards for **explicit knowledge about language** concern three main areas among "the conventions of standard English":

- Various aspects of grammar (e.g., prepositions, conjunctions, and verb tenses)
- Punctuation and capitalization
- Expanding and combining sentences, as well as comparing and contrasting dialects and registers

The Standards that demand explicit knowledge about language are accompanied by additional requirements for knowledge of academic vocabulary and figurative language (pp. 28–29):

- "Determine or clarify the meaning of unknown and multiple-meaning words and phrases based on grade 5 reading and content, choosing flexibly from a range of strategies."
- "Demonstrate understanding of figurative language, word relationships, and nuances in word meanings."

In Grade 5, all ELA students, including ELLs, are expected to achieve the Language Standards (CCSS, ELA, L.5.1–6). The Language Standards for Grade 5 (L.5.1–6) are presented in Table 2.6.

The Standards strongly emphasize the knowledge and usage of standard—albeit sometimes relatively unimportant—grammar rules, as well as academic vocabulary. There are no definitions or guidelines regarding what represents grade-appropriate Greek and Latin affixes and roots or grade-appropriate general

TABLE 2.6 Language Standards for Grade 5

[For teaching principles and techniques, see chapters 7, 8, and 9.]

Conventions of Standard English

What's Valued: Explicit Knowledge about Standard Grammar and Selected Constructions, and Punctuation

Demonstrate command of the conventions of standard English grammar and usage when writing or speaking.
- Explain the function of conjunctions, prepositions, and interjections in general and their function in particular sentences.
- Form and use the perfect (e.g., *I had walked; I have walked; I will have walked*) verb tenses.
- Use verb tense to convey various times, sequences, states, and conditions.
- Recognize and correct inappropriate shifts in verb tense.
- Use correlative conjunctions (e.g., *either/or, neither/nor*)."

Demonstrate command of the conventions of standard English capitalization, punctuation, and spelling when writing.
- Use punctuation to separate items in a series.
- Use a comma to separate an introductory element from the rest of the sentence.
- Use a comma to set off the words yes and no (e.g., *Yes, thank you*), to set off a tag question from the rest of the sentence (e.g., *It's true, isn't it?*), and to indicate direct address (e.g., *Is that you, Steve?*).
- Use underlining, quotation marks, or italics to indicate titles of works.
- Spell grade-appropriate words correctly . . .

Knowledge of Language

What's Valued: Knowledge of Language Conventions and Sentence Structure

Use knowledge of language and its conventions when writing, speaking, reading, or listening.
- Expand, combine, and reduce sentences for meaning, reader/listener interest, and style.
- Compare and contrast the varieties of English (e.g., *dialects, registers*) used in stories, dramas, or poems.

Vocabulary Acquisition and Use

What's Valued: Extensive Academic and Domain-Specific Vocabulary & Metaphors

Determine or clarify the meaning of unknown and multiple-meaning words and phrases based on grade 5 reading and content, choosing flexibly from a range of strategies.
- Use context (e.g., *cause/effect relationships and comparisons in text*) as a clue to the meaning of a word or phrase.
- Use common, grade-appropriate Greek and Latin affixes and roots as clues to the meaning of a word (e.g., *photo-graph, photo-syn-thesis*).

Demonstrate understanding of figurative language, word relationships, and nuances in word meanings.
- Interpret figurative language, including similes and metaphors, in context.
- Recognize and explain the meaning of common idioms, adages, and proverbs.
- Use the relationship between particular words (e.g., *synonyms, antonyms, homographs*) to better understand each of the words.

Acquire and use accurately grade-appropriate general academic and domain-specific words and phrases, including those that signal contrast, addition, and other logical relationships (e.g., *however, although, nevertheless, similarly, moreover, in addition*).

academic and domain-specific words and phrases. However, a large number of lists and work-sheets on all manner of Greek and Latin affixes and roots are available online free of charge or for purchase.

These work-sheets include parts of words that range from *in-/un-* (not) to *omni-* (all—*all things, ways, and places*) to *-orium* (*forming nouns denoting a place for a particular function—auditorium*, but possibly not *moratorium*, which is not a place). Speculation is often heard that what constitutes grade-appropriate Greek and Latin affixes and roots or grade-appropriate general academic vocabulary may be easier to identify only in retrospect, depending on what items appear on the assessments.

The Language Standards clearly place the heaviest burden of grammar, punctuation, and spelling instruction on Grades 1–5 teachers. Given the degree of specificity regarding what constructions to teach and at what grade, the only aspect of instruction not addressed in the Standard is how to do it.

> Since the rationale for acquiring explicit knowledge about specific language constructions is not provided, unfortunately, it is unclear why these constructions were selected for learning in Grades 1–5.

Some of the selected constructions, such as the future perfect tense (e.g., *will have walked*), are actually dated and rarely found in Standard American English (Hinkel, 2004, 2013).

A great deal of research has demonstrated that, for both L1 and L2 learners, the range of academic vocabulary and expanding the vocabulary base play a vital role across all language skills, and especially in reading (see an extensive discussion in chapter 7). In simple terms, without a solid vocabulary base, it may be impossible to learn well at school.

However, what is surprising is that the "rules" of standard English, and particularly its elements, such as capitalization, punctuation, and spelling, seem to occupy higher priority on the Standards than vocabulary acquisition. Whether this order of priorities has any curricular and instructional implications remains to be seen (IRACCSS, 2012).

The separation of vocabulary learning and use into its own Standard also represents a significant shift in the curricular and instructional perspective currently adopted in many English-speaking settings. Since at least the 1970s, the explicit, direct, and focused teaching and learning of vocabulary has been largely abandoned in favor of "picking up" vocabulary (also called *incidental learning*) in the context of other instructional or language-related activities, such as reading or listening (Krashen, 1993, 1994, 2003; Nagy, Anderson, & Herman, 1987; Nagy, Herman, & Anderson, 1985).

During those decades, many vocabulary specialists have continued to demonstrate by means of research that incidental vocabulary learning is slow, sporadic, unsystematic, and ineffective (Laufer & Hulstijn, 2001; Nation, 2013; Rott, 2000). However, despite this large body of evidence, instructional biases in favor of contextual vocabulary learning have remained dominant in curricular thinking.

> The Common Core Standards reflect an enormous change in how vocabulary learning is seen and done in the context of schooling: from incidental to direct explicit instruction.

To be sure, the development of learners' vocabulary base is still considered to be a part of language usage in other school domains, such as reading, math, history, and science.

It appears that the long-standing emphasis on contextual incidental vocabulary learning is now much diminished. The old claim that engaging in extensive reading can lead to a steady growth of vocabulary knowledge has all but disappeared, and particularly so with the new emphasis on reading for information and writing from research and sources.

Action Point

Frequent words (e.g., *line, circle*) are easy to learn because they occur in daily conversations. On the other hand, academic vocabulary is less frequent, and it occurs predominantly in more formal (but not necessarily strictly academic) speech and writing. Domain-specific vocabulary is words and phrases that are used in specialized texts, such as math (e.g., *perpendicular, fraction*), the sciences (e.g., *glacier, femur*), or history (e.g., *pharaoh, musket*).

For teachers, the ability to identify the differences between the three types of vocabulary is important. Most educated speakers of any language can usually identify conversational, general academic, and domain-specific vocabulary based on their own experience. In the text below, classify words and phrases according to the three types of vocabulary. There is probably more than one possible classification for some words.

Weather is the state of the atmosphere, to the degree that it is hot or cold, wet or dry, calm or stormy, clear or cloudy. Weather has effects on humans in different situations and locations. Therefore, weather is something people often communicate about. Weather is driven by air pressure (temperature and moisture) differences between one place and another. These pressure and temperature differences can occur due to the sun angle at any particular spot, which varies by latitude from the tropics.

> On Earth, common weather phenomena include wind, cloud, rain, snow, fog, and dust storms. Weather forecasting is the application of science and technology to predict the state of the atmosphere for a future time and a given location. There are a variety of end users to weather forecasts. Weather warnings are important forecasts because they are used to protect life and property.
>
> Forecasts based on temperature and precipitation are important to agriculture. Temperature forecasts are used by utility companies to estimate demand over coming days. On an everyday basis, people use weather forecasts to determine what to wear on a given day. Since outdoor activities are severely curtailed by heavy rain, snow and the wind chill, forecasts can be used to plan activities around these events, and to plan ahead and survive them. (Adapted from http://en.wikipedia.org/wiki/Weather)
>
> Compare your findings with those of your colleagues. What may be the reasons for various vocabulary classifications?

In Grades 11–12, all ELA students, including ELLs, are expected to achieve the Language Standards (CCSS, ELA, L.11–2.1–6). A summary of the Grades 11–12 Standards is presented in Table 2.7.

To implement vocabulary instruction required by the Standards, it is the teacher's job to identify what academic vocabulary needs to be taught and learned. Fortunately, after many decades of research, currently, a great deal is known about general academic and domain-specific vocabulary commonly encountered in schooling and education. See chapter 7 for details on vocabulary instruction.

> Now that academic vocabulary has once again become an important focus of teaching and the Standards, academic vocabulary instruction needs to take place throughout all grades and across all curricular areas.

TABLE 2.7 Summary of the Language Standards, Grades 11–12

[For teaching principles and techniques, see chapters 7, 8, and 9.]

Conventions of Standard English

<u>What's Valued: Grammar and Punctuation of Standard English</u>

Demonstrate command of the conventions of standard English grammar and usage when writing or speaking.

- Apply the understanding that usage is a matter of convention, can change over time, and is sometimes contested.

- Resolve issues of complex or contested usage, consulting references.

(Continued)

TABLE 2.7 (Continued)

Demonstrate command of the conventions of standard English capitalization, punctuation, and spelling when writing.

- Observe hyphenation conventions.
- Spelling

Knowledge of Language

<u>What's Valued: Understanding and Using Grammar in Context</u>

Apply knowledge of language to understand how language functions in different contexts, to make effective choices for meaning or style, and to comprehend more fully when reading or listening.

- Vary syntax for effect, consulting references as needed; apply an understanding of syntax to the study of complex texts when reading.

Vocabulary Acquisition and Use

<u>What's Valued: Extensive Academic Vocabulary, Word Forms, and Metaphors</u>

Determine or clarify the meaning of unknown and multiple-meaning words and phrases based on reading and content, choosing flexibly from a range of strategies.

- Use context (e.g., the overall meaning of a sentence, paragraph, or text; a word's position or function in a sentence) as a clue to the meaning of a word or phrase.
- Identify and correctly use patterns of word form changes that indicate different meanings or parts of speech (e.g., *conceive, conception, conceivable*).
- Consult general and specialized reference materials to find the pronunciation of a word or to determine or clarify its precise meaning, its part of speech, its etymology, or its standard usage.
- Verify the preliminary determination of the meaning of a word or phrase.

Demonstrate understanding of figurative language, word relationships, and nuances in word meanings.

- Interpret figures of speech (e.g., hyperbole, paradox) in context and analyze their role in the text.
- Analyze nuances in the meaning of words with similar denotations.

Acquire and use accurately general academic and domain-specific words and phrases, sufficient for reading, writing, speaking, and listening at the college and career readiness level; demonstrate independence in gathering vocabulary knowledge when considering a word or phrase important to comprehension or expression.

Talking Shop

Metaphors and figurative language are famously culture-bound and can be incomprehensible outside the language and culture in which they are used. A few metaphors and figures of speech from various languages are listed below. See if you can figure out—at least approximately—what these expressions might mean. The answer key is provided later in this chapter.

1. Skillful hawks hide their talons. (Japanese)
2. Teaching is carving a jade. (Chinese)
3. There's no truth in one's feet. (Russian)
4. Water beneath hay. (Arabic)
5. A word becomes a seed. (Korean)
6. Things are looking up. (English)

Metaphors and figure of speech are words or phrases for one thing (e.g., a hawk) that is used to refer to another thing (e.g., a person) in order to show or suggest that they are similar. Metaphors are so numerous that most L1 users of any language do not even notice them.

What types of teaching suggestions can you come up with (note that this is a metaphor) to explain to L2 learners how to use them in their writing? Can you think of a few examples?

In 1984, Nagy and Anderson published their highly regarded study to create a reliable estimate of how many words there are in print school books. To obtain a good estimate, they investigated a compilation of the words occurring in books and other printed materials used by children in Grades 3–9. As a result of their study, Nagy and Anderson concluded that printed school English contains about 88,000 word families (e.g., *word, words, wording, wordy* comprise one word family).

According to Graves, August, and Mancilla-Martinez (2012), as a follow-up to the original study, Nagy and Herman (1987) recalibrated earlier estimates and concluded that 3rd-graders have a reading vocabulary range of 10,000 words, on average, and that high school graduates have average reading vocabularies of about 40,000 words. Nagy and Herman also indicated that L1 schoolchildren learn approximately 3,000 words each year. More recent estimates, based on a synthesis of research since the 1980s, are that average 12th-graders' vocabulary is along the lines of 50,000 word families and that school-age learners add from 3,000 to 4,000 words each year.

Most ELLs have much smaller vocabularies when they begin their schooling. Thus, many ELLs start with a significant disadvantage, not to mention that there is a great deal of variability in ELLs' vocabulary ranges depending on their L1s, education levels, and socio-economic backgrounds. As has been mentioned earlier in this chapter, only 2% of ELLs who are "far off track" in their reading skills can and do catch up to their grade-level reading.

There is no doubt that the overarching goal of the schooling and CCSS is to provide ELLs as many opportunities as possible to develop a solid vocabulary base before they finish their education.

> For ELLs, the vocabulary learning burden (Nation, 1990) at school is enormous. And there's not a moment to lose.

> Answer Key to Metaphors and Figures of Speech
>
> 1. People who are modest hide their great talents.
> 2. Teaching is a laborious, slow, intensive, but rewarding process that requires great deal of skill.
> 3. Take a seat and get off your feet.
> 4. Someone or something appears solid on the surface but is not trustworthy.
> 5. What you say is what you get.
> 6. The situation is improving.

Common Core Standards for ELLs

In the Common Core, the development of language skills represents a separate area of learning Standards that all school-age learners are expected to attain. One of the fundamental elements of CCSS is that all learners, including ELLs, have to have writing skills and language capacities to understand and apply the content of instructional materials in a range of academic subjects, such as ELA, math, and science. To put it another way, ELLs need to attain sufficient language proficiency to work with the content of schooling.

The document titled *Application of Common Core State Standards for English Language Learners* (CCSS, 2010), which is not very elaborate, consists of two and a half pages on both English and math. It states that "the development of native-like proficiency in English takes many years and will not be achieved by all ELLs, especially if they start schooling in the US in the later grades" (p. 1). The text additionally points out that "Teachers should recognize that it is possible to achieve the standards for reading and literature, writing & research, language development and speaking & listening without manifesting native-like control of conventions and vocabulary."

In all, CCSS stipulates that the standards apply to all students, who must meet "rigorous grade-level expectations in the areas of speaking, listening, reading, and writing to prepare all students to be college and career ready, including English language learners." Further, L2 learners "also will benefit from instruction . . . so they are able to participate on equal footing with native speakers in all aspects of social, economic, and civic endeavors." It seems pretty clear that not much practical information can be found specifically in regard to what and how L2 learners need to be taught and what they need to learn to attain the language proficiency expected in the Common Core Standards.

In many cases, ELLs can be fully or highly proficient in casual daily conversations and have highly developed interactional skills. However, the language required for conversational interactions with peers or family members represents only a fraction of that needed for school learning that entails a great deal of reading and writing academic text.

> In the case of most ELLs, academic language requires intensive, extensive, and systematic instruction because it does not occur in daily interactions and conversational exchanges. Without academic language elements, such as grammar, vocabulary, and punctuation, it is not possible for these learners to read, achieve the knowledge of the content, or produce written academic prose.

When it comes to vocabulary teaching and learning, a number studies have demonstrated that although ELL vocabulary ranges are typically two to three years behind L1 students, their growth rates are similar to and may even surpass those of L1 school-age learners (Mancilla-Martinez & Lesaux, 2011b).

> It is absolutely vital that ELLs receive early, systematic, and intensive vocabulary instruction to enable them to catch up. The ultimate goal of vocabulary learning at school is to enable them to take advantage of grade-appropriate instruction in the content and subject areas (Graves et al., 2012).

The Standards place a great deal of emphasis on developing students' academic language skills. The Language benchmarks focus almost entirely on grammar, sentence structure, and academic vocabulary and linguistic devices (e.g., figurative language and metaphors) of standard English.

The CCSS requirements of all students include two main learning foci:

- The academic content and school subjects.
- The development of academic proficiency in spoken and written English, without which the Standards cannot be achieved.

> The greatest challenge for ELLs is that the learning of the academic language and the academic content need to take place intensively and simultaneously.

The Common Core State Standards for the ELA represent a major shift in the philosophy and focus of school education in the United States. These standards mark the emergence of foundationally and qualitatively different social expectations of ELLs, together with other school learners.

Teaching ELLs and providing them with opportunities to learn and accomplish the learning goals outlined in the Standards requires significant shifts in teacher education and educational practices at all levels of school curriculum and instruction. As Silva (1993) puts it, ELLs need more of everything: the development of academic speaking skills, oral and pronunciation skills, reading fluency and comprehension, grammar, vocabulary, and writing. All that—in addition to learning academic literacy and content. ELLs also need excellent, well-prepared, and high quality teachers.

> An educational shift of this magnitude requires a significant re-thinking of teacher education and teacher-education programs to provide teachers with the necessary knowledge and skills as well as the essential materials and technology.

The necessary components of ELL classroom instruction must include the following objectives in each and every lesson (Coleman & Goldenberg, 2012):

- Specific learning objectives for language and content
- Clear, understandable, focused, and systematic instruction
- Varied teaching techniques and materials, including visuals to aid comprehension
- Suitable and grade-appropriate reading materials
- Practice, practice, and more practice

Chapter Summary

The Common Core Standards represent the greatest philosophical and practical shift in schooling and education in the country in the past century. The Standards are a set of learning goals and guidelines, but they are not a curriculum. The impact of the Standards on the population of the United States cannot be overestimated.

In addition to the foundations for the Common Core Standards in writing and the attendant language skills, the NAEP framework, adopted in the Standards, promotes three types of texts and writing skills: **to persuade, to explain,** and **to convey real or imagined experience**. These are the simplest pointers to the types of student writing and text.

What Is Valued in Student Writing in Schooling and in the Common Core:

- Text types and purposes—argumentation, information/explanation, and some narrative
- Writing attributes—clarity, standard academic organization, research, evidence, and more evidence
- Students' skills—editing, technology, collaboration, and writing from sources

What Is Valued in Student Language in Schooling and in the Common Core:

- Grammar and punctuation of standard English, as well as some knowledge of sentence structure
- Formal and informal language uses in appropriate context
- Extensive academic and disciplinary vocabulary and metaphors
- More academic grammar and vocabulary—as much as possible

Notes

1 ACT, founded in 1959, was originally an acronym that stood for American College Testing. However, in 1996, the name of the organization was changed to simply ACT to account for its changing focus and function.
2 In CCSS, the learning goals for Grades 9–10 and Grades 11–12 are grouped to cover a period of two years each.

Further Reading

Bex, T., & Watts, R. (1999). *Standard English: The widening debate*. London: Routledge.
Blau, S. (2006). College writing, academic literacy, and the intellectual community: California dreams and cultural oppositions. In P. Sullivan & H. Tinberg (Eds.), *What is "college-level" writing?* (pp. 358–377). Urbana, IL: NCTE.
Christensen, L. (1990). Teaching standard English: Whose standard? *The English Journal, 79*(2), 36–40.
Coxhead, A. (2000). The new academic word list. *TESOL Quarterly, 34,* 213–238.
Edwards, D., & Mercer, N. (1987). *Common knowledge: The development of understanding in the classroom*. London: Methuen.
ICAS. (2002). *Academic literacy: A statement of competencies expected of students entering California's public colleges and universities*. Sacramento, CA: Intersegmental Committee of the Academic Senates of California Colleges and Universities.

Kendall, J. (2011). *Understanding Common Core State Standards*. Alexandria, VA: Association for Supervision & Curriculum Development.
Liu, D. (2012). The most frequently-used multi-word constructions in academic written English: A multi-corpus study. *English for Specific Purposes, 31*, 25–35.
Rothman, R. (2011). *Something in common: The Common Core Standards and the next chapter in American education*. Cambridge, MA: Harvard University Press.
Zwiers, J. (2014). *Building academic language: Meeting Common Core Standards across disciplines, Grades 5–12* (2nd ed.). San Francisco: Jossey-Bass.
Zwiers, J., O'Hara, S., & Pritchard, R. (2014). *Common Core Standards in diverse classrooms: Essential practices for developing academic language and disciplinary literacy*. Portland, ME: Stenhouse.

References

ACT. (2010). *A first look at the common core and college and career readiness*. Iowa City, IA: Author.
ACT. (2013). *The condition of college and career readiness 2013* [On-line]. Retrieved from www.act.org/research/policymakers/cccr13/pdf/CCCR13-NationalReadinessRpt.pdf
Addison, J., & McGee, S. (2010). Writing in high school/Writing in College: Research trends and future directions. *College Composition and Communication, 62*(1), 147–179.
Applebee, A. (1981). *Writing in the secondary school*. Urbana, IL: National Council of Teachers of English.
Applebee, A. (1983). *A study of writing in the secondary school*. Urbana, IL: National Council of Teachers of English.
Chastain, K. (1990). Characteristics of graded and ungraded compositions. *Modern Language Journal, 74*, 10–14.
Christensen, L. (1990). Teaching standard English: Whose standard? *The English Journal, 79*(2), 36–40.
Coleman, R., & Goldenberg, C. (2012). The common core challenge for English language learners. *Principal Leadership, 12*(1), 46–51.
Common Core State Standards. (2010). Retrieved from www.corestandards.org/
Dougherty, C. (2014). *Catching up to college and career readiness: The challenge is greater for at-risk students*. Iowa City, IA: ACT.
Gallagher, K. (2006). *Teaching adolescent writers*. Portland, ME: Stenhouse.
Graff, G., & Birkenstein-Graff, C. (2009). An immodest proposal for connecting high school and college. *College Composition and Communication, 61*(1), 409–416.
Graves, M., August, D., & Mancilla-Martinez, J. (2012). *Teaching vocabulary to English-language learners*. New York: Teachers College Press.
Greenberg, J., McKee, A., & Walsh, K. (2013). *Teacher prep review: A review of the nation's teacher preparation programs*. Washington, DC: National Council on Teacher Quality.
Hairston, M. (1982). The winds of change: Thomas Kuhn and the revolution in the teaching of writing. *College Composition and Communication, 33*, 76–88.
Hairston, M. (1986). On not being a composition slave. In C. W. Bridges (Ed.), *Training the new teacher of college composition* (pp. 117–124). Urbana, IL: NCTE.
Hinkel, E. (2004). *Teaching academic ESL writing: Practical techniques in vocabulary and grammar*. Mahwah, NJ: Lawrence Erlbaum Associates.
Hinkel, E. (2013). Research findings on teaching grammar for academic writing. *English Teaching, 68*(4), 3–21.

International Reading Association Common Core State Standards (CCSS) Committee. (2012). *Literacy implementation guidance for the ELA Common Core State Standards* [On-line]. Retrieved from www.reading.org/Libraries/association-documents/ira_ccss_guidelines.pdf

Jago, C. (2011). *With rigor for all: Meeting Common Core Standards for reading literature* (2nd ed.). Portsmouth, NH: Heinemann.

Kendall, J. (2011). *Understanding Common Core State Standards.* Alexandria, VA: Association for Supervision & Curriculum Development.

Kinsella, K. (2012). Cutting to the Common Core: Communicating on the same wavelength. *Language Magazine, XX,* 18–25.

Knoblauch, C., &Brannon, L. (1984). *Rhetorical traditions and the teaching of writing.* Upper Montclair, NJ: Boynton/Cook.

Krashen, S. (1993). *The power of reading.* Englewood, CO: Libraries Unlimited.

Krashen, S. (1994). The pleasure hypothesis. In J. Alatis (Ed.), *Georgetown University round table on languages and linguistics* (pp. 299–322). Washington, DC: Georgetown University Press.

Krashen, S. (2003). *Explorations in language acquisition and use.* Portsmouth: Heinemann.

Laufer, B., & Hulstijn, J. (2001). Incidental vocabulary acquisition in a second language: The construct of task-induced involvement. *Applied Linguistics, 22*(1), 1–26.

Mancilla-Martinez, J., & Lesaux, N. K. (2011a). Early home language use and later vocabulary development. *Journal of Educational Psychology, 103,* 535–546.

Mancilla-Martinez, J., & Lesaux, N. K. (2011b). The gap between Spanish-Speakers' word reading and word knowledge: A longitudinal study. *Child Development, 82,* 1544–1560.

McLaughlin, M., Glaab, L., & Carrasco, H. (2014). *Implementing Common Core State Standards in California: A report from the field.* Palo Alto, CA: California State Department of Education.

Nagy, W., & Anderson, R. (1984). How many words are there in printed school English? *Reading Research Quarterly, 19,* 304–330.

Nagy, W., Anderson, R., & Herman, P. (1987). Learning word meanings from context during normal reading. *American Educational Research Journal, 24,* 237–270.

Nagy, W., & Herman, P. A. (1987). Breadth and depth of vocabulary knowledge: Implications for acquisition and instruction. In M. McKeown & M. Curtis (Eds.), *The nature of vocabulary acquisition* (pp. 19–59). Hillsdale, NJ: Erlbaum.

Nagy, W., Herman, P. A., & Anderson, R. (1985). Learning words from context. *Reading Research Quarterly, 20,* 233–253.

Nation, I. S. P. (2013). *Learning vocabulary in another language* (2nd ed.). Cambridge: Cambridge University Press.

National Assessment of Educational Progress. (2011). *Writing framework for the 2011 National Assessment of Educational Progress. Washington, D.C.: National Assessment Governing Board, U.S. Department of Education* [On-line]. Retrieved from www.nagb.org/content/nagb/assets/documents/publications/frameworks/writing-2011.pdf

National Center for Education Statistics. (2011). *The Nation's Report Card: Writing 2011.* Washington, DC: Author. Retrieved from http://nces.ed.gov/nationsreportcard/pdf/main2011/2012470.pdf

National Center for Education Statistics (2013). *The Nation's Report Card: A first look: 2013 Mathematics and Reading* (NCES 2014-451). Washington, DC: Institute of Education Sciences, U.S. Department of Education,

National Governors Association (NGA) & Council of Chief State School Officers (CCSSO). (2010a). *Common Core State Standards for English Language Arts & Literacy in History/Social Studies, Science, and Technical Subjects.* Washington, DC: Author.

National Governors Association (NGA) & Council of Chief State School Officers (CCSS). (2010b).Common Core State Standards Key Considerations. Washington, DC: Author.

Palacios, M., Casserly, M., & Corcoran, A. (2013). *Implementing the Common Core State Standards: Year two progress report from the Great City Schools.* Washington, DC: Council of the Great City Schools.

Rott, S. (2000). Relationships between the process of reading, word inferencing, and incidental word acquisition, in assigning meaning to form. In J. Lee & A. Valdman (Eds.), *Form and meaning: Multiple perspectives* (pp. 255–282). Boston: Heinle & Heinle.

Samson, J., & Collins, B. (2012). *Preparing all teachers to meet the needs of English Language Learners: Applying research to policy and practice for teacher effectiveness.* Washington, DC: Center for American Progress.

Silva, T. (1993). Toward an understanding of the distinct nature of L2 writing: The ESL research and its implications. *TESOL Quarterly, 27,* 657-677.

Slater, C. (1982). Writing: The experience of one school district. *Journal of Reading, 26*(1), 24–32.

Stewart, M., & Leaman, H. (1983). Teachers' writing assessments across the high school curriculum. *Research in the Teaching of English, 17*(2), 113–125.

Sullivan, P., & Tinberg, H. (Eds). (2006). *What is "college-level" writing?* Urbana, IL: NCTE.

Sullivan, P., Tinberg, H., & Blau, S. (Eds.). (2010). *What is "college-level" writing?* Urbana, IL: NCTE.

Zwiers, J., O'Hara, S., & Pritchard, R. (2014). *Common Core Standards in diverse classrooms: Essential practices for developing academic language and disciplinary literacy.* Portland, ME: Stenhouse.

3
WHAT'S VALUED IN COLLEGE AND UNIVERSITY ACADEMIC WRITING?

This chapter discusses:

- The findings of studies on typical student academic writing tasks
- The features of student writing, discourse, and text that are valued in the academy
- The types of writing and text that are not universally valued
- What the TOEFL rubrics actually mean in terms of student writing quality

Introduction

Since at least the 1980s, a large number of studies have investigated the types of writing and written assignments expected of students in colleges and universities and on standardized tests of L2 writing skills. All these studies report empirical data and findings that directly address a range of academic tasks and skills important in academic writing in colleges and universities in English-speaking countries, such as the U.S. and Canada. Some of these investigations pivot on narrowly focused data, and others are relatively broad in scope (e.g., Hale et al., 1996; Hinkel, 2005, 2011; Horowitz, 1986; ICAS, 2002; Rosenfeld, Leung, & Oltman, 2001). Still additional reports refer to the specific characteristics of student writing that are routinely evaluated on large-scale assessments and tests of writing abilities (e.g., Weigle, 2002). When it comes to the assessment and testing of writing, for instance, the elements of written discourse and text that are typically considered to be desirable or disadvantageous are relatively easy to identify because their scoring rubrics are widely disseminated. In this light, it is clear that the features of writing considered to be important in evaluations of L2 writing quality have to find their way into the curricula for teaching L2 writing.

The goal of this chapter is to provide a grounded perspective on what is valued or not valued in student academic writing in colleges and universities and on assessments in the U.S. and Canada. To begin, a review of the findings of three broad-based reports takes a detailed look at the written assignments commonly required of students in a diverse array of academic disciplines, including humanities, the fine arts, natural sciences, and engineering, as well as in general education courses. Then the discussion moves to the discourse and language skills required to produce satisfactory academic prose at the college and university level. Like the overview of the academic assignments, the overview of the requisite incremental writing skills reports on the findings of four empirical studies, which together encompass over 60 U.S. and Canadian universities. In keeping with its overall purpose, the chapter also considers the criteria for evaluating student writing on international standardized tests, such as the Writing Section in the Test of English as a Foreign Language (TOEFL) iBT and the TOEFL Test of Written English (TWE). The two distinct TOEFL tests of writing evolved as an outcome of two different means for test delivery: TOEFL iBT is Internet-based while TWE is a component of the paper-based version. Further distinctions between them are discussed later in the chapter.

Academic Writing Tasks and Student Texts

In 1982, a few decades ago, Arthur Applebee (1982) undertook a study of the incremental skills emphasized in school writing in the 9th- and 11th-grade classrooms (i.e., when students prepare for admission to college/university), in six subject areas: English, science, social science, math, business education, and foreign language. Applebee's study took place in two high schools during an entire school year, logging in about 300 hours of instruction. To confirm his original findings, Applebee also sent out questionnaires to 200 principals nationwide to request that the best teachers in the six subject areas comment on the ways writing was taught in their classes. Applebee's findings are as follows (pp. 372–374):

- The primary purpose of academic writing dealt directly with "evaluation of subject-area learning," with the greatest attention being devoted to relevant information "synthesized through lectures and textbooks."
- Written language skills at the word and sentence level were extensively underscored by teachers in all subject areas.
- Information (discourse) organization skills took up less attention and instruction than the elements of language work in terms of time and effort.

In academic writing in the disciplinary courses, little seems to have changed since Applebee's study took place.

Although not directly relevant to the focus on the writing skills in this overview, the findings of the studies on the most important factors in students' academic survival still place knowledge of the subject matter above all other considerations. The recurrent themes in faculty surveys (such as those summarized in Tables 3.1

and 3.2 later in the chapter) point directly to the following essential gauges of academic performance:

1. Students must have close familiarity with the content of their courses, pay detailed attention to the material, and come to class prepared.
2. Written work serves as an almost universal measure of students' level of understanding of the course material.
3. The quality of the written product (i.e., content organization, grammatical accuracy and polish, and academic vocabulary) is commonly interpreted as a reflection of students' attitudes to the class and about learning.

In regard to the quality of students' language specifically, the Intersegmental California Academic Senate (ICAS, 2002, p. 22) report, for instance, sums up the results of its broad-based faculty survey across California's 109 colleges and 33 universities: "Students must use varied sentence structure, appropriate vocabulary for an academic audience, and produce finished and edited papers that follow standard English conventions of grammar, capitalization, punctuation, and spelling, and are relatively free of error" (p. 22).

Currently, it is an established fact that a majority of undergraduates and many graduate students in U.S. colleges and universities are likely to be poorly prepared for their academic writing tasks. For instance, as noted, the report ICAS (2002) prepared by the joint Academic Senate state-wide indicates this explicitly:

> "Only 1/3 of entering college students are sufficiently prepared for the two most frequently assigned writing tasks: analyzing information ... and synthesizing information from several sources" (ICAS, 2002, p. 4). These findings are closely aligned with those identified in the ACT study of 256,765 test takers in various states (see chapter 2).

Many ESL teachers and faculty in the disciplines recognize that at practically all levels of instruction, academic writing is integral to the learning process in colleges and universities. As was noted in chapter 2, the purpose of academic writing, beginning at least in middle school, is to display knowledge, and in schooling, students' written work represents the crucial means of measuring and evaluating their understanding of what is taught. To succeed in the academy, students have to be prepared to display their knowledge of the course material in their assignments that are at the core of their studies (Christie, 1998; Schleppegrell, 2004). That is, in their secondary and post-secondary schooling alike, students are required to take courses in a wide range of disciplines, such as the sciences or the humanities, when they need to read widely and produce large amounts of academic writing.

Practically all course assignments consist of more than one writing task. For example, a brief exposition in the introduction can lead to an analysis, possibly with a cause/effect rhetorical structure, and followed by a summary in the conclusion. All formats of academic writing require information structuring, paraphrasing, and restatement skills, as well as a passable command of relevant vocabulary and sentence structure.

The findings of the three studies summarized in Table 3.1 below present an encompassing view of academic writing requirements in U.S. and Canadian colleges and universities. The first study (Hale et al., 1996), commissioned by the Educational Testing Service (ETS), surveyed academic writing tasks in eight universities and in such diverse disciplines as English, history, economics, chemistry, engineering, and computer science. The second (ICAS, 2002) reported the results of faculty surveys on the characteristics of academic literacy and writing abilities necessary for students in California post-secondary education systems, the only study of its kind. The third investigation does not deal with the particular lengths or types of students' written assignments; instead, it focuses on their rhetorical modes and academic task types.

TABLE 3.1 Academic Writing Tasks Required in North American Colleges and Universities

8 U.S./Canadian Universities (Hale et al., 1996)	California Universities (33) & Community Colleges (109) (ICAS, 2002)	33 U.S. Universities (Rosenfeld, Courtney, & Fowles, 2004)
Writing Tasks		
Essay 52% (5–10+ pp)	Long essays (8+ pp) 1–2/term	
Short tasks 46% (0.5–1 pp)	Short essays (4–6 pp) 2–3/term	
Report with interpretation 20% (3–10+ pp)	In-class essay exams 2–3/term	
Research paper 12% (9–10+ pp)		
Rhetorical modes		
Cause/effect 39%	Analysis 60%	Analysis/synthesis, from multiple sources (3.8 of 5)
Analysis 18%	Synthesis of info from several sources 58%	
Classification 16%	Factual description/short answer 50%	Extraction/summary of essential info (3.8 of 5)
Comp./contrast 11%	Brief summaries 38%	Observations (e.g., events, behaviors, experiments) (3.8 of 5)
Exemplification +definition 8%		
Not typically found in academic assignments		*Least important*
Process 6%	Personal info/essay 10% (Comp & Writing courses)	Persuasive writing, appeals to a reader's emotions, experiences, or values (2.2 of 5)
Argument 3%		
Narrative 0%		Descriptions/evaluations of rhetorical techniques (2.2 of 5)

The surveys of written assignments at the post-secondary level (Table 3.1) show that long papers of between 5 and 10 (or more) pages are a mainstay of the student writing requirements in humanities and social sciences courses, while extensive lab and experiment reports are required in the sciences. In many assignments, students are asked to carry out library research; extract and synthesize information from multiple sources; carry out interviews; produce reviews, annotations, and abstracts of published works; and submit business, project, or study proposals. Written assignments of varied lengths are required in practically all disciplines, including undergraduate and graduate courses in computer sciences, physics, mathematics, and engineering. Short writing assignments (e.g., computer program documentation or short answers) are significantly more frequent in undergraduate than graduate courses and more frequent in in-class than out-of-class assignments (Hale et al., 1996).

Typically, 30% of the final course grade in general education courses is based on the out-of-class assignments (ICAS, 2002). However, only 20% of the faculty who teach courses other than composition indicate that they provide assistance with assignments and instruction in research.

Types of Tasks in College and University Writing

A number of key factors about student assignments are immediately noticeable in Table 3.1. Regardless of whether a particular survey of the important writing skills was carried out in the mid-1990s or mid-2000s, the essential writing tasks expected of students remain very similar and consistent. Numerous researchers of the types of academic writing and the criteria for the evaluations of writing in the academy have actually commented that these have largely remained unchanged since at least the 1960s (e.g., Coffin et al., 2003; Curry & Lillis, 2004; ICAS, 2002; Jordan, 1997; Lea & Street, 1998).

Valued and Ubiquitous Writing Tasks in the Academy

- *Analytical writing* predominates in the academy. Around 60% of the faculty who participated in the Hale et al. (1996) study assigned analytical and causal analysis papers, as did a similar proportion of the respondents in the ICAS (2002) survey. According to the Rosenfield et al. (2004), a majority of teaching faculty in the U.S. see analytical/synthesis writing as crucial for academic success in their undergraduate classes (ranked 3.8 of 5, "very important").

- *Extracting information and summarizing important points* is also common when students work with texts (e.g., textbooks, supplemental articles, or additional readings): 38% of the faculty in the ICAS (2002) survey required brief summaries regularly. In general terms, many disciplinary faculty ranked extracting information from several sources as "very important" in academics (Rosenfield et al., 2004).

- ***Reports with or without interpretation*** (also called "descriptions of observations" or "factual descriptions" in various studies–e.g., of lab experiments, behaviors, or events) occupy an important place in academic student writing. These are noted in all three studies in Table 3.1 and are seen as important as analysis/synthesis or summative writing in terms of student academic success.

Another prominent finding, however, pertains to the types of writing that are hardly ever found in the academy, outside composition classes. These are extensively discussed in the three reports outlined in Table 3.1. In fact, the ICAS (2002, p. 23) report points to "a mismatch between students' preparation and the abilities needed to complete typical college writing tasks."

Writing Tasks NOT Common in the Academy

- ***Personal essay/information*** assignments are encountered predominantly in composition and English department courses, including writing courses.
- ***Argumentation essays,*** probably the most popular in English for Academic Purposes classes, rarely show up outside these and other composition assignments. The ICAS (2002, p. 23) report also specifically notes the prevalence of argumentation essays exclusively in composition classes, while "only about one-third of the students are sufficiently prepared" to write on analysis and synthesis tasks.
- ***Process descriptions*** are assigned by only 6% of the faculty who teach academic courses (Hale et al., 1996).
- ***Persuasive writing,*** likely taught in every L1 or L2 composition program in North America, is not considered to be important to students' success outside these courses.

On the whole, a great deal of agreement has been identified among the disciplinary faculty across the many dozens of institutions in the three studies. A majority commented that the following discourse/information organization elements are essential in students' written work (ICAS, 2002; Rosenfeld et al., 2004):

- An effective thesis
- Well-chosen examples

- Substantiated and logical reasoning
- A thorough examination of topic/issues

> In regard to L2 students specifically, the dominant view among the teaching faculty is that many of these "students are not prepared to meet college level academic demands": 64% of the faculty stated that L2 students experience difficulties in reading or writing at the college level (ICAS, 2002, p. 29).

Talking Shop

In your own experience as a student, what types of writing tasks have you been able to identify in your course work? When you write a course assignment or paper, how do you structure information to present your ideas or findings? If you have worked with others on group projects, what have you been able to observe in how your peers approach their writing tasks?

Action Point

Construct a questionnaire that you can use to gather written or spoken responses in, say, an email message or a scheduled interview. Ask 3 or 4 professors in your department or school regarding the types of written projects they assign in their courses and what their expectations are of student writing quality. Your questions can be relatively specific—e.g., do you expect that a piece of writing contains a thesis statement—or general—e.g., what do you consider to be good or not-so-good writing?

Analyze the responses you collect from the faculty and summarize the information in a way that allows you to make reasonable generalizations in terms of what in fact represents a common writing task, a good student paper, or high quality writing.

Academic Writing Skills: Discourse Organization and Language

To complement the focus on the prevalent types of writing and written assignments, the surveys (Table 3.1) also investigated the essential discourse and language abilities needed for a satisfactory completion of these writing tasks. While their findings on the specific writing skills are detailed in Table 3.2, a fourth investigation

TABLE 3.2 Discourse and Language Skills Valued or Not Valued in Academic Writing

8 U.S./Canadian Universities (Hale et al., 1996)	22 U.S./Canadian Universities (Rosenfeld et al., 2001)	California Universities (33) & Community Colleges (109) (ICAS, 2002)	33 U.S. Universities (Rosenfeld et al., 2004)
Most Important Discourse Skills (in declining order of importance)			
Thesis-driven writing. Specific and factual supporting info.	Organized writing that conveys major and supporting ideas. (4.19 of 5)	Effective thesis. Logical reasoning. Well-chosen examples.	Organized and coherent ideas/information. (4.1 of 5) Clear writing with smooth idea Transitions. (3.8 of 5)
Reasoned interpretation of facts (report with interpretation).	Relevant reasons and examples to support ideas. (4.09 of 5)	Structure ideas in a sustained way. Support main points with precise facts/examples.	Focused, supported discussion with relevant examples/reasoning. (3.8 of 5) Logical reasoning. (3.8 of 5)
Least Important Discourse Skills			
Summary/evaluation of readings.★ Definition/illustration. Unstructured writing (e.g., journals, observation notes).	Writing to a particular audience or reader. Sufficient quantity of writing.	Argumentation/persuasive essays. Informal/personal responses. Evaluations of others' work.★ Casual/informal language and tone in writing.	Uses of conventions of a particular genre. Expressing original or novel ideas. Evaluations of others' work.★ Uses of analogy or comparison to describe concepts to a general audience.

Language Skills (in declining order of importance)

A command of standard written English: grammar, phrasing, effective sentence structure, spelling, punctuation. (3.70 of 5)	Varied sentence structure. Correct grammar and punctuation. (86% of faculty) Accurate spelling. (75% of faculty) Writing that is edited and relatively free of error.	Grammar and rules of standard written English. (4.1 of 5) Accurate spelling/punctuation. (4.0 of 5) Writing has to be edited for clarity, coherence, and correctness. (3.9 of 5)
Appropriate academic vocabulary. (3.62 of 5)	Appropriate academic vocabulary. (88% of faculty)	Precise vocabulary without empty/vague phrases. (3.9 of 5) Effective choice of words. (3.8 of 5)

*Although these discourse skills are not considered to be important in writing in practically all disciplines, they are valued in English departments and composition courses.

is also added to the data. The survey by Rosenfeld et al. (2001), based on faculty questionnaires, reports on the highly valued elements of students' writing that are vital for academic survival.

As with the overview in Table 3.1, it is easy to note the similarities among the typical requirements in dozens of colleges and universities in the 1990s and 2000s (Table 3.2). In identifying priorities in student writing, practically all disciplinary courses emphasize the importance of content (subject matter) knowledge. In this context, (1) the development of an effective thesis (2) supported by content points and factual reasoning (4.1 of 5, "very important"), combined with (3) the quality of language are valued just as highly as subject matter. At the college and university level, based on these reports, the importance rating of appropriate "academic vocabulary" and "precise vocabulary" closely follows that of "edited writing, relatively free of error."

Valued and Required Elements of University Writing

Discourse Structuring

- Clear organization of information and a well-supported thesis
- Specific supporting points accompanied by good examples
- Reasoned interpretation of facts

Language Skills

- The use of standard written English
- Grammatical accuracy
- Correct spelling and punctuation
- Developed and effective academic vocabulary
- Relatively few language errors

While the faculty appraisals of the essential student skills correlated highly across an array of disciplines, such as education, psychology, natural sciences, physical sciences, and engineering, the four reports point out that in practically all surveyed institutions, a great deal of attention and discussion is devoted to the fact that "English [as a discipline] was the one area with different profiles" of ratings (Rosenfeld et al., 2004, p. 33). In fact, the study also found the student writing tasks considered to be valuable and top priority in English classes often correlated negatively with those in other subject areas.

Similarly, the ICAS (2002) report, for example, emphasizes repeatedly that composition assignments and curricula do not focus on the types of writing similar to those in other disciplines. Composition faculty and the disciplinary faculty in California colleges and universities, for example, "agree that students are best prepared to write personal essays, informal responses, short answer essay questions, and brief summaries of readings" (p. 23). As the ICAS faculty members comment, "even when [students] are essentially very good students, they seem to arrive at" disciplinary courses "under-prepared in writing by their previous academic work."

Not Particularly Important Discourse and Writing Skills

- Argumentation writing and analyzing arguments; persuasive writing
- Personal or informal responses to readings
- Evaluations of others' work (e.g., a book or a writer's effectiveness)
- Writing to a particular audience or reader, or to a general audience
- Using the conventions of a particular genre

In addition to the expectations of writing quality that apply to all students, many survey findings pertain to L2 learners directly. The four studies in Table 3.2 outline a number of language and writing skills that are paramount for L2 students. The conclusions to the Rosenfeld et al. (2004, p. 50) survey state:

> "Writing was judged by undergraduate faculty to be *important* for competent performance in a variety of subject areas . . . for undergraduate students. This was true at both minority and nonminority schools." (emphasis in the original)

Critical Academic Writing Skills

Almost all conclusions regarding the students' crucial language abilities and preparatory work focus directly on students' *academic* English, which is required to meet the demands of college writing.

- **Language abilities**—Proficiency in academic English, beyond conversational fluency, including competencies in:
    - The grammar of standard written English
    - Complex sentence structure
    - Developed academic vocabulary
    - Punctuation conventions
- **Preparatory work**—Specific direct and explicit instruction in academic English with an emphasis on self-correction and editing skills considered to be paramount in academic writing.

The ICAS (2002, p. 80) statement of the essential student competencies also underscores that "L2 learners at the high school level need extensive focused instruction and practice attending to forms—both grammatical structures and vocabulary—to express ideas appropriately in academic English." To put it in another way, in 108 California state universities, the teaching faculty view L2 writers' skills in grammar and vocabulary so important that an emphasis is placed on this instruction beginning in high school. In many cases, by the time when L2 students arrive in universities, the amount of time and work required to attain the fundamentals may be simply daunting, if at all possible (Hinkel, 2002, 2004).

> **Talking Shop/Action Point**
>
> What do you think the foundations of a curriculum should be? Create a set of the three (or four or five) essential and foundational elements for building a curriculum. What do they need to be and what factors should they be take into account? How can these foundational elements be made flexible and dynamic to change with the times, places, learners, and teaching content?

Academic Writing Valued on the TOEFL and the Test of Written English

The TOEFL is probably the most widely administered measure of student language proficiency and skills, including academic writing, and its outcomes for test takers affect a large number of people—for example, students, teachers, school administrators, parents, and college admission officers. In many cases, the TOEFL represents the most commonly employed language assessment for nonnative speakers who apply for admission to colleges, universities, or other schools, or those who seek professional licensing, various types of certification, employment, on-the-job promotions, or funding. The TOEFL is a high stakes assessment of language and writing proficiencies because much depends on the outcomes of the standardized measurements for the individuals who are required to take them. The CCSS Writing assessment, along with the TOEFL iBT Writing Section, are probably the most well-known, established, and researched assessments of writing proficiency (see also chapter 2).

The remainder of this chapter will take a look at what specific properties of writing are assessed in L2 academic writing on the TOEFL. By identifying similar properties of writing evaluated on this widely known test, it may be possible to determine what features of writing are valued above others (see also Hinkel [2005, 2012] for a discussion).

What's Valued in the TOEFL iBT Writing

Like CCSS, NAEP, and other types of assessments of student writing, the TOEFL has undergone periodic revisions. Since the mid-1990s, modifications in the test have been driven primarily by evolutions of technology and the Internet. The most recent changes in how the TOEFL is delivered, administered, and scored have also led to revisions of the evaluative rubrics designed for the Writing Section (originally created for the Test of Written English; Educational Testing Service [ETS] 2004, 2005). The most recent version of the rubrics was developed for the TOEFL iBT Writing Section, introduced in late 2006.

The overview of the current edition of the TOEFL Tips (ETS, 2008, pp. 22 & 26) explains that the purpose of the Writing Section is to measure "a test taker's ability to write in an academic setting" and that "the students must be able to present their ideas in a clear, well-organized manner." Although the test of L2 writing has been in development since 1963, the original version of the Test of Written English (TWE) was formally added to the TOEFL in 1986. In the intervening decades, the TOEFL Writing Section has had numerous opportunities for modification and fine-tuning. At present, the TOEFL Writing test is considered to be one of the most established and reliable measures of L2 written proficiency for academically bound nonnative speakers.

In general terms, the ETS TOEFL program has a extensive research basis that also includes an array of foundational and validity studies that have played a key role in TWE and Writing Section development (e.g., Frase, Faleti, & Ginther, 1999; Henning, 1992; Lee, Breland, & Muraki, 2004; Sakyi, 2000; Weigle, 2010). Because TOEFL essay prompts, writing tasks, and rubrics have been subjected to extensive scrutiny over a period of many years, a number of validation studies afford the writing portion of the test a great deal of credibility with admission offices and the teaching faculty in colleges and universities around the world. According to the test guide (ETS, 2011a, p. 4), the Writing Section "measures the ability to write in a way that is appropriate for college and university course work."

At present, two types of writing tasks are administered on the test: integrated writing and independent writing. In these two tasks, test takers are required "to write a response to material they have heard and read" or "compose an essay in support of an opinion" (ETS, 2008, p. 5). In the former writing task, it appears that test-takers are expected to deal with a more complex test that demands both listening and reading comprehension integrated with writing. On the other hand, in the writing tasks that deal with "supporting an opinion," the test of writing is unchanged from the traditional task that has been administered on TWE for the past more than half century: "This is the same type of task on the TOEFL and the

Test of Written English" (p. 23). More specifically, the purpose of TWE and the Writing Section of TOEFL iBT is "to assess the various factors that are generally considered crucial components of written academic English" (ETS, 2004, p. 10) and to "measure test takers' ability to write in an academic environment" (ETS, 2005, p. 20).

Other important variables that seem rather constant across all versions of the TOEFL writing portion are the evaluation criteria that continue to occupy a high priority. Specifically, the criteria for evaluating the quality of L2 writing have remained the same as they were traditionally outlined:

- The response to the integrated writing task is scored on the quality of writing (organization, appropriate and precise use of grammar and vocabulary) and the completeness and accuracy of the content.
- The independent writing essay is scored on the overall quality of the writing: development, organization, and appropriate and precise use of grammar and vocabulary.

(ETS, 2008, p. 26)

The stated educational objective of the test is defined as follows (ETS, 2004, p. 6): "The purpose of TWE is to give examinees whose native language is not English an opportunity to demonstrate their ability to express ideas in acceptable written English in response to an assigned topic. Topics are designed to be fair, accessible, and appropriate to all members of the international TOEFL population." To this end, the TOEFL essays are evaluated based on "lexical and syntactic standards of English and the effectiveness with which the examinee, organizes, develops, and expresses ideas in writing." The two descriptions of quality in L2 writing presented above and its main properties are very similar, and they strongly resemble those expected of student academic writing noted in the studies of university writing (as discussed earlier). The qualities of good L2 writing rather predictably consist of good organization, "appropriate and precise use of grammar and vocabulary," and completeness of content/development. As has been noted throughout this chapter, in the standardized tests of student writing, not much has changed, despite the changes in how writing is taught and assessed in the classroom.

Three TOEFL writing rubrics are presented in Table 3.3, side by side, from highest to lowest to simplify comparisons of the testing criteria for L2 writing. Two of these reflect the newest modifications in the rubrics introduced in late 2006 together with the Internet TOEFL (iBT), and the other set of the evaluation criteria was originally created in the 1970s and 1980s. As with the rubrics for the NAEP assessment of school writing, the evaluative frameworks for TWE have changed little after many validation studies and content (topic/prompt) modifications.

The specific differences between the rubrics for the writing portion of the TOEFL implemented between 1986 and 2006 include only a few adjustments.

TABLE 3.3 TOEFL Writing Rubrics and TWE Scoring Guide1

Score	Task Description		
			TOEFL iBT/Next Generation
	Test of Written English (TWE)	Independent Writing	Integrated Writing
24–30 5 iBT 6 TWE	Demonstrates clear competence on both the rhetorical and syntactic levels, though it may have occasional errors. A paper in this category: • effectively addresses the writing task • is well organized and well developed • uses clearly appropriate details to support a thesis or illustrate ideas • displays consistent facility in the use of language • demonstrates syntactic variety and appropriate word choice	An essay at this level largely accomplishes all of the following: • effectively addresses the topic and task • is well organized and well developed, using clearly appropriate explanations, exemplifications, and/or details • displays unity, progression, and coherence • displays consistent facility in the use of language, demonstrating syntactic variety, appropriate word choice, and idiomaticity, though it may have minor lexical or grammatical errors	A response at this level successfully selects the important information from the lecture and coherently and accurately presents this information in relation to the relevant information presented in the reading. The response is well organized, and occasional language errors that are present do not result in inaccurate or imprecise presentation of content and connections.

(Continued)

TABLE 3.3 (Continued)

Score	Task Description		
	Test of Written English (IWE)	TOEFL iBT/Next Generation	
		Independent Writing	Integrated Writing
17–23 4 iBT 5 TWE	Demonstrates competence in writing on both the rhetorical and syntactic levels, though it will probably have occasional errors. A paper in this category • may address some parts of the task more effectively than others • is generally well organized and developed • uses details to support a thesis or illustrate ideas • displays facility in language • demonstrates some syntactic variety and range of vocabulary	An essay at this level largely accomplishes all of the following: • addresses the topic and task well, though some points may not be fully elaborated • is generally well organized and well developed, using appropriate and sufficient explanations, exemplifications, and/or details • displays unity, progression, and coherence, though it may contain occasional redundancy, digression, or unclear connections • displays facility in the use of language, demonstrating syntactic variety and range of vocabulary, though it will probably have occasional noticeable minor errors in structure, word form, or use of idiomatic language that do not interfere with meaning	A response at this level is generally good in selecting the important information from the lecture and coherently and accurately presents this information in relation to the relevant information presented in the reading, but it may have minor omission, inaccuracy, vagueness, or imprecision of some content from the lecture or in connection to the points made in the reading. A response is also scored at this level if it has more frequent or noticeable language errors as long as such usage and grammatical structures do not result in anything more than an occasional lapse of clarity or the connection of ideas.

10–16	Demonstrates minimal competence in writing on both the rhetorical and syntactic levels. A paper in this category	An essay at this level is marked by one or more of the following:	A response at this level contains some important information from the lecture and conveys some relevant connection to the reading, but it is marked by one or more of the following:
3 iBT			
4 TWE	• addresses the writing topic adequately but may slight parts of the task	• addresses the topic and task using somewhat developed explanations, exemplifications, and/or details	• Although the overall response is definitely oriented to the task, it conveys only vague, global, unclear, or somewhat imprecise connection of the points made in the lecture to points made in the reading.
	• is adequately organized and developed	• displays unity, progression, and coherence, though connection of ideas may be occasionally obscured	• The response may omit one major key point made in the lecture.
	• uses some details to support a thesis or illustrate an idea	• may demonstrate inconsistent facility in sentence formation and word choice that may result in lack of clarity and occasionally obscure meaning	• Some key points made in the lecture or the reading, or connections between the two, may be incomplete, inaccurate, or imprecise.
	• demonstrates adequate but possibly inconsistent facility with syntax and usage	• may display accurate but limited range of syntactic structures and vocabulary	• Errors of usage and/or grammar may be more frequent or may result in noticeably vague expressions or obscured meanings in conveying ideas and connections.
	• may contain some serious errors that occasionally obscure meaning		

(Continued)

TABLE 3.3 (Continued)

Score	Task Description		
		TOEFL iBT/Next Generation	
	Test of Written English (TWE)	Independent Writing	Integrated Writing
0–9 TWE 2 iBT 3 TWE	Demonstrates some developing competence in writing, but it remains flawed on either the rhetorical or syntactic level, or both. A paper in this category may reveal one or more of the following weaknesses: • inadequate organization or development • inappropriate or insufficient details to support or illustrate generalizations • a noticeably inappropriate choice of words or word forms • an accumulation of errors in sentence structure and/or usage	An essay at this level may reveal one or more of the following weaknesses: • limited development in response to the topic and task • inadequate organization or connection of ideas • inappropriate or insufficient exemplifications, explanations, or details to support or illustrate generalizations in response to the task • a noticeably inappropriate choice of words or word forms • an accumulation of errors in sentence structure and/or usage	A response at this level contains some relevant information from the lecture, but it is marked by significant language difficulties or by significant omission or inaccuracy of important ideas from the lecture or in the connections between the lecture and the reading; a response at this level is marked by one or more of the following: • The response significantly misrepresents or completely omits the overall connection between the lecture and the reading. • The response significantly omits or significantly misrepresents important points made in the lecture. • The response contains language errors or expressions that largely obscure connections or meaning at key junctures or that would likely obscure understanding or key ideas for a reader not already familiar with the reading and the lecture.

1 iBT **2 TWE**	Suggests incompetence in writing. A paper in this category is seriously flawed by one or more of the following weaknesses: • failure to organize or develop • little or no detail or relevant specifics • serious and frequent errors in usage or sentence structure • serious problems with focus	An essay at this level is seriously flawed by one or more of the following weaknesses: • serious disorganization or underdevelopment • little or no detail, or irrelevant specifics, or questionable responsiveness to the task • serious and frequent errors in sentence structure or usage	A response at this level is marked by one or more of the following: • The response provides little or no meaningful or relevant coherent content from the lecture. • The language level of the response is so low that it is difficult to derive meaning.
0 iBT **1 TWE**	Demonstrates incompetence in writing. A paper in this category • may be incoherent • may be undeveloped • may contain severe and persistent writing errors	An essay at this level merely copies words from the topic, rejects the topic, or is otherwise not connected to the topic, is written in a foreign language, consists of keystroke characters, or is blank.	The response at this level merely copies sentences from the reading, rejects the topic or is otherwise not connected to the topic, is written in a foreign language, consists of keystroke characters, or is blank.

Scores 4 and 5 (24–30) TOEFL iBT (5 and 6 TWE)—The highest level of L2 writing skills, labeled Good:

- The addition of the "displays unity, progression, and coherence" or accuracy criteria
- An allowance for minor/occasional "lexical or grammatical errors" (Score 5), "occasional noticeable minor errors," or "more frequent or noticeable language errors" in grammar, vocabulary, and usage (Score 4)

Score 3 (17–23) TOEFL iBT (4 TWE)—Fair L2 written proficiency:

- A similar addition of the "displays unity, progression, and coherence" category, or "only vague, global, unclear, or somewhat imprecise connections" of the points
- An added definition regarding the expected quality of language: "accurate but limited range of syntactic structures and vocabulary" (vs. "some serious errors that occasionally obscure meaning" in the earlier rubric), or specification of errors "of usage and/or grammar" and "noticeably vague expressions or obscured meanings . . . and connections"

Scores 1 and 2 (0–16) TOEFL iBT (0 and 1 TWE)—Two lowest tiers of L2 writing abilities:

- A substitution of the disorganization and underdevelopment category with "little or no meaningful or relevant coherent content from the lecture" in response to the topic
- A replacement of a content criterion ("serious problems with focus") with a language-related measure ("serious and frequent errors in sentence structure or usage" or "the language level of the response is so low that it is difficult to derive meaning"

Based on the TOEFL writing rubrics, it seems relatively easy to figure out the essential characteristics of L2 writing that are considered to be important on the test and probably beyond it in the academic world. As has been mentioned, the primary purpose of the TOEFL writing component is to "measure" students' essential academic writing skills.

The booklet on TOEFL iBT Tips (ETS, 2008, p. 22) also offers the following outline of written discourse properties that students need to address in their test preparation, "in all types of writing":

- Identify one main idea and its main supports
- Plan how to organize the essay (e.g., with an outline)
- Develop it by using "reasons, examples, and detail" (p. 22)

- Express information in an organized way
- Use effective linking words (transitional phrases) to connect ideas and help the reader understand the connections in the flow of ideas
- Use a range of grammar structures and vocabulary for effective expression
- Use grammar and vocabulary accurately; use idiomatic expressions appropriately
- Follow the conventions of spelling, punctuation, and layout

In light of all these helpful suggestions, it seems relatively easy to summarize the features of L2 writing that are valued on the assessment of L2 written proficiency.

What's Valued and Measured in L2 Written Proficiency
(see also the discussion of student university writing earlier in this chapter)

- An essay that mostly stays close to the task/prompt/content without too many digressions (the subject matter)
- A relatively rigid discourse structure (organization) that follows a classical form with an overtly stated central idea (the thesis) and directly relevant supports
- Developed language skills (grammar and vocabulary)
- Close adherence to the conventions of standard written English
- To the extent possible, error-free text

To identify the valued characteristics of L1 or L2 student writing, however, a far more interesting perspective can be gained from examining the common and shared criteria in the rubrics for evaluating writing quality. A large number of publications on L2 writing by ETS, which is solely in charge of the TOEFL and L2 writing tests, as well as reports, analyses, and guides for L1 school writing produced by the NAEP (the National Assessment Governing Board that oversees and develops its framework and test specifications) make clear expectations of writing quality in education (see chapter 2 for a detailed discussion). A vast body of public and proprietary works similarly and consistently refers to the processes entailed in constructing writing, as well as the purposes of academic writing and its features. The writing processes, expressivity, creative ideas, and "shaping" writing seem to be emphasized in the publications on the assessment and testing of L1 and L2 alike.

For example, NAEP Writing Framework (2011), ETS, and TOEFL/TWE publications (1996, 2001, 2004, 2005, 2008) and Cumming, Kantor, and Powers (2001), refer to writing as a process for communicating meaning and note the complexity of the writing process, with its recursive development, drafting, evaluating, revising, and polishing. Some of the reports, in fact, find that the goal of writing assessment is to enable test-takers to produce "purposeful texts" and to "facilitate a variety of writing processes" (Cumming, Kantor, Powers, Santos, Taylor, 2000, pp. 7–9). Most, if not all, reports on the standardized assessment and testing of writing also emphasize the academic validity of their tasks and topics, as well as reliability in measuring the students' abilities to organize their discourse and ideas and use standard written English.

For L2 writers and their teachers, however, an analysis of the writing rubrics adopted on the TOEFL sheds a great deal of light on what is actually considered to be crucially, vitally important in academic writing across various instruments for measuring written proficiency in the academy.

Action Point

What do you think the connections between tests and writing curricula should be? Given that in many cases, tests drive how a curriculum is developed, can this in effect lead to "teaching to the test"? Compare the views of university faculty on the essentials of student writing and see if you can identify the differences and similarities between them and the evaluation points in the TOEFL rubrics. Are the requirements of university writing also valued on the test? What elements that are important in university writing are not noted on the test? And vice versa?

The Least that Academic L2 Writers Must Be Able to Do

Many L2 students and their teachers disdain the TOEFL and its writing component and consider it an evil not particularly necessary. These individuals also believe that the test is idiosyncratic and flawed and that it does not reflect the actual skills needed for success in academics, nor the students' abilities to produce passable academic prose. However, as Table 3.4 demonstrates, the proportion of L2 students who can produce a good quality text in English, based on the ETS definitions of good writing, is actually quite small: 15% and 10%, respectively, in the Writing Section of TOEFL iBT and TWE.

Even at first glance, it seems clear from the data in Table 3.4 that L2 academic writers have a less complex and cognitively demanding task with a 30-minute time limit and one piece of writing that they are required to produce in order to support an opinion on TWE than on two writing tasks that take 50 minutes. It is also apparent that the 30 minutes allotted for the writing task on TWE is larger than the 25 minutes allocated for each writing task on TOEFL iBT.

TABLE 3.4 Score Distributions on TOEFL iBT Writing Section and TWE2

TOEFL Writing Section	Score		
	Good	Intermediate/Fair	Low/Limited
	24–30 (3.75–5) iBT or 5–6 TWE	17–23 (2.50–3.50) iBT or 3.5–4.5 TWE	1–16 (1–2.25) iBT or 1.0–3.0 TWE
TOEFL iBT (2 writing tasks; 50 minutes	15%	29%	54%*
TWE (1 writing task; 30 minutes)	10%	65%	25%*

Based on TOEFL and TWE Rubrics, ETS (2004, 2011a, 2011b)
*A total of 98% for TOEFL iBT is the maximum value provided in ETS (2011a, 2011b).

In comparison, the proportion of the test-takers with Good writing skills is 5% higher on TOEFL iBT than on TWE. The Fair/Intermediate writing scores of 17–23 on TOEFL iBT and 3.5–4.5 on TWE is more than twice as large at 29% on the former and 65% on the latter. The same can be said for the group of Limited/Low L2 writers with the 54% and 25% disparity. The data in Table 3.4 also point to the fact that a great majority of L2 writers (i.e., more than 85%) obtain writing scores below the "Good" writing category (i.e., between 1 and 23 on TOEFL iBT and between 1 and 3 on TWE, respectively) (ETS, 2004, 2005, 2011b).

> Based on the Educational Testing Service (2011b) data, it seems rather obvious that the Writing Section on TOEFL iBT represents a much loftier goal than the writing assignment on TWE in terms of the necessary language proficiency, as well as vocabulary and grammar skills. The difference in the writing task complexity is in fact entailed in the very nature of the test. Both receptive skills (i.e., reading and listening) and productive skills (i.e., writing) are requisite in the Writing Section on TOEFL iBT. However, only productive language skills are in demand on the TWE writing.

The rubric (ETS, 2008, p. 47) for the Good test scores (24–30) consists of four main and highlighted components:

1. The topic and task are effectively addressed; or the content information is coherently and accurately presented.
2. The information is well organized with well developed explanations, exemplifications, and details; or important content is successfully selected.
3. The text is unified and coherent.

72 Curriculum Foundations

4. The language facility is displayed consistently with varied word choice and grammar, and relatively few errors in lexis and grammar; or language usage is accurate and precise, save for "occasional" minor errors.

The rubrics (ETS, 2008, p. 47) for Fair/Intermediate scores, 17–23, similarly include four main evaluative points:

1. The topic and task are largely well addressed with a few unelaborated points; or the content information is "generally good" in coherently and accurately presented, although it may contain "minor omission,. . ., vagueness, or imprecision" of content.
2. The information is generally well organized with sufficient explanations, exemplifications, and details.
3. The text is unified and coherent, with occasional redundancies and digressions; or contains "occasional lapse of clarity on in the connection of ideas."
4. The language facility is demonstrated by means of syntactic variety and a range of vocabulary, although occasional errors are noticeable in word form, grammar usage or structures, and idiomatic expressions.

The TOEFL descriptors of Writing with scores of 1–16 (i.e., the lowest of the ratings), provide the detailed criteria for what is valued in L2 academic writing.

Four crucial rating points include:

1. The topic and task are addressed, with "somewhat" developed explanations, exemplifications, and details; or "although response is definitely oriented to the task it provides only vague, . . . unclear, or somewhat imprecise connection" to the content.
2. Unity and coherence are demonstrated, although connections between ideas are occasionally obscured; or major key points in the content are overlooked.
3. The language usage is inconsistent in sentence structure and word choice that may make the ideas occasionally difficult to understand; or connections between ideas in the content "may be incomplete, inaccurate, or imprecise."
4. Accurate but limited grammar and vocabulary; or frequent errors in grammar, vague expressions, or "obscured meanings."

To Conclude

Based on the information contained in faculty surveys and the research carried out by ETS in regard to the TOEFL, L2 curricula in practically all language teaching needs to establish the following objectives for student learning:

- Overall receptive language proficiency: academic vocabulary and grammar needed to comprehend formal spoken and written text and interpret information

- Discourse organization skills needed to parse spoken and written text (receptive skills) and to produce formal academic prose (productive skills), including a focus on a clear and systematically supported thesis
- Developed and varied academic vocabulary and advanced grammar required to construct complex and reasonably sophisticated sentences (productive skills)
- Editing skills that require identification and eradication of at least some of the frequent errors
- Reasonable punctuation and spelling in accordance with the conventions of standard written English

According to the perspectives of the teaching faculty in universities, the academic tasks that require both reading and writing are particularly daunting for practically all L2 students (ICAS, 2002). Neither is actually possible without a substantial range of academic vocabulary and grammar, and both of these require extensive and intensive instruction. Academic vocabulary and grammar cannot be learned in conversational discourse simply because they do not occur there. In this regard, just as native speakers do in the process of schooling (see chapter 2), L2 learners have to undertake the serious task of learning the elements of the academic language (Hinkel, 2002, 2003, 2004). In such undertakings, the role of the curriculum is paramount: what to study and learn is of crucial importance. For example, although it is commonly believed that reading large amounts of fiction necessarily leads to the acquisition of an extensive academic vocabulary, many studies have demonstrated that this is not always the case for either type of learners, L1 or L2 (e.g., Hu & Nation, 2000; Nation & Webb, 2011; Schmitt & Carter, 2000; Schmitt & Zimmerman, 2002; Stanovich & Cunningham, 1992; Waring & Nation, 2004). Academic vocabulary typically consists of technical—and often discipline-related—words and phrases, and they are not prevalent in fiction or other kinds of popular literature. That is, academic language skills are specific to the academy, and a curriculum for academic learners needs to concentrate on their academic needs. Corpus studies shed a great deal of light on this subject, and chapter 7 identifies some of these, as well as how to address them.

An important factor in teaching academic writing skills is requiring students to read like a writer (Nation, 2008). Substantial evidence exists that this ability can assist L2 writers in developing discourse and organization skills that seem to be highly valued in the academy and on the tests of writing, such as the TOEFL. Reading like a writer calls for a careful analysis of the discourse structure and text. However, for the analysis to be successful and productive, the curriculum and instruction need to focus on the valued features of coherent and accurate prose and how it is constructed. It is difficult to learn to write without a clear understanding of the structure of writing, information sequencing, and key points. Much research has shown that L2 writers usually experience difficulty in reading and writing, and these are the cornerstones of education.

The remainder of this book is devoted to the incremental steps of how these enormous objectives can be accomplished. Two points can be made with certainty, however:

1. Developing academic writing skills requires a persistent effort on the behalf of both teachers and learners.
2. These objectives can be accomplished over a bit of time.

Chapter Summary

Since at least the 1980s, a large number of studies have investigated the types of writing and written assignments expected of students in colleges and universities and on standardized tests of L2 writing skills. Currently, it is an established fact that a majority of undergraduates and many graduate students in U.S. colleges and universities are likely to be poorly prepared for their academic writing tasks.

Practically all course assignments consist of more than one writing task. For example, a brief exposition in the introduction can lead to an analysis, possibly with a cause/effect rhetorical structure, and followed by a summary in the conclusion. All formats of academic writing require information structuring, paraphrasing, and restatement skills, as well as a passable command of relevant vocabulary and sentence structure.

Almost all conclusions regarding the students' crucial language abilities and preparatory work focus directly on students' academic English, which is required to meet the demands of college writing—that is, the language skills that extend beyond conversational fluency and proficiency in academic English. The essential elements of L2 academic writing skills include the grammar of standard written English, complex sentence structure, developed academic vocabulary, and punctuation conventions. In addition, specific, direct, and explicit instruction in academic English is necessary, with an emphasis on the self-correction and editing skills considered paramount in L2 academic writing.

Notes

1 TOEFL iBT test materials and TWE materials excerpted from Test of Written English Guide, 5th edition, Educational Testing Service, 2004, are reprinted by permission of Educational Testing Service, the copyright owner. No endorsement of this publication by Educational Testing Service should be inferred.
2 According to the ETS website, TOEFL Paper-based Test (TOEFL Pbt), of which TWE is a part, was to be phased out in mid-2012. However, it was originally scheduled for discontinuance in 2005.

Further Reading on L2 Academic Writing Skills

Campbell, C. (1990). Writing with others' words: Using background reading text in academic composition. In B. Kroll (Ed.), *Second language writing* (pp. 211–230). New York: Cambridge University Press.

Hinkel, E. (2003). Simplicity without elegance: Features of sentences in L2 and L1 academic texts. *TESOL Quarterly, 37,* 275–301.
Hinkel, E. (2004). *Teaching academic ESL writing: Practical techniques in vocabulary and grammar.* Mahwah, NJ: Lawrence Erlbaum Associates.
Horowitz, D. (1986). What professors actually require: Academic tasks for the ESL classroom. *TESOL Quarterly, 20,* 445–462.
Jordan, R. (1997). *English for academic purposes.* Cambridge: Cambridge University Press.
Lea, M., & Street, B. (1998). Student writing in higher education: An academic literacies approach. *Studies in Higher Education, 23,* 157–172.
Santos, T. (1988). Professors' reactions to the academic writing of nonnative-speaking students. *TESOL Quarterly, 22,* 69–90.

References

Applebee, A. (1982). Writing and learning in school settings. In M. Nystrand (Ed.), *What writers know* (pp. 365–381). New York, NY: Academic Press.
Christie, F. (1998). Learning the literacies of primary and secondary schooling. In F. Christie & R. Misson (Eds.), *Literacy and schooling: New directions* (pp. 47–73). London: Routledge.
Coffin, C., Curry, M., Goodman, S., Hewings, A., Lillis, T., & Swann, J. (2003). *Teaching academic writing: A toolkit for higher education.* London: Routledge.
Cumming, A., Kantor, R., & Powers, D. (2001). *Scoring TOEFL essays and TOEFL 2000 prototype writing tasks: An investigation into raters' decision making and development of a preliminary analytic framework.* Monograph Series 22. Princeton, NJ: Educational Testing Service.
Cumming, A., Kantor, R., Powers, D., Santos, T., &Taylor, C. (2000). *TOEFL 2000 writing framework: A working paper.* Princeton, NJ: Educational Testing Service.
Curry, M., & Lillis, T. (2004). Multilingual scholars and the imperative to publish in English: Negotiating interests, demands, and rewards. *TESOL Quarterly, 38*(4), 663–688.
Educational Testing Service. (1996). *Test of Written English instructional guide* Princeton, NJ: Author.
Educational Testing Service. (2001). *TOEFL 2000–2001, Information bulletin for computer-based testing.* Princeton, NJ: Author.
Educational Testing Service. (2004). *Test of written English guide* (5th ed.). Princeton, NJ: Author.
Educational Testing Service. (2005). *TOEFL iBT tips: How to prepare for the next generation TOEFL test and communicate with confidence.* Princeton, NJ: Author.
Educational Testing Service. (2008). *TOEFL iBT tips.* Princeton, NJ: Author.
Educational Testing Service. (2011a). *Test and score data summary for TOEFL Internet-based and Paper-based tests.* Princeton, NJ: Author.
Educational Testing Service. (2011b). *TOEFL 2011–12 Information and registration bulletin.* Princeton, NJ: Author.
Frase, L., Faletti, J., Ginther, A., & Grant, L. (1999). *Computer analysis of the TOEFL test of written English* [Research report 64]. Princeton, NJ: Educational Testing Service.
Hale, G., Taylor, C., Bridgeman, B., Carson, J., Kroll, B., & Kantor, R. (1996). *A study of writing tasks assigned in academic degree programs* [Research Report 54]. Princeton, NJ: Educational Testing Service.
Henning, G. (1992). *Scalar analysis of the test of written English: TOEFL Research Report 38.* Princeton, NJ: Educational Testing Service.
Hinkel, E. (2002). *Second language writers' text.* Mahwah, NJ: Lawrence Erlbaum Associates.

Hinkel, E. (2004). *Teaching academic ESL writing: Practical techniques in vocabulary and grammar.* Mahwah, NJ: Lawrence Erlbaum Associates.

Hinkel, E. (2005). Analyses of L2 text and what can be learned from them. In E. Hinkel (Ed.), *Handbook of research in second language teaching and learning* (pp. 615–628). Mahwah, NJ: Lawrence Erlbaum Associates.

Hinkel, E. (2011). What research on second language writing tells us and what it doesn't. In E. Hinkel (Ed.), *Handbook of research in second language teaching and learning* (Vol. 2, pp. 523–538). New York: Routledge.

Hinkel, E. (2012). Cultures of learning in the U.S.A. In M. Cortazzi & J. Cortazzi (Eds.), *Cultures of learning* (pp. 21–35). London: Palgrave-McMillan.

Horowitz, D. (1986). What professors actually require: Academic tasks for the ESL classroom. *TESOL Quarterly, 20,* 445–462.

Hu, M., & Nation, P. (2000). Unknown vocabulary density and reading comprehension. *Reading in a Foreign Language 13*(1), 403–430.

ICAS. (2002). *Academic literacy: A statement of competencies expected of students entering California's public colleges and universities.* Sacramento, CA: Intersegmental Committee of the Academic Senates of California Colleges and Universities.

Jordan, R. (1997). *English for academic purposes.* Cambridge: Cambridge University Press.

Lea, M., & Street, B. (1998). Student writing in higher education: An academic literacies approach. *Studies in Higher Education, 23,* 157–172.

Lee, Y.-W., Breland, H., & Muraki, E. (2004). *Comparability of TOEFL CBT prompts for different native language groups.* Princeton, NJ: Educational Testing Service.

Nation, I. S. P. (2008). *Teaching vocabulary.* Boston: Heinle & Heinle.

Nation, I. S. P., & Webb, S. (2011). Content-based instruction and vocabulary learning. In E. Hinkel (Ed.), *Handbook of research in second language teaching and learning* (Vol. 2, pp. 631–644). New York: Routledge.

Rosenfeld, M., Courtney, R., & Fowles, M. (2004). *Identifying the writing tasks important for academic success at the undergraduate and graduate level.* Princeton, NJ: Educational Testing Service.

Rosenfeld, M., Leung, S., & Oltman, P. (2001). *The reading, writing, speaking, and listening tasks important for academic success at undergraduate and graduate levels* (MS 21). Princeton, NJ: Educational Testing Service.

Sakyi, A. (2000). Validation of holistic scoring for ESL writing assessment: How raters evaluate ESL compositions. In A. Kunnan (Ed.), *Fairness and validation in language assessment* (pp. 129–152). Cambridge: Cambridge University Press.

Schleppegrell, M. (2004). *The language of schooling.* Mahwah, NJ: Lawrence Erlbaum.

Schmitt, N., & Carter, R. (2000). The lexical advantages of narrow reading for second language learners. *TESOL Quarterly, 9*(1), 4–9.

Schmitt, N., & Zimmerman, C. (2002). Derivative word forms: What do learners know? *TESOL Quarterly, 36*(2), 145–171.

Stanovich, K. E., & Cunningham, A. E. (1992). Studying the consequences of literacy within a literate society: The cognitive correlates of print exposure. *Memory & Cognition, 20,* 51–68.

Waring, R., & Nation, P. (2004). Second language reading and incidental vocabulary learning. *Angles on the English Speaking World, 4,* 11–23.

Weigle, S. (2002). *Assessing writing.* Cambridge: Cambridge University Press.

Weigle, S. (2010). Validation of automated scores of TOEFL iBT tasks against non-test indicators of writing ability. *Language Testing, 27*(3), 335–353.

4
SECOND LANGUAGE WRITING AND LANGUAGE LEARNING

This chapter discusses:

- Some reasons for the neglect of language in the teaching of writing
- The baseline in L2 reading, writing, and vocabulary
- Studies of L2 academic writing and text: issues of language quality
- L2 academic writing and areas of difficulty
- Error gravity studies
- Learning to organize ideas and the language needed to structure discourse (L1-based top-down approach)

Introduction: Some Reasons for Neglect of Language Quality

In the U.S. and some other English-speaking countries, one of the prominent characteristics of pedagogy and methods for teaching L2 composition to nonnative speakers of English is that much of it has little to do with the learning needs of L2 students specifically. In the 1970s and 1980s, the teaching of composition to native speakers was becoming established as a discipline separate from the teaching of literature in English departments.

Since that time and to this day, L2 writers have largely received instruction in the same range of writing skills and composition as have "basic" native speaker writers. Typically, L1 composition courses focus on such ubiquitous aspects of composing as planning, drafting, developing an argument, organizing ideas and discourse, as well as the uses of sentence transitions, precision in word choices, and documenting published sources. Ordinarily, composition curricula do not make an attempt to develop L2 learners' incremental and essential language skills (see, for example, Zamel [1987] and ICAS [2002], for a discussion of the absent—but essential—teaching of language to L2 writers). In addition to the self-evident fact that L2 learners need to learn the language before they can write in it, ideological windstorms have swept composition studies away from the mainstream academic disciplines and their time-honored and somewhat rigid way of teaching students and evaluating student writing (Blau, 2006; Hinkel, 2011; Leki, Cumming, & Silva, 2008; Sullivan & Tinberg, 2006; Weigle, 2002; see also chapter 3).

Since the time when rhetoric and composition studies first set out to separate from and philosophically distinguish themselves from practically all other disciplinary mindsets on any campus in North America, their goals have been effectively accomplished. Today, the objectives and methods for teaching English Language Arts (ELA) at school and undergraduate composition have effectively become an area of instruction fundamentally and functionally different from any other such area (e.g., Anson & Forsberg, 1990; Bazerman, 1988; McCarthy, 1987; North, 1986; Rosenfeld, Courtney, & Fowels, 2004). For example, Lester Faigley (1992) one of the key figures in composition teaching, refers to "the peculiarly North American discipline of composition studies" (p. 13) and comments that "scholarship in composition studies . . . is chaotic like the weather—a phenomenon difficult to predict, but one that follows certain regularities at particular sites" (p. 16).

Until very recently, ELA and composition pedagogy for native and nonnative speakers alike followed its own particular fashions and highly politicized trends that have for decades predominated in many English departments in North American education. In 1970s and 1980s, and to this day, the somewhat extreme politization of rhetoric and composition studies has fragmented their pedagogical focus. The political bandwagons and fragmentation have also led to a wide disparity in what is taught, how, and for what purpose (Berkenkotter, Huckin, & Ackerman, 1988; Herrington, 1985; Langer, 1992). In the past several decades, disparate and often haphazard political agendas in ELA and composition teaching have also subsumed the what, the how, and the why in the teaching of ESL writing.

At present, occasional L2 writers can be found in practically any ELA and composition classroom in the U.S. and Canada, for example. As an outcome, practically all composition teachers have encountered L2 writers among their students (see, for example, NCTE slogans, such as "Every writing teacher is a second language writing teacher" or "Every teacher is a teacher of English language learners"). Such incidental experiences have also been powerfully validated by a number of case studies published between the late 1980s and early 2000s on the real or imagined parallels between the writing skills of undergraduate L1 and L2 students. Although published cases discuss the writing and learning processes of only one to half a dozen students, these works proved to be highly influential during the heyday of the "paradigm shift" in the teaching of composition. These publications, combined with teachers' occasional encounters with L2 writers, have persuaded most—if not all—L1 composition teachers that they are fully qualified to teach L2 writing without much background in L2 learning processes or L2 instruction (e.g., Kutz, Groden, & Zamel, 1993; Nelson, 1991; Zamel, 1995; for a particularly poignant discussion of the issue, see Silva, 1990).

Because the discipline of composition studies deals with L1 writers almost exclusively, virtually all methods and practices for teaching L2 writing have been simply "borrowed" or derived from those developed for native speakers.

> There is little doubt that L2 writers need to attain an extensive range of writing skills, which L1 novice writers also have to acquire in the process of schooling. However, a crucial distinction between the L1 and L2 writers is that native speakers already have highly developed (native) language proficiencies.

The writing skills that both L1 and L2 writers have to learn may apply to organizing ideas into coherent discourse or structuring their writing in some sort of principled way. In addition, however, developed and relatively advanced language skills are fundamental and mandatory to enable L2 writers to produce competent (or at least passable) discourse and text in L2. To allude to an old saying, just as it is impossible to bake a cake without the necessary ingredients and knowing how to use them, it is not likely that L2 writers can cook up an academic paper without the requisite essential language skills or knowing how to be able to produce academic prose.

This chapter takes a look at studies of learner language in writing. By and large, these consist of research into the persistent and difficult issues in L2 writing and its language quality, including that at the college and university levels (i.e., the written academic prose produced by schooled L2 writers). A number of extensive and detailed research reports have been published that shed light on L2 writers' productive language skills. These investigations typically analyze an array of L2 writing features, including L2 uses of grammar, vocabulary, rhetorical markers, errors, or the conventions for organizing ideas, which have greatly influenced L2 writing instruction.

The research into the integral elements of L2 writing quality has traditionally concentrated on the three main characteristics of L2 academic prose:

- The language features employed (or not employed) in L2 academic writing (e.g., academic language, vocabulary, or complex sentences)
- The types of prevalent and damaging L2 errors and their hierarchies of importance (e.g., subject-verb agreement or verb tense shifts)
- Discourse organization and idea structuring

Taken together, the findings of these investigations lay the foundation for developing instruction and curricula with an ultimate goal of improving students' language range and quality.

The objective of this chapter is to identify curricular domains of L2 language and writing (i.e., the systematic studies of the learner), as was noted in chapter 1. While chapters 2 and 3 examine socially valued features of school and academic writing, this chapter identifies the language and discourse properties of L2 writing, including the de-valued characteristics of L2 prose, such as errors, that must be addressed in curriculum design and instruction.

Along these lines, the next chapter zeros in on the indispensable elements of L2 language base required to produce at least passable academic writing (i.e., the recommendations of the specialists).

Action Point

In practically all colleges and universities, composition courses for first- or second-year undergraduate students are offered every term. In many cases, course syllabi or course descriptions are available online or can be easily obtained, on request, from the English department, where such courses are typically offered. Collect 4 or 5 syllabi for various composition classes and identify specifically what writing skills represent the foci of teaching. How much instruction and attention is devoted to the development of academic language and writing? What priorities can be identified in the teaching of writing at your institution (or some other college or university)?

Analyze the information you glean from these syllabi and course descriptions and determine what undergraduate writing skills can be improved as a result of taking these composition courses and what cannot be.

The Baseline: L2 Reading, Writing, and Vocabulary

At present, research has clearly and unambiguously demonstrated that L2 writers' skill level in vocabulary and grammar disadvantage the quality of their formal prose. A large number of studies report that, even after several years of language learning, L2 writers' text continues to differ significantly from that of novice L1 writers in regard to a broad range of vocabulary and grammar properties. The results of dozens of analyses indicate that even advanced and highly educated L2 writers, such as doctoral students enrolled in universities in English-speaking countries and professionals, have a severely limited lexical and syntactic repertoire compared to their native speaker (NS) peers. In many cases of undergraduate L2 writers, for example, a restricted access to advanced language features results in simple texts that rely on the most common language features that occur predominantly in conversational discourse (e.g., Carson, 2001; Hedgcock, 2005; Hinkel, 2009, 2011; Jenkins & Hinds, 1987; North, 1986). Currently, in light of a large body of research findings obtained after about a half a century of comparative L1 and L2 text analyses, this conclusion seems rather obvious and clear-cut.

In regard to the lexical range required to produce competent written prose, a great deal of disagreement accompanies the amount of vocabulary necessary for or known by university-educated native and nonnative speakers. One of the key issues in the debate is whether the amount of vocabulary should be measured in terms of individual words or word families. The difference between the two types of measurements is substantial: counting words is crucially different than counting word families, which consists of base words and their derived forms (e.g., *child, children, childhood, childish*).

Although the vocabulary counts undertaken by researchers in the 1970s and 1980s relied on individual words, in the past three decades, practically all measurements of vocabulary have largely dealt with word families. Nonetheless, since much of the research into L2 reading and writing deals with the counts of words and word families, both types of studies are briefly discussed here.

Practically all researchers of L2 reading and vocabulary agree that high frequency words are easy to learn, and they allow learners to do a great deal in a second language. These are required in all forms of language usage: speaking, listening, reading, and writing. High frequency lists consist mostly of function words (e.g., articles; prepositions; pronouns; and common content words, such as *make, time, state, year*, or *new*). West's (1953) General Service List includes about 2,000 words, and 80% of these are function words.[1] These essential and most common words are easy to learn simply because they are so common.

On the other hand, even common academic words (e.g., *authority, democracy*, or *random*) do not occur nearly as often, and these need to be actively taught—and learned (Nation, 2005, 2011, 2013). For example, when, over the course of a week-long vacation, tourists repeatedly ask for directions in an unfamiliar city where a new language is spoken, the words required, such as *straight, left*, or *right*, are easy to learn even in just two or three interactions with the locals. However, the words that are even slightly less common, such as *a traffic light* or *intersection*, may take a little more exposure. Of course, listening, like reading, is a receptive skill, and, asking for directions requires a lot more vocabulary and language control than being able to get a bit of an idea what the locals are saying in response. Writing a request for street directions in another language, for example, is another story entirely (see the discussion below).

> Early vocabulary learning is easy because early learning includes highly frequent words, but less frequent words, such as those in basic academic vocabulary, are harder to learn, and they need to be taught.

Given that the most common 500 high frequency words on West's (1953) list, for example, consist of *a, the, and, by, but, in, out, we, you, I, do, this,* and the like, the scale in Table 4.1 seems to be readily understandable. For instance, to use an earlier example, a tourist who can ask for and understand basic street directions in a foreign country may not be able to read a newspaper or even a newspaper advertisement. That is, a vocabulary range of 500 words, pictures, illustrations, or street signs (as in letters or letter strings) are essential for most basic comprehension. On the other hand, a vocabulary of 500 to 1,000 words can allow learners to "pick out" a few familiar words in newspaper headlines.

TABLE 4.1 Reading Skill Levels and L2 Vocabulary Size

0–500 word families
- Pictures and illustrations are required for comprehension.
- Only a few content words recognized in unsimplified (native-level) L2 text.
- Only extremely simplified texts (such as those for very young children) can be understood.
- Identifying letters or letter strings (words and phrases) immediately can be difficult.
- Reading takes place letter by letter or word by word.
- The beginnings of the sentences are often forgotten when the end is reached.

500–1,000 word families
- Native speaker texts can be completely incomprehensible.
- Dictionary use represents the main reading strategy.
- Reading is word by word, followed by re-reading when meaning continuity is lost.
- Making text-based inferences is not possible.
- The meaning of the message is difficult to retain, and the content of reading is soon forgotten.
- Slow and predictable plots in graded readers can be comprehensible.
- Overall, reading is slow, laborious, and exhausting.

1,000–2,000 word families
- Dictionary usage is the main reading strategy, with the exception of highly predictable texts.
- Unsimplified texts remain so complex that they are soon abandoned.
- Content words can be occasionally identified in stretches of text.
- Humor and textual irony are inaccessible.
- Most texts are processed at the sentence level, and complex story plots can be difficult to follow.

2,000–5,000 word families
- Most words in text are understood but not immediately.
- Dictionary use is frequently required.
- Text structure can become accessible at the discourse level.

5,000 +
- Most unsimplified L2 text at the level of general interest can be understood, but not when the topic is specialized.
- Introductory academic texts may require occasional use of a dictionary.

(Adapted from Waring, 2002)

Researchers use a variety of tests to measure students' vocabulary sizes. Some of these are rough and approximate instruments, but some are normed and standardized with a relatively high degree of accuracy (see Nation, 1990, for a thorough discussion of such tests). However, as a general rule of thumb, when L2 readers and writers display language skills such as those in outlined Tables 4.1 and 4.3, their vocabulary size is probably in the range indicated.

Scanning a newspaper page and deriving bits of basic news reports can be possible with a vocabulary range of 1,000 to 2,000 words, even though the details of news stories will not be understood. To read a newspaper and to be able to understand at least some of the news stories, learners would require familiarity with 2,000 to 3,000 or 4,000 words, and attaining this much vocabulary takes a bit of work. Along these lines, most L2 students who aspire to academic studies in a country where another language represents the medium of instruction—and is required for all academic writing tasks—need to have a vocabulary of over 5,000 words, which includes academic words that have to be systematically and persistently learned.

> A vocabulary size of approximately 5,000 word families is requisite for relatively fluent L2 reading, even though a dictionary is still necessary at this level (e.g., Hirsh & Nation, 1992; Hu & Nation, 2000).

Talking Shop

Have you studied or learned another language? For how many years? Can you scan newspaper headlines and understand—at least approximately—what they say? Are you able to read a newspaper article closely and understand its contents in detail?

Do you have a sufficient language base to write a summary of a newspaper article and formulate your position on the topic discussed in it? And how about an academic paper on a topic addressed in several journal articles?

In your estimation, how many more years would attaining academic language proficiency take, compared to an ability to engage in a conversation?

Table 4.2 demonstrates the vocabulary size and the number of words required to read in English at school and illustrates the difficulty of being able to understand L2 text without knowing many content words. The term *text coverage* is the percentage of text words known by the reader or the number of words needed to cover the text.

TABLE 4.2 Vocabulary Size and Text Coverage

Number of Words	% Text Coverage
86,741	100.0
43,831	99.0
12,448	95.0
5,000	89.4
4,000	87.6
3,000	85.2
2,000	81.3
1,000	74.1
100	49.0
10	23.7

(Carroll, Davis, & Richman, 1971)

According to Hu and Nation (2000), with text coverage of 80% (20 out of every 100 words unknown to the readers, at a vocabulary range of slightly over 1,000 words), reading and comprehending text may be difficult. Typical non-academic or general interest L2 texts—for instance, a newspaper article—cannot be understood adequately enough for learners to answer comprehension questions.

In general, 98% text coverage (1 unknown word in 50) is needed for most L2 learners to understand what they are reading. Based on the results of several experiments, Hu and Nation (2000) conclude that it is possible for some learners in the 90% and a few more in the 95% group to have adequate or close to adequate comprehension, but for a majority of learners this accessible vocabulary is too small to understand the text well enough to account for its contents.

L2 Vocabulary and Writing

The data in Table 4.3 below highlight the types of written text that nonnative speakers can produce, depending on their accessible vocabulary range. As has been mentioned, knowing 500 or 1,000 of the most frequent English words does not allow L2 learners to produce a piece of writing, however simple, because these common words consist of articles, prepositions, pronouns, and basic nouns and adjectives (e.g., *now, study, away, start, room, enough, best, some*). As is apparent from the outline of the writing skills at various vocabulary levels in Table 4.3, clearly, L2 learners with vocabulary sizes of 500 or 1,000 words cannot be expected to produce much text.

In fact, basic written prose can begin to emerge only when the learner's vocabulary range exceeds 2,000 words. Typically, the descriptions of student writing found at the level of over 5,000 words seem to be pretty typical of what is considered to be relatively advanced in advanced ESL classes or many community

TABLE 4.3 L2 Vocabulary Size and Writing Skill Levels

0–500 word families
- Only very basic sentences with extremely poor choice of words.
- Series of correct or incorrect phrases without sentences.
- Translated phrases and sentences.

500–1,000 word families
- A small number of compound sentences (e.g., *Bob left, and Mike went home.*).
- The use of only basic phrase and sentence conjunctions (e.g., *and, but, then*).
- Translated sentences that consist of largely translated phrases.

1,000–2,000 word families
- Complete dependence on a bilingual dictionary when writing longer texts.
- Poor word choice.
- Occasional collocations (words that often co-occur together in discourse as in *strong wind* or *big wind*, but not *large wind*), but many awkward and strange phrases.
- Disjointed ideas/incoherent in spots.

2,000–5,000 word families
- Highly pre-patterned and predictable texts can be produced without a dictionary (e.g., *This is a big problem in my country*).
- Spontaneous writing and writing on new topics are almost completely dependent on bilingual dictionary use.

5,000 +
- A bilingual dictionary is used only rarely in routine types of writing, mostly for the purpose of identifying subtle differences in word meanings or looking up specific terms.
- Extensive reliance on a bilingual dictionary in writing specialized texts, such as homework assignments.
- Consistent and repeated errors and misused words.
- Un-idiomatic text, short on collocations.

(Adapted from Waring, 2002)

colleges. At this juncture, it is important to note that the text produced by L2 writers with such a high level of vocabulary (i.e., around 5,000 words) seems to be far from impressive, as many L2 teachers know from experience.

Analyses of L2 Academic Text and Writing: Identifying Curricular Domains

> Academic vocabulary must be taught simply because it does not occur in daily interactions and conversational exchanges.

Hu and Nation (2000, p. 406) point out that "the relationship between text coverage and vocabulary size is strongly affected by the kind of text that is looked at." That is, knowing high frequency English words does not enable the readers to understand academic text well.

TABLE 4.4 Vocabulary Size and Text Types

Text Type	First 1000 Most Frequent Words	Second 1000 Most Frequent Words	Academic Vocabulary (Coxhead, 2000)
Conversation	84%	6%	2%
Juvenile fiction	85%	6%	—
Academic texts	71%	5%	10%

(Adapted from Hu & Nation, 2000)

On the other hand, the first 1,000 most frequent words can enable learners to get a handle on portions of conversations. The most rare of the first 1,000 include, for example, *ideal, warm, miss, familiar, guest, everyone, duty, perfect, flow, kitchen, dust,* or *admit,* which occur more frequently in conversations than any other types of discourse. Notably, however, as Table 4.4 shows, only 6% of the second 1,000 most common words have a bit of substance to add to the learner's ability to comprehend conversational exchanges, with content words, such as *flood, distant, decrease, complicate, consumer,* or *harvest,* all of which would seem rather basic to most native speakers.

It is easy to conclude from these data in Table 4.4 that conversational vocabulary does not occur in academic texts, and academic vocabulary cannot be learned by means of attaining conversational fluency.

The fundamental distinctions between conversational and academic vocabulary and grammar represent the impetus for several studies carried by Hinkel (2002a, 2003a, 2004a, 2005). Hinkel's (2002b) study focused on 68 linguistic and rhetorical features of text (e.g., vocabulary and grammar) in a corpus of 1,457 essays (434,768 words) written by native and nonnative speakers of English enrolled in degree studies in U.S. universities. The purpose of her corpus analysis was to identify the frequency counts of language features that occur or do not occur in student writing and compare those in L1 text to those in L2 learner prose. The objective of such comparisons is usually to provide empirical information about similarities and distinctions between the language uses and types of language features in native and nonnative student writing to guide L2 teaching and curricula.

The language features addressed in Hinkel's analysis included both advanced academic vocabulary (e.g., *account, anticipate, controversy, occurrence*) and syntactic constructions such as complex sentences with various types of subordinate clauses (e.g., *²Things I have learned will not be only for my benefit but also to increase the business quality in the country* or *Interacting with people that [are] already successful will help you decide weather looking into future opportunities a must or not*), passive voice constructions (e.g., *It can be seen on my experience, such as at high school and college*), and the uses of English tenses (e.g., *After our graduation, most of us have been adults*).

A large majority of the L2 students whose writing was included in the study were not new arrivals. These writers had spent a few years in the U.S. while they were learning L2 and working their way through the first two years in general education courses in colleges and universities. This particular demographic characteristic of the learners in Hinkel's 2002 investigation highlights the extent and the kinds of students' language exposure.

> Conversational vocabulary and grammar provide poor coverage for academic text, and having a large conversational range does not necessarily enable L2 learners to read and write academic prose.

The results of Hinkel's (2002b, 2003a, 2003b, 2004b, 2005, 2009) investigations are summarized in Table 4.5. The language features identified in students' L2 writing are divided into two broad classes: those that need to be persistently and intensively taught and those that should be un-taught. Relative to the writing of novice first-year students who are native speakers of English, the vocabulary and language features of L2 students with years of exposure to conversational interactions in English leads to their developed conversational language skills but a prominent lack of academic vocabulary and advanced grammar construction (as in the examples above).

> The written prose of experienced L2 writers contains important shortfalls of academic vocabulary and grammar. On the other hand, however, the language of conventionally skilled L2 writers includes an extensive range of colloquial and conversational constructions, such as *guys, a lot, everyone, like he has a problem, dude, someone, thing, something, everything, never, nothing,* and *always*.

Studies of vocabulary, grammar, and morphological (word form) characteristics of L2 text, as well as error analyses (see a discussion later in this chapter), are typically quantitative. Such investigations allow for identifying statistically significant differences between the textual properties of L1 and L2 prose. A large body of research reports has been published in the past several decades. These deal with a broad range of lexical and syntactic characteristics of L2 prose, such as the uses of personal and other types of pronouns, sentence structure (e.g., subordination and coordination), phrase and sentence conjunctions (e.g., sentence transitions), prepositional phrases, concrete and abstract nouns, verb tenses and aspects, cohesive devices (e.g., lexical repetition), lexical synonyms and ties, active and passive voice constructions, and lexical and grammatical errors. Many studies, for example, have investigated the uses of discourse markers (e.g., *well, you know,* or *I mean*), cohesion and coherence devices (e.g., *so, the cause of, a result*), modal verbs, hedges, and modifiers in L1 and L2 prose (Field & Oi, 1992; Flowerdew, 2000; Hinkel, 1995, 2001b, 2002a, 2004b; Johnson, 1992; Khalil, 1989; Mauranen, 1996; Swales, 1990).

For this purpose, researchers may compare the frequencies and contexts of sentence conjunctions (e.g., *furthermore, however,* and *thus*), coordinating conjunctions (e.g., *and, but, yet,* and *so*), and/or summary markers (e.g., *in short* and *in sum*) (e.g., Field & Oi, 1992; Hinkel, 1999, 2001b, 2003; Schleppegrell, 2002). Similarly, to analyze the uses of modal verbs, usage measurements can be computed separately or together for possibility and ability modals (e.g., *can, may*) or obligation and necessity modals (e.g., *must, should*).

Overall, based on a vast body of research, limited vocabulary and grammar are the most frequently cited/noted properties of L2 text. Some of these examinations are summarized in Table 4.5, and the curricular guidelines presented below are based on the data discussed in Hinkel (1999, 2002c, 2005, 2009). Speaking generally, the vocabulary and grammar constructions that need to be intensively taught are those that fall dramatically short in L2 writing but are found in the prose of basic L1 writers. The academic vocabulary and grammar constructions outlined in Table 4.5 are frequently found in virtually all academic writing of L1 students

TABLE 4.5 The Vocabulary and Grammar Features That Need to Be Intensively Taught

Top and Urgent Priorities

Vocabulary

Academic collocations and formal idiomatic phrases (e.g., *The purpose of this essay/paper/ analysis/overview is to . . . The main emphasis/focus/goal/purpose of this essay/paper/project is to . . .*)

Academic nouns of all types, such as:

- Abstract and academic nouns, and nominalizations (nouns ending in *-ion, -ity, -ness, -ment*) and gerunds (nouns ending in *–ing*)
- Commonplace and catch-all academic nouns (e.g., *advantage, approach, aspect, category, characteristic, class, method*)

Grammar

- Complex sentences with subordinate clauses of all types

Second Priorities

Grammar

- Highly prevalent and academic impersonal *it*-constructions (e.g., *it seems/it appears/it is clear that . . .*)
- Descriptive adjectives (e.g., *an important project* vs., for example, predicate adjectives, as in *this project is important*)
- Passive voice (e.g., *the article was published*)

Third Priorities

- Hedges of all types, such as:
  - Frequency adverbs (e.g., *frequently, occasionally, often, usually*)
  - Contextual and possibility hedges (e.g., *comparatively, likely, possible(-ly), probable(-ly), relative(-ly)*)
  - Modal verbs[3] as hedges (e.g., *can, may, could*)
  - Conditional clauses (e.g., *if the author shows facts . . .*)

beginning in the 8th grade and are usually well established in the range of high school writing (NCES/NAEP, 2003; Schleppegrell, 2004).

Academic collocations and formal idiomatic phrases have to be taught to both L1 and L2 writers simply because these advanced expressions do not occur in naturalistic settings. That is, just like abstract nouns, these constructions are found predominantly in textbooks or academic prose. The difference between L1 and L2 writers, however, is that by the time L1 learners reach the 8th grade, they have encountered and had numerous opportunities to acquire such nouns as *democracy, random,* or *monarchy*. For many—if not all—L2 writers, impersonal *it-* constructions, extensive uses of passives, and hedging represent new, and often difficult, domains of language that have to be explicitly taught. According to Schleppegrell (2004, p. 81), many L2 writers in schools and colleges "haven't had the opportunity to develop academic registers in their first languages" (register is a variety of language used for a particular purpose or in a particular social setting; e.g., academic language includes formal grammar or formal words). In addition to learning conversational English, L2 academic writers have to learn an entirely new range of grammar and vocabulary that do not occur in casual speech. On the other hand, many L1 writers develop an ability to distinguish between spoken and formal written registers between 4th and 6th grades, and sometimes even earlier (Kress, 1994, 1996).

Talking Shop

Can you identify some of the grammar and vocabulary features of casual conversations or formal writing? How can you tell the difference between conversational and formal grammar and vocabulary? When and where did you learn the differences between the two styles?

In your experience, what are the most prominent characteristics that distinguish the two? What are the reasons that conversational register often finds its way into academic writing?

Many people hold the view that the informal written style is not necessarily out of place in academic writing. So, why is it important for L1 and L2 students to learn to use academic grammar and vocabulary? Discuss your views with your classmates.

As has been mentioned, colloquial and conversational vocabulary and grammar constructions dominate in L2 academic prose because many L2 writers have far more exposure to conversational discourse than they do to standard and formal writing in English. In many cases, however, L2 writers may not be aware, for example, that such vocabulary as *dude, stuff, guy,* or *gal*, or constructions such as *he's gonna be late because he is always late* are inappropriate in academic writing. Much research has demonstrated that the distinctions between academic language and that found in casual conversations needs to be emphasized throughout the teaching of formal writing required in schooling at any level (e.g., Chang & Swales, 1999; Hinkel, 2002a, 2003a; Schleppegrell, 2002, 2004; Shaw & Liu, 1998). However, an additional reason that colloquialisms are typically found in L2 academic prose is that L2 writers simply lack vocabulary and grammar essential for producing written academic text.

Vocabulary and grammar constructions outlined in Table 4.6 rarely occur in academic writing and need to be "un-taught"—i.e., students need to be taught not to use these features in their academic writing. Alternative and more academic

TABLE 4.6 Conversational Vocabulary and Grammar Constructions That Need NOT Be Taught

Top and Urgent Priorities

Vocabulary
- Indeterminate and vague nouns (e.g., *human(s), human being(s), people, society, world, stuff, thing(y), -ever* nouns such as *whoever* and *whatever*)
- Tentative verbs (e.g., *like, plan, try, want*)
- Thinking/feeling verbs that rarely occur in informational texts (e.g., *believe, feel, forget, guess, hear, know, learn, love, prove, remember, see, think*)
- Phrase conjunctions (*and, or, but* vs., for example, *in addition* or *however*)
- Repeated and simplistic sentence transitions (e.g., *moreover, furthermore, thus, therefore*)

Grammar
- First and second person pronouns and contexts that require their uses (e.g., personal narratives/examples/experiences) in lieu of rhetorical support

Second Priorities

Vocabulary
- Intensifiers and emphatics of any type (e.g., *absolutely, a lot, complete(-ly), deeply, for sure, hugely, total(-ly)* or *I do agree that this method is better*)
- Indirect pronouns (e.g., *everyone, no one, nothing; anyone, some, something*)

Grammar
- *Be* as a main verb and predicative adjectives (e.g., *John is tall*)
- Modals of obligation (*must, have to*)
- Contractions (*don't, can't*)

Third Priorities

Grammar
- Future tense verb uses (e.g., *the income of these people is going to/will rise if they get education*)
- Progressive verb uses (e.g., *I am explaining my point of view clearly*)
- *Some-, any-, no-* (indefinite) pronouns (*some-/any-/every-/no-* words, e.g., *somebody, nothing, everyone, anything*)
- Rhetorical questions (e.g., *Do you know what the purpose of life is?*)
- Causative constructions (e.g., *because, because of*)
- *by*-phrase passives (*the depth is determined by the technician during the experiment*)

lexical and syntactic means of constructing text and discourse have to be taught (see Table 4.5).

Many L2 learners can engage in fluent and unconstrained conversational discourse. In a great number of cases, when listening to a conversation between two individuals it is not possible to tell the difference between those to have access to academic language in English and those who do not. As an outcome, such academic L2 writers need to attain proficiency in academic language simply because without it they are unable to succeed in their academic tasks.

However, for L2 writers to produce academic prose, intensive vocabulary work is required. To replace the occurrences of *human beings, thing, people,* and *whoever,* more formal vocabulary needs to be taught and learned. For example, contextually appropriate vocabulary is relatively easy to find:

> <u>People</u>—*adults, employees of local businesses, individuals, persons, population, the public, residents, community/group members, workers*

To replace personal narratives as evidence, instruction in what represents evidence is also requisite, as well as how to build arguments and evidence for persuasion (see chapter 3 for additional discussion), and how to structure information in writing. Causative constructions, such as *because* and *because of* can be substituted by *reason* and other words a great deal better suited for academic writing:

> <u>Reason</u>—*aim, basis, cause, consideration, expectation, explanation, goal, purpose, thinking, understanding*

Similarly, asking rhetorical questions does not replace providing informed answers based on sound facts. These curricular considerations will be addressed in chapter 5.

Action Point

Writing samples of school age children are relatively easy to find online. Or maybe you can locate pieces of writing produced by your own children, nieces, nephews, or second cousins. How old are these children? What type of writing do they need to produce?

In these writing samples, identify and count the number of occurrences of formal grammar features or formal vocabulary, and then do the same for the occurrences of informal grammar or vocabulary. Count the number of words in each sample. The easiest way to approximate this number is to locate a typical single written line, count the number of words in it, and multiply it by the number of complete lines in the sample.

> Then to determine the rate of occurrences of formal or informal grammar constructions and vocabulary, divide the number of occurrences by the approximate number of words in a writing sample. For example, 8 formal grammar features divided by 40 words = 0.2. Then multiply this number by 100 to get a percentage. For example, 0.2 times 100 = 20%.
>
> As the next step, locate the writing sample of an academic L2 writer—of any age—but not a university student writing a class paper (say, an email message), and repeat the procedure. Are these rates similar or different? For writers of similar or different ages? What would such a mini research project demonstrate? What conclusions can be made based on your computations?

L2 Academic Writing and Areas of Difficulty

As early as the mid-1980s, specialists in the teaching of L2 writing and language began to sound the alarm regarding the applicability of methods and techniques adopted for teaching L1 writing to the instruction of L2 learners. Many researchers investigated the range and types of the language learning needs of L2 students in the U.S. academy (e.g., Hinkel, 2003a; Horowitz, 1986a, 1986b; Leki, 2007; Santos, 1988; Swales & Feak, 2012). Their studies, as well as those of other L2 writing experts, have shown clearly that academic ESL and EAP programs do not adequately prepare their L2 students for the writing tasks that predominate in the academy (e.g., Hinkel, 2002b, 2004b, 2011; ICAS, 2002; Rosenfeld et al., 2004). A great deal of research carried out in the 1980s and 1990s has determined unambiguously that the expectations of academic and assessment writing have remained consistently focused on the quality of the student prose that invariably includes such considerations as the vocabulary range and sophistication, the type and complexity of the sentence structure, phrase-level grammar, word order, word morphology, inflections, verb tenses and voice, and pronoun uses, as well as spelling and punctuation.

To demonstrate that L1 approaches to writing instruction cannot and should not be used for teaching L2 writers, Silva (1993) synthesized the findings of 72 empirical studies that compared an extensive spectrum of characteristics of L1 and L2 prose, including language features, discourse structure, rhetorical development, elaboration, persuasion, clarity, specificity, and audience orientation, among many others. His synthesis showed that while L1 and L2 writing "are similar in their broad outlines, they are different in numerous and important ways" (p. 671). Specifically, Silva underscores that a great number of disparities exist between L1 and L2 uses of language. He emphasized that the language learning needs of L2 writers were crucially distinct from those of basic or proficient L1 writers. Silva further states that L2 writing pedagogy requires special and systematic approaches that take into account the linguistic, rhetorical, and cultural differences between

L1 and L2 writers (see also Silva, 1997, for a discussion of the ethical issues that accompany the applications of teaching methods for L1 writers to L2 learners).

According to Silva (1993), pronounced and crucial differences manifest themselves in practically all facets of L1 and L2 language usage: fluency, accuracy, range, quality, and structure. Producing L2 text is far more work- and time-consuming, and revision is demonstrably more difficult. To summarize Silva's conclusions specifically as they pertain to text and language quality, empirical comparisons of L1 novice college-level writing with L2 prose of university students have identified numerous systematic and significant disparities. Silva concludes his overview of research by saying that L2 writers have needs that are "distinct from those of L1 writers, whether they be basic or skilled." The author also points out that it is necessary "for L2 teachers to work to enhance their L2 writers' grammatical and lexical resources" that can allow students to build syntactic and lexical repertoire. That is, instruction must provide students the language options indispensable for producing competent text.

Along these lines, Schleppegrell (2002, 2004) undertakes an extensive and thorough investigation of the language (i.e., grammar and vocabulary range) as well as discourse features L2 students need to learn and deploy for success in their schooling. Her analysis identifies the challenges that academic language presents to L2 learners who are often unfamiliar with the typical "literate" variety of features employed at school. Like Silva, Schleppegrell finds that L2 learners and speakers of nonstandard dialects often have no access to opportunities for advanced literacy development outside of school. For such learners, an explicit focus on language is critical if they are to do well in their subjects.

According to Schleppegrell's (2004) conclusions, in schooling, students attain new knowledge through language, and in practically all contexts of schooling, the language is complex, dense, and abstract. In particular, in various subject areas, such as science, history, and social studies, the linguistic features of writing require students to identify, understand, and construct disciplinary meanings by means of which knowledge is shared and developed. To this end, to be able to come to knowledge and demonstrate it, L2 learners have to achieve a level of language that enables them to obtain education. That is, in order for students to "engage in critical dialogues with institutions and social forms," they need to understand how ideas and beliefs comprise a world view, a political outlook, or literacy practices, all of which are expressed and conveyed through language. Schleppegrell calls for an increased awareness among teachers of language expectations entailed in schooling and the linguistic elements that are valued in school.

Talking Shop

According to several authors cited in this chapter, in the schooling and education of L2 learners, a lack of emphasis on the development of their language proficiency seems to lead to continued and persistent social inequalities. In your view, how can these be overcome? What can be the reasons that language proficiency continues to be neglected in teaching?

If you were designing a curriculum for an ELA class in, say, elementary or junior high levels, how would you undertake to incorporate language teaching? For your consideration:

- What should be short-term and long-term priorities in language teaching?
- What does research have to contribute to creating strategic language teaching priorities?
- What specific areas of language development would your curriculum emphasize?
- What additional training would the teachers of L2 learners need to enable them to add a language focus?
- How does language education at your institution prepare you for working to overcome long-standing inequalities in the education of L2 learners?

Speaking broadly, virtually all studies to date have identified fundamental and pronounced differences between all facets of writing in L1 and L2 discourse and text. For example, the process of constructing L2 discourse is consistently and significantly different from that involved in producing L1 written prose. Based on the findings of hundreds of studies, compared to the discourse structuring and ideational development in L1 writing, the following characteristics of L2 writing seem to be prominent:

- Organization and structuring of discourse moves and their contents inconsistently with the conventions of formal written English
- The unsystematic construction or placement of thesis statements, as well as their complete omission
- A failure to account for counterarguments and anticipate audience reactions
- The support for contextual arguments and claims by means of statements of personal opinions and beliefs in lieu of more substantive information
- A preponderance of unsupported argumentation
- Reliance on simple grammar, conversational vocabulary, and short sentences
- Preponderance of text-level errors of practically all types (i.e., grammar, word-form, vocabulary usage and meaning, verb and noun usage, meaning, and form, preposition, and article errors)
- Non-academic language, style and tone that can include, for example, direct and authoritative admonitions, warnings, superlatives, rhetorical questions, ornate analogies, and direct appeals to the reader

- A lack of clarity, developed coherence, and consistent specificity, explicitness, and cohesion
- Weak lexical/semantic ties and theme connections, and a prevalence of overt phrase and sentence conjunctions, such as *and, first/second/third*, or *moreover*
- Ineffective strategies for exemplification, extracting and citing information from sources, as well as paraphrasing, quoting, and incorporating source material

To date, a large number of studies have focused on a broad range of lexical and syntactic features of L2 text, such as the uses of personal and other types of pronouns, modal verbs, sentence structure (e.g., subordination and coordination), phrase and sentence conjunctions (e.g., sentence transitions), prepositional phrases, concrete and abstract nouns, verb tenses and aspects, cohesive devices (e.g., lexical repetition), lexical synonyms and ties, active and passive voice constructions, and lexical and grammatical errors (e.g., Flowerdew, 2000; Hinkel, 1995, 2001a, 2002a, 2004a; Johnson, 1992; Khalil, 1989; Mauranen, 1996; Swales, 1990).

Overall, based on a vast body of research, limited vocabulary and grammar are the most frequently cited/noted properties of L2 text, noted in declining order in Table 4.7.

At present, research has clearly and unambiguously demonstrated that L2 writers' skill level in vocabulary and grammar disadvantage the quality of their formal prose. A number of studies report that, even after several years of language learning, the grammar and vocabulary in L2 academic text continues to differ significantly from that of novice L1 writers in regard to a broad range of properties. In many

TABLE 4.7 Grammar and Vocabulary in L2 Writing

Compared to L1 written text, L2 formal prose exhibits the following prominent characteristics:
- Significantly fewer academic and collocational expressions
- High rates of incomplete or inaccurate sentences (e.g., missing sentence subjects or verbs; incomplete verb phrases; sentence fragments)
- Repetitions of content words more often (i.e., nouns, verbs, adjectives, and adverbs)
- Frequent simple paraphrases or a lack of paraphrasing
- Uses of shorter words (fewer words with two or more syllables), and conversational vocabulary, and high frequency words (e.g., *good, bad, ask, talk*)
- A limited repertoire of modifying and descriptive prepositional phrases, as well as a higher rate of misused prepositions
- Little subordination, but two to three times more coordination
- Inconsistent uses of verb tenses and few passive constructions
- High rates of personal pronouns (e.g., *I, we, he*) and personal narratives, as well as low rates of impersonal/referential pronouns (e.g., *it, this, one*)
- Markedly reduced rates of abstract and interpretive nouns, and nominalizations (e.g., *rotation, cognition, analysis*)
- A preponderance of conversational intensifiers, emphatics, exaggeratives, and overstatements (e.g., *totally, always, huge, for sure*) and conversational hedges (e.g., *sort of, in a way*), together with few possibility/probability hedges (e.g., *apparently, perhaps*)

cases of undergraduate L2 writers, for example, a restricted access to advanced language features results in simple texts that rely on the most common language features that occur predominantly in conversations. Currently, in light of a large body of research findings obtained after about a half a century of L2 text analyses, this conclusion seems rather obvious (Carson, 2001; Hedgcock, 2005; Hinkel, 2009, 2011; Leki et al., 2008; Paltridge, 2004).

> The ultimate goal of developing L2 writers' language skills is to give them "an equal chance to succeed in their writing-related personal or academic endeavors" (Silva, 1993, pp. 670–671).

In his extensive book-length survey of the language skills required in higher education in a number of English-speaking countries, Jordan (1997) presents the following summary of language areas that students consider to be most difficult. The participants of the studies included mostly undergraduate, as well as a few graduate, students. These learners ranked speaking in front of small groups as most difficult (participating in seminars), followed by two writing tasks (written assignments and note-taking), and noted that their receptive skills—understanding lectures and reading at an adequate speed—were least difficult.

Jordan's investigation further looks into the elements of students' writing skills to identify those most in need of improvement to enable students to succeed in their studies. The responses to questionnaires were solicited from both students and faculty, and it appears that, despite a few minor differences, these are similar overall.

The results of Jordan (1997) show clearly that, although the order of language learning priorities identified by university students and faculty are not identical, in general terms, they seem rather uniform. The areas of difficulty include the student's ability to write in an appropriate academic style that in fact consists of a solid range of academic vocabulary, grammar, and punctuation skills. A close look at the elements of writing skills that are difficult for L2 students enrolled in colleges and universities in Jordan's survey is also largely similar to that found in the study of the California college and university faculty, discussed in detail in

TABLE 4.8 Rank Order of Language Difficulty in College/University Studies

Rank Order of Difficulty	Percentage of Students That Assigned #1 Rank to Most Difficult L2 Skills
Participating in seminars	28%
Writing	23%
Taking lecture notes	11%
Understanding lectures	9%
Reading at a satisfactory speed	4%

(Adapted from Jordan, 1997)

TABLE 4.9 Rank Order of Language Difficulty in Academic L2 Writing

Elements of Writing Skills	Students' Ranks of Most Difficult L2 Skills	Faculty Ranks of Most Difficult L2 Skills
Vocabulary	1 (62%)	3 (70%)
Academic style	2 (53%)	1 (92%)
Spelling	3 (41%)	5 (23%)
Grammar	4 (38%)	2 (77%)
Punctuation	5 (18%)	4 (23%)

(Adapted from Jordan, 1997)

chapter 2. According to that survey (ICAS, 2002; see chapter 3), the quality of students' language in the state's 109 colleges and 33 universities required intensive and extensive work on the following elements of writing:

- Sentence structure
- Appropriate academic vocabulary
- Error correction/editing
- Spelling and punctuation

Action Point

Do you have access to a few (4 or 5) L2 learners? Possibly at your institution? Or among students at a local language-teaching program or school? If so, you can ask them several questions, similar to those in Jordan's (1997) study. Your questionnaire does not have to be extensive, but it would be interesting to find out if the responses of the learners you are familiar with align with or differ from the responses in Jordan's investigation.

Some examples of the questions you can ask are listed below:

For you, what are the most difficult aspects of writing in English? Spelling? Punctuation? Grammar? Academic vocabulary? Correcting/editing errors in writing?

In addition, you can ask these learners about the curriculum in their classes:
- What aspects of language receive a great deal of attention and which ones less?
- If these learners could change what they are taught language, what would the changes be?
- If they could alter how they are taught language, what would such changes be?

Error Gravity, Frequency, and Pattern Studies: The Editing Focus

Primarily due to the prevailing research interest in contrastive and error analyses in the 1960s, 1970s, and 1980s, an enormous body of work has been published on the types, patterns, and causes of learner error in speech and writing. The early interest of researchers in error analyses has also been taken up more recently in the 1990s and 2000s with the goal of developing L2 course curricula and enhancing learner error identification and editing skills in writing.

Some of the error analysis studies also set out to determine the severity and importance of L2 errors in the perceptions of university faculty who evaluate—and grade—L2 writers' work (e.g., Raimes, 1991; Santos, 1988). Other researchers similarly focused on the gravity of L2 errors in large-scale assessments and ratings of writing (e.g., Sakyi, 2000; Vann, Meyer, & Lorenz, 1984; Vann, Lorenz, & Meyer, 1991; Vaughan, 1991). Pedagogically oriented publications build on this foundation to refine and supplement course curricula for L2 writing instruction and develop L2 writers' error awareness. All these studies attempt to prioritize errors and establish a hierarchy of L2 errors in writing to help teachers and learners focus on the most important of these (Bates, Lane, & Lange, 1993; Ferris, 2002, 2003, 2004; Ferris & Roberts, 2001; Holt, 1997).

A summative overview of key error gravity studies presents a relatively complete picture of what is, in effect, de-valued in student academic prose. Table 4.10 consolidates the findings of several influential studies, based on large sets of data and faculty survey research. Bates, Lane, and Lange (1993) provide guidelines for teachers that are intended to supplement a textbook on error awareness and editing. Ferris (2002, 2003, 2004) develops a detailed and comprehensive program for teachers to deal with learner errors systematically and thoroughly. Ferris' program is based on the results of her earlier study on the severity and frequency of L2 errors in writing (Ferris & Roberts, 2001). Raimes (1991) conducted a similar study of L2 errors in compositions and the evaluations of these errors by composition faculty. The findings of Raimes' study are reflected in her textbook for students (*Grammar Trouble Spots*, 2nd ed., 1999). Vann et al. (1984) reported the hierarchical severity of 12 common ESL errors in the perceptions of over 320 faculty in 8 disciplines, such as biology, education, engineering, humanities, physical and mathematical sciences, and social sciences, in a large U.S. university. The summary of research on the severity of errors in L2 writing is presented in Table 4.10.

It is important to note at the outset that L2 writers' abilities to identify and correct grammar and vocabulary errors is a developmental process at least to some extent. That is, as their experience with constructing L2 text grows, the frequency of errors in many instances of L2 writing can decline.

TABLE 4.10 Types of Errors in Declining Order of Severity

Bates, Lane, and Lange (1993)	Ferris (2002, 2003) and Ferris and Roberts (2001)	Vann et al. (1984)	Raimes (1991, 1999)
Most Egregious Errors			
Verb tense form modals	Sentence structure: boundaries, unnecessary/missing elements; unidiomatic expression	Word order	Sentence structure
Conditional sentence/clause	Word choice: meaning, prepositions, pronouns	*It*-deletion	Sentence transitions, coordinating conjunctions
Active/passive voice	Verb tense form	Verb tense	Punctuation
Dependent clauses	Noun endings, singular and plural	Relative clauses	Verb tense
Sentence structure	Punctuation	Active/passive voice	Subject-verb agreement
Word order	Articles/determiners	Word meaning	Active/passive voice
Sentence transitions	Word form: morphology	Subject-verb agreement	Modal verbs
Less Severe Errors			
Subject-verb agreement	Spelling	Pronoun agreement	Verb form
Articles	Run-on sentences	Prepositions	Nouns and quantifiers
Noun endings, singular and plural	Pronouns	Spelling	Articles
Word choice: morphology, meaning	Subject-verb agreement	Run-on sentences	Pronoun reference
Prepositions	Sentence fragments	Articles	Adjective/adverb form
	Miscellaneous: idioms, inappropriate register		Prepositions
Other Types of Errors			
Nonidiomatic expressions			Relative clauses
Wrong word meaning			Conditional sentences
Inappropriate register/ conversational style			Quotations, citing sources
Lack of coherence/ unity			
Unclear/illogical expressions, text			

> However, researchers have also found that, for a majority of L2 learners, eliminating all grammar and vocabulary errors is virtually impossible. Furthermore, while some types of sentence- and phrase-level errors can be reduced with experience, other classes of errors are a great deal more difficult to eliminate.

Although studies of L2 writing have shown that errors can occur in the L2 uses of a broad range of language constructions, the following error types have been recognized as highly common and pervasive (e.g., Cutting, 2000; Ferris, 1995, 1997, 2002; Ferris & Roberts, 2001; McCretton & Rider, 1993).

Examples of Frequent Error Types in L2 Writing

- Sentence divisions, fragmented and clipped sentences, and run-ons (e.g., *And he brings. *Because of creative teacher.*)
- Subject and verb agreement (e.g., *Good education support students in their studies.*)
- Verb tenses and aspects, and verb phrases (e.g., *To find a good technician was very difficult at present. *It also important in process teaching.*)
- Word-level morphology (i.e., absent or incorrect affixes) and incorrect word forms (e.g., *using limited budgetary, *High standard educator want to have a higher prices to pay for their service*)
- Incomplete or incorrect subordinate clause structure (e.g., missing subjects, verbs and clause subordinators, as in *when some of teacher teach learning language, *an engineer who design creative can't taught at school*)
- Misuses (or under-uses and over-uses) of coherence and cohesion markers, such as coordinating conjunctions and demonstrative pronouns (e.g., *To begin with, this is my conclusion. *Adding, many surveys find this result.*)
- Singular or plural nouns and pronouns (e.g., *Western parents works with the child to find out the problems. *They know how marriage are important to rise kids when the average age of marriage are 25 to 27.*)
- Incorrect or omitted prepositions (e.g., *from my opinion, *At some time there is this young businessman who just about takes a taxi of the airport.*)
- Incorrect or omitted articles (e.g., *Treasure hunter found gold in bottom of a hole, but he maybe closing on treasure. *Many people use cellphone to make phone call to family, but some use internet.*)
- Incorrect modal verbs (e.g., *The feature of those technology can be discussed in my paper in following paragraphs. *Meaningless work will make people feel boring, which must lead to poor performance.*)
- Spelling errors

(All examples in this list are from actual L2 student writing.)

Since the 1980s, analyses of L2 language errors have become a familiar venue in investigations of written computer corpora of learner writing (Granger, 1998; Granger & Tribble, 1998; Green, Christopher, & Lam, 2000; Nesselhauf, 2005). In general terms, the analysis of grammatical and lexical errors in L2 prose is rooted in the contrastive (error) analysis that predominated in L2 learning research between the 1950s and 1970s.

One of the most popular comments on the studies of errors in L2 writing is that L1 writers who are native speakers of English also make mistakes. This observation is unquestionably true. A recent empirical study of L1 undergraduate writing in 24 U.S. universities (Lunsford & Lunsford, 2008) identified the most frequent types of L1 errors (in declining order):

- Wrong word
- Spelling (including homonyms)
- Incomplete or missing documentation
- Mechanical error with a quotation
- Missing comma after an introductory element
- Missing word
- Unnecessary or missing capitalization
- Vague pronoun reference
- Unnecessary comma
- Unnecessary shift in verb tense
- Missing comma in a compound sentence

It seems clear from this list that the L1 errors in formal prose are fundamentally distinct from those in L2 university writing because the former are unlikely to impede comprehension (see also studies of error gravity in L2 writing, e.g., Vann et al. (1991), Vann et al. (1984), and Santos (1988)).

Talking Shop

Most work on the severity of L2 errors in writing was carried out between the mid-1980s and early 2000s. Looking at the summary of several investigations from a contemporary perspective, do you agree with the rankings of errors, as they are classified in Table 4.9? Why or why not? Discuss your views with your classmates.

How would you re-order the ranks of error severity in L2 writing? Would your ranked order stay the same if the purpose of writing were social (e.g., an email message or a journal entry) rather than academic?

> In the list of Examples of Frequent Error Types in L2 Writing, each L2 text excerpt includes errors of more than one type. In these excerpts, which types of errors are more severe than others? Do you agree with the classification of the errors in the example list? Why or why not?

Applications of L1 Composition Pedagogy to Teaching L2 Writing

Extensive research in the teaching of composition to native speakers of English began in earnest in the early 1960s. At that time, large numbers of students started to enter U.S. colleges and universities without much formal preparation for writing papers in the canonical courses in literature and the history of Western civilization. Faced with increasing numbers of students from all walks of life, the teaching faculty in English departments across the U.S. began to realize that in fact little research had been undertaken into how coherent writing was achieved or how best to teach academic writing skills to students with diverse backgrounds in schooling.

The process approach to the teaching of writing took the composition world by storm in the 1960s and 1970s. The process-based method pivots on an ideal that each individual writer can and should be encouraged to create their own original discourse and style. Such a democratic philosophy for teaching composition to students with limited experience in writing presented a world of opportunities.

When composition instruction can focus on developing the writer's personal and academic maturity and their own unique process for constructing an essay, then the need to teach and require students to learn such restrictive features of academic writing as rigid and formulaic patterns of discourse organization, sentence structure, or text cohesion is greatly reduced. Thus, both the teacher and the students can in fact enjoy the process of writing and composition classes where creativity, invention, and the development of the students' writing processes are valued above the artificial and outmoded features of formal writing such as paragraphing or constructing a thesis statement.

In addition to a diverse population of native speakers, however, in the 1970s and 1980s, large groups of nonnative speakers also arrived in the academic arena. For the next three decades or so, the process approach for teaching composition to native speakers has been widely and practically exclusively adopted in the teaching of second language writing to students who often did not have the essential language proficiencies to enable them to construct school-based prose.

Applying the writing and composition pedagogy for native speakers to teaching L2 writers appealed to many ESL instructors. The teaching of L1 composing skills and processes relied on the research and experience of the full-fledged and mature discipline of rhetoric and composition, which continues to occupy a prominent place in the U.S. academy (Krapels, 1990; Reid, 1993; Zamel, 1982, 1983). Thus, in the teaching of L2 writing, it was possible to find a few short-cuts that, theoretically, could allow ESL teachers and curriculum designers to accomplish their instructional goals based on solid research findings and pedagogical frameworks (Leki, 1995). However, the L1 composition pedagogy was developed for a different type of learner. In addition, because many ESL practitioners were trained based on methodologies for teaching the L1 composition and writing process, employing these approaches, techniques, and classroom activities entailed working with known and familiar ways of teaching.

A number of prominent experts in language learning and development began to voice concerns that L2 learners were in fact being short-changed in their foundational need to develop a language base and skills, without which it may simply not be possible to produce competent academic text. L2 researchers, teacher trainers, and teachers have argued that a lack of explicit and thorough language teaching serves to exacerbate the social, economic, and vocational disadvantages of minorities and L2 learners and ultimately reduces their options (e.g., Christie, 2012; Cope & Kalantzis, 2000; Martin, 1989). These specialists have repeatedly noted that, for these types of learners, social access and inclusion can be achieved through a facility with language and writing. Like native speakers, L2 writers have to achieve proficiency in writing because their linguistic repertoire and writing skills often determine their social, economic, and political choices.

> However, as the studies discussed in chapters 2 and 3 demonstrate, the defining characteristics of socially valued writing skills crucially hinge on a developed facility in grammar and vocabulary (e.g., a command of standard written English). For many a student, the incremental skills that undergird a demonstrable written proficiency require instruction.

For instance, Frodesen (2001, p. 234) states that "the wholesale adoption of L1 composition theories and practices for L2 writing classes seems misguided in light of the many differences between first and second language writers, processes, and products." According to Frodesen, the neglect of language instruction for L2 writers is most prevalent in the U.S., where many continue to believe that comprehensible input is sufficient for language acquisition. Frodesen and other experts, such as Birch (2005), Byrd (2005), Byrd and Reid (1998), and McKay (1993) point out that curriculum design in L2 writing instruction has to include grammar and vocabulary to enable L2 writers to communicate meaningfully and appropriately.

# Action Point

A short excerpt from an L2 academic paper written for a class assignment in an undergraduate psychology course is presented below. What types of errors can you identify, count, and classify? Can you correct all of these? Can you explain the errors and how to correct them to the L2 writer? What do you think the reasons are that an advanced academic learner enrolled in a university degree program has continued to make so many errors?

The Excerpt

It has been criticized that the Internet generation spents much time to surfing the web, watching television, and playing game. A concern, which are mostly mentioned about this generation is that the youngs adults in the generation a lack of concentration, or have trouble to read long text. Its decreased reading ability is interupted as the result of increase uses of the internet and other media platforms. However, it required to consider that there is only negative effect on the Internet generation's reading skill. Also, if so, there a need to find how to handle the problem.

To begin with, it is necessary to check the currency status. Two main focuses to analyze the situations are: (1) Are there a true negative effect coming from the increase Internet uses? (2) Does it only consider the young adults? It is hardly able to say that here is a clear relationship between decrease reading habit and Internet. However, it is time that less people are reading than the past.

L1-Based Analysis of Learning Needs: Discourse Organization Skills

Because much of the L2 instructional methodology is derived from the prevalent approaches to teaching L1 composition to native speakers, the analysis of L2 learning needs similarly stems from the research on L1 writing (Ferris, 2002, 2003). Typically, in the teaching of L2 writing, discourse organization skills can be found under the labels of "rhetorical shaping," "essay form," "shaping ideas," "logical organization," or "global organization." In practically all cases, the idea shaping or form metaphors applied to writing are not easy for L2 writers to grasp because in real terms little is in fact "shaped" in L2 academic prose such as that presented in the "Action Point" feature in the previous section.

The summary of a large body of work on discourse organization and text structuring skills is presented in Table 4.11. Practically all academic writers who have experienced the struggle of organizing their own ideas in text or helping

TABLE 4.11 Teaching Priorities in Discourse Organization Skills

The Structure of the Text

Overall: writing fluency, the development and specificity of ideas/examples/illustrations
- Introduction: the thesis/position to signal the structure, order, and flow of information/ideas
- Conventionalized discourse organization: the structure, order, and flow of information/ideas
- Connectedness of ideas/cohesion: globally to the thesis and locally to the main points
- Supporting information/ideas/facts: globally related to the thesis and locally to the main point; explicitly stated
- Major supporting points/arguments
  - Paragraphing: division (coherence) and connectedness (cohesion)
  - Cohesion and cohesive ties: lexical—rephrased ideas, phrases, and words (synonyms); pronoun reference
- Avoiding: digressions, repetitions, and interruptions
- Conclusion/Closing statement(s)

Academic discourse-driven vocabulary and grammar
- Conventionalized and discourse-functional collocations (e.g., *the purpose of this paper is to/this essay will discuss, the main point, to conclude*)
- Various types of academic hedges (e.g., *often, usually, possibly, perhaps, may, seem, appear*)
- Grammar accuracy (sentence construction and word forms)
- Complex sentences with subordinate clauses
- Editing and error identifications skills

---

others produce formal and structured prose may have little trouble concurring with these priorities for teaching learners how to organize their ideas in written prose.

All textbooks for teaching writing, writing handbooks for students, and manuals for professional writers are likely to emphasize clarity of the discourse structure. It is considered to be a top—if not the top—priority in spoken discourse, such as lectures, presentations, explanations, and discussions. In formal written discourse, where the writer's idea organization can be scrutinized and examined, there is probably no priority higher than the clarity of the structure. The old mantra that every piece of academic writing has to include a thesis statement has remained a consistent characteristic of formal prose since time immemorial (see chapter 3).

> The vital need for a thesis statement and its supports has endured as a mainstay of all writing in schooling and education.

106 Curriculum Foundations

The rigid and conventionalized discourse structuring along the lines of the thesis statement has also been an abiding expectation of how academic writing is constructed. What represents major supporting points and fact-based argumentation has been a matter of some debate among academic writing specialists. Nonetheless, their presence in formal academic pieces of writing has continued to be a high priority in the teaching of writing to L1 and L2 students alike. The critical need for accurate and edited text cannot be over-emphasized in teaching L2 academic writing.

Action Point

Below, another short portion is extracted from an L2 academic assignment in philosophy on whether schools and colleges should teach ethical and social values. Can you re-organize the text to make it easier to follow? What types of problems with the discourse organization can you observe? Can you build a mini-lesson on how to organize the ideas in writing? Can you demonstrate how written academic discourse in English has to be constructed?

And most importantly, can you explain to the L2 writer the reasons that written discourse in an academic paper has to be structured in a particular way?

The Excerpt

Walking on campus of the University, I do feel that it looks like a city. In every city, it would be essential for people living there to know ethical and social values. Schools are not only a place for learning academic subjects, but also for learning ethical and social values. That is because students live in school every day in a very prominent stage in their lives, because they live with variety of personalities and characters, and because there is no other place where it teaches these value.

These days, people spend a main part of their lives in school. For one thing, it is a very good time for students to learn ethical and social values, since they are young enough and their personalities are flexible and ready to accept values. For another, they spend most of their time in school. Sometimes, they do not have time to attend other social events. Furthermore, they usually stay long enough in school to practice those values and get ready for a real society.

Chapter Summary

A vocabulary size of approximately 5,000 word families is requisite for relatively fluent L2 reading, even though a dictionary is still necessary at this level. In fact, basic written prose can begin to emerge only when the learner's vocabulary range exceeds 2,000 words. Conversational vocabulary and grammar provide poor coverage for academic text, and having a large conversational range does not necessarily enable L2 learners to read and write academic prose. The written prose of experienced L2 writers contains important shortfalls of academic vocabulary and grammar. On the other hand, however, the language of conventionally skilled L2 writers includes an extensive range of colloquial and conversational constructions.

For L2 writers to produce academic prose, intensive vocabulary work is required. Academic L2 writers need to attain proficiency in academic language simply because without it they are unable to succeed in their academic tasks.

Hundreds of studies have identified fundamental and pronounced differences between all facets of writing in L1 and L2 discourse and text. Based on their findings, compared to the discourse structuring and ideational development in L1 writing, a broad range of characteristics of L2 writing seem to be urgent, important, and prominent. Research has clearly and unambiguously demonstrated that L2 writers' skill level in vocabulary and grammar disadvantage the quality of their formal prose.

In addition, error gravity studies and other pedagogically oriented publications have the goal of refining and supplementing course curricula for L2 writing instruction and developing L2 writers' error awareness. A summative overview of key error gravity studies presents a relatively complete picture of what is, in effect, de-valued in student academic prose. However, researchers have also found that, for a majority of L2 learners, eliminating all grammar and vocabulary errors is virtually impossible. It is important to note that L1 errors in formal prose are fundamentally distinct from those in L2 university writing because the former are unlikely to impede comprehension. Furthermore, while some types of sentence- and phrase-level errors can be reduced with experience, other classes of errors are a great deal more difficult to eliminate.

The L1 composition pedagogy that dominates in teaching writing at the college and university level was developed at a different time and for a different type of learners. The defining characteristics of socially valued writing skills crucially hinge on a developed facility in grammar and vocabulary. For many a student, the incremental skills that undergird a demonstrable written proficiency require instruction. Research on basic L1 and academic L2 writing has also established clear baselines in terms of curricular and instructional needs of learners.

Notes

1. Full citations of Michael West's (1953) General Service List, which consists of over 2,000 of the most frequent words, are easily available online.
2. According to the linguistic tradition of data designation, * (an asterisk) designates data and examples that are ungrammatical or otherwise incorrect. A question mark (?) designates questionable—but not necessarily incorrect—data.
3. A few terms as they occur here are based on the definitions and Glossary of Terms of the California Department of Education Draft of ELD Standards (2012), found at www.cde.ca.gov/sp/el/er/documents/caleldstdintro.pdf and retrieved on July 21, 2012.

Further Reading on L2 Writing and Language Learning

Chang, Y., & Swales, J. (1999). Informal elements in English academic writing: Threats or opportunities for advanced non-native speakers. In C. Candlin & K. Hyland (Eds.), *Writing texts, processes and practices* (pp. 145–167). London: Longman.

Frodesen, J. (2014). Grammar in writing. In M. Celce-Murcia, D. Brinton, & M. Snow (Eds.), *Teaching English as a second or foreign language* (4th ed., pp. 233–248). Boston: Heinle & Heinle.

Hinkel, E. (2003). Simplicity without elegance: Features of sentences in L2 and L1 academic texts. *TESOL Quarterly, 37,* 275–301.

Hinkel, E. (2004). *Teaching academic ESL writing: Practical techniques in vocabulary and grammar.* Mahwah, NJ: Lawrence Erlbaum Associates.

Hinkel, E. (2011). What research on second language writing tells us and what it doesn't. In E. Hinkel (Ed.), *Handbook of research in second language teaching and learning* (Vol. 2, pp. 523–538). New York: Routledge.

Nation, I. S. P. (2009). *Teaching ESL/EFL reading and writing.* New York: Routledge.

Further Reading on Error Correction and Editing Skills

Ferris, D. (2003). *Response to student writing: Implications for second language students.* New York: Routledge.

Ferris, D. (2004). The grammar correction debate in L2 writing: Where are we, and where do we go from here (and what do we do in the meantime . . .?). *Journal of Second Language Writing, 13*(1), 49–62.

Ferris, D., & Roberts, B. (2001). Error feedback in L2 writing classes: How explicit does it need to be? *Journal of Second Language Writing, 10,* 161–184.

Santos, T. (1988). Professors' reactions to the academic writing of nonnative-speaking students. *TESOL Quarterly, 22,* 69–90.

Schleppegrell, M. (2002). Challenges of the science register for ESL students: Errors and meaning-making. In M. Schleppegrell & M. Colombi (Eds.), *Developing advanced literacy in first and second languages* (pp. 119–142). Mahwah, NJ: Lawrence Erlbaum Associates.

References

Anson, C., & Forsberg, L. (1990). Moving beyond the academic community: Transitional stages in professional writing. *Written Communication, 7*(2), 200–231.

Bates, L., Lane, J., & Lange, E. (1993). *Writing clearly: Responding to ESL compositions.* Boston: Heinle & Heinle.

Bazerman, C. (1988). *Shaping written knowledge: The genre and activity of the experimental article in science.* Madison, WI: University of Wisconsin Press.

Berkenkotter, C., Huckin, T., & Ackerman, J. (1988). Conventions, conversations, and the writer: Case study of a study in a rhetoric Ph.D. program. *Research in the Teaching of English, 22*(2), 9–44.

Birch, B. (2005). *Learning and teaching English grammar, K-12.* White Plains, NY: Prentice Hall.

Blau, S. (2006). College writing, academic literacy, and the intellectual community: California dreams and cultural oppositions. In P. Sullivan & H. Tinberg (Eds.), *What is "college-level" writing?* (pp. 358–377). Urbana, IL: NCTE.

Byrd, P. (2005). Instructed grammar. In E. Hinkel (Ed.), *Handbook of research in second language teaching and learning* (pp. 545–562). Mahwah, NJ: Lawrence Erlbaum Associates.

Byrd, P., & Reid, J. (1998). *Grammar in the composition classroom.* Boston: Heinle & Heinle.

Carroll, J. B., Davies, P., & Richman, B. (1971). *The American Heritage word frequency book.* Boston: Houghton Mifflin.

Carson, J. (2001). Second language writing and second language acquisition. In T. Silva & P. Matsuda (Eds.), *On second language writing* (pp. 191–199). Mahwah, NJ: Lawrence Erlbaum Associates.

Chang, Y., & Swales, J. (1999). Informal elements in English academic writing: Threats or opportunities for advanced non-native speakers. In C. Candlin & K. Hyland (Eds.), *Writing texts, processes and practices* (pp. 145–167). London: Longman.

Christie, F. (2012). *Language education throughout the school years: A functional perspective.* Malden, MA: Wiley-Blackwell.

Cope, B., & Kalantzis, M. (Eds.). (2000). *Multiliteracies: Literacy learning and the design of social futures.* New York: Routledge.

Cutting, J. (2000). Written errors of students in higher education and English native speaker students. In G. M. Blue, J. Milton, & J. Saville (Eds.), *Assessing English for academic purposes* (pp. 97–113). Oxford: Peter Lang.

Faigley, L. (1992). *Fragments of rationality: Postmodernity and the subject of composition.* Pittsburgh, PA: University of Pittsburgh Press.

Ferris, D. (1995). Can advanced ESL students be taught to correct their most serious and frequent errors? *CATESOL Journal, 8*(1), 41–62.

Ferris, D. (1997). The influence of teacher commentary on student revision. *TESOL Quarterly, 31,* 315–339.

Ferris, D. (2002). *Treatment of error in second language student writing.* Ann Arbor, MI: University of Michigan Press.

Ferris, D. (2003). *Responding to student writing.* Mahwah, NJ: Lawrence Erlbaum Associates.

Ferris, D. (2004). The grammar correction debate in L2 writing: Where are we, and where do we go from here? (and what do we do in the meantime...?) *Journal of Second Language Writing, 13*(1), 49–62.

Ferris, D., & Roberts, B. (2001). Error feedback in L2 writing classes: How explicit does it need to be? *Journal of Second Language Writing, 10,* 161–184.

Field, Y., & Oi, Y. L. M. (1992). A comparison of internal conjunctive cohesion in the English essay writing of Cantonese speakers and Native speakers. *RELC Journal, 23,* 15–28.

Flowerdew, L. (2000). Using a genre-based framework to teach organizational structure in academic writing. *ELT Journal, 54,* 369–378.

Frodesen, J. (2001). Grammar in writing. In M. Celce-Murcia (Ed.), *Teaching English as a second and foreign language* (3rd ed., pp. 233–248). Boston: Heinle & Heinle.

Granger, S. (1998). The computer learner corpus: A versatile new source of data for SLA research. In S. Granger (Ed.), *Learner English on computer* (pp. 3–18). London: Longman.

Granger, S., & Tribble, C. (1998). Learner corpus data in the foreign language classroom: Form-focused instruction and data-driven learning. In S. Granger (Ed.), *Learner English on computer* (pp. 199–209). London: Longman.

Green, C., Christopher, E., & Lam, J. (2000). The incidence and defects on coherence of marked themes in interlanguage texts: A corpus-based enquiry. *English for Specific Purposes, 19,* 99–113.

Hedgcock, J. (2005). Taking stock of research and pedagogy in L2 writing. In E. Hinkel (Ed.), *Handbook of research in second language teaching and learning* (pp. 597–614). Mahwah, NJ: Lawrence Erlbaum Associates.

Herrington, A. (1985). Writing in academic settings: A study of the contexts for writing in two college chemical engineering courses. *Research in the Teaching of English, 19*(3), 331–359.

Hinkel, E. (1995). The use of modal verbs as a reflection of cultural values. *TESOL Quarterly, 29,* 325–343.

Hinkel, E. (1999). Objectivity and credibility in L1 and L2 academic writing. In E. Hinkel (Ed.), *Culture in second language teaching and learning* (pp. 90–108). Cambridge: Cambridge University Press.

Hinkel, E. (2001a). Giving examples and telling stories in academic essays. *Issues in Applied Linguistics, 12,* 149–170.

Hinkel, E. (2001b). Matters of cohesion in L1 and L2 academic texts. *Applied Language Learning, 12,* 111–132.

Hinkel, E. (2002a). Expressing L1 literacy in L2 writing. In D. S. Li (Ed.), *Discourses in search of members: Festschrift in honor of Ronald Scollon's 60th birthday* (pp. 465–482). Greenwood, CT: Ablex.

Hinkel, E. (2002b). *Second language writers' text*. Mahwah, NJ: Lawrence Erlbaum Associates.

Hinkel, E. (2002c). Teaching grammar in writing classes: Tenses and cohesion. In E. Hinkel & S. Fotos (Eds.), *New perspectives on grammar teaching in second language classrooms* (pp. 181–198). Mahwah, NJ: Lawrence Erlbaum Associates.

Hinkel, E. (2003a). Adverbial markers and tone in L1 and L2 students' writing. *Journal of Pragmatics, 35,* 1049–1068.

Hinkel, E. (2003b). Simplicity without elegance: Features of sentences in L2 and L1 academic texts. *TESOL Quarterly, 37,* 275–301.

Hinkel, E. (2004a). *Teaching academic ESL writing: Practical techniques in vocabulary and grammar.* Mahwah, NJ: Lawrence Erlbaum Associates.

Hinkel, E. (2004b). Tense, aspect, and the passive voice in L1 and L2 writing. *Language Teaching Research, 8,* 5–29.

Hinkel, E. (2005a). Analyses of L2 text and what can be learned from them. In E. Hinkel (Ed.), *Handbook of research in second language teaching and learning* (pp. 615–628). Mahwah, NJ: Lawrence Erlbaum Associates.

Hinkel, E. (Ed.). (2005b). *Handbook of research in second language teaching and learning.* Mahwah, NJ: Lawrence Erlbaum.

Hinkel, E. (2009). The effect of essay prompts and topics on the uses of modal verbs in L1 and L2 academic writing. *Journal of Pragmatics, 41*(4), 667–683.

Hinkel, E. (2011). What research on second language writing tells us and what it doesn't. In E. Hinkel (Ed.), *Handbook of research in second language teaching and learning* (Vol. 2, pp. 523–538). New York: Routledge.

Hirsh, D., & Nation, P. (1992). What vocabulary size is needed to read unsimplified texts for pleasure? *Reading in a Foreign Language 8*(2), 689–696.

Holt, S. L. (1997). Responding to grammar errors. In D. L. Sigsbee, B. W. Speck, & B. Maylath (Eds.), *Approaches to teaching non-native English speakers across the curriculum* (pp. 69–76). San Francisco: Jossey-Bass.

Horowitz, D. (1986a). Process, not product: Less than meets the eye. *TESOL Quarterly, 20,* 141–144.

Horowitz, D. (1986b). What professors actually require: Academic tasks for the ESL classroom. *TESOL Quarterly, 20,* 445–462.

Hu, M., & Nation, P. (2000). Unknown vocabulary density and reading comprehension. *Reading in a Foreign Language 13*(1), 403–430.

ICAS. (2002). *Academic literacy: A statement of competencies expected of students entering California's public colleges and universities.* Sacramento, CA: Intersegmental Committee of the Academic Senates of California Colleges and Universities.
Jenkins, S., & Hinds, J. (1987). Business letter writing: English, French, and Japanese. *TESOL Quarterly, 21,* 327–349.
Johnson, P. (1992). Cohesion and coherence in compositions in Malay and English. *RELC Journal, 23,* 1–17.
Jordan, R. (1997). *English for academic purposes.* Cambridge: Cambridge University Press.
Khalil, A. (1989). A study of cohesion and coherence in Arab EFL college students' writing. *System, 17,* 359–371.
Krapels, A. (1990). An overview of second language writing process research. In B. Kroll (Ed.), *Second language writing* (pp. 27–56). Cambridge: Cambridge University Press.
Kress, G. (1994). *Learning to write.* London: Routledge.
Kress, G. (1996). *Before writing: Rethinking paths to literacy.* London: Routledge.
Kutz, E., Groden, S., & Zamel, V. (1993). *The discovery of competence: Teaching and learning with diverse student writers.* Portsmouth, NH: Boynton/Cook.
Langer, J. (1992). Speaking of knowing: Conceptions of understanding in academic disciplines. In A. Herrington & C. Moran (Eds.), *Writing, teaching, and learning in the disciplines* (pp. 69–85). New York: MLA.
Leki, I. (1995). Coping strategies of ESL students. *TESOL Quarterly, 29,* 235–260.
Leki, I. (2007). *Undergraduates in a second language: Challenges and complexities of academic literacy development.* New York: Lawrence Erlbaum.
Leki, I., Cumming, A., & Silva, T. (2008). *A synthesis of research on second language writing in English.* New York: Routledge.
Lunsford, A., & Lunsford, K. (2008). Mistakes are a fact of life: A national comparative study. *College Composition and Communication, 59*(4), 781–806.
Martin, J. (1989). *Factual writing: Exploring and challenging social reality.* Oxford, UK: Oxford University Press.
Mauranen, A. (1996). Discourse competence: Evidence from thematic development in native and non-native texts. In E. Ventola & A. Mauranen (Eds.), *Academic writing: Intercultural and textual issues* (pp. 195–230). Amsterdam/Philadelphia: John Benjamins.
McCarthy, L. (1987). A stranger in strange lands: A college student writing across curriculum. *Research in the Teaching of English, 21*(3), 233–267—meta analysis?.
McCretton, E., & Rider, N. (1993). Error gravity and error hierarchies. *International Review of Applied Linguistics, 31*(3), 177–188.
McKay, S. (1993). *Agendas for second language literacy.* New York: Cambridge University Press.
Nation, I. S. P. (1990). *Teaching and learning vocabulary.* New York: Newbury House.
Nation, I. S. P. (2005). Teaching and learning vocabulary. In E. Hinkel (Ed.), *Handbook of research in second language teaching and learning* (pp. 581–595). Mahwah, NJ: Lawrence Erlbaum Associates.
Nation, I. S. P. (2011). Research into practice: Vocabulary. *Language Teaching, 44,* 529–539.
Nation, I. S. P. (2013). *Learning vocabulary in another language* (2nd ed.). Cambridge: Cambridge University Press.
National Center for Education Statistics. (2003). *The Nation's Report Card: The NAEP writing achievement levels* [On-line]. Retrieved from HTTP: nces.ed.gov/nationsreportcard/writing/achieveall.asp
Nelson, M. (1991). *At the point of need: Teaching basic and ESL writers.* Portsmouth, NH: Boynton/Cook.
Nesselhauf, N. (2005). *Collocations in a learner corpus.* Amsterdam: John Benjamins.

North, S. (1986). Writing in philosophy class: Three case studies. *Research in the Teaching of English, 20*(3), 225–262.

Paltridge, B. (2004). Academic writing. *Language Teaching, 37*(2), 87–105.

Raimes, A. (1991). Errors: Windows into the mind. *College ESL, 1,* 55–64.

Raimes, A. (1999). *Grammar troublespots: An editing guide for students* (2nd ed.). Cambridge: Cambridge University Press.

Reid, J. (1993). *Teaching ESL writing.* Englewood Cliffs, NJ: Prentice Hall.

Rosenfeld, M., Courtney, R., & Fowles, M. (2004). *Identifying the writing tasks important for academic success at the undergraduate and graduate level* [GRE RR 00]. Princeton, NJ: Educational Testing Service.

Sakyi, A. (2000). Validation of holistic scoring for ESL writing assessment: How raters evaluate ESL compositions. In A. Kunnan (Ed.), *Fairness and validation in language assessment* (pp. 129–152). Cambridge: Cambridge University Press.

Santos, T. (1988). Professors' reactions to the academic writing of nonnative-speaking students. *TESOL Quarterly, 22,* 69–90.

Schleppegrell, M. (2002). Challenges of the science register for ESL students: Errors and meaning-making. In M. Schleppegrell & M. Colombi (Eds.), *Developing advanced literacy in first and second languages* (pp. 119–142). Mahwah, NJ: Lawrence Erlbaum Associates.

Schleppegrell, M. (2004). *The language of schooling.* Mahwah, NJ: Lawrence Erlbaum Associates.

Shaw, P., & Liu, E. (1998). What develops in the development of second language writing. *Applied Linguistics, 19,* 225–254.

Silva, T. (1990). Second language composition instruction: Developments, issues, and directions in ESL. In B. Kroll (Ed.), *Second language writing* (pp. 11–23). New York: Cambridge University Press.

Silva, T. (1993). Toward an understanding of the distinct nature of L2 writing: The ESL research and its implications. *TESOL Quarterly, 27,* 657–677.

Silva, T. (1997). On the ethical treatment of ESL writers. *TESOL Quarterly, 31,* 359–363.

Sullivan, P., & Tinberg, H. (Eds.). (2006). *What is "college-level" writing?* Urbana, IL: NCTE.

Swales, J. (1990). *Genre analysis.* Cambridge: Cambridge University Press.

Swales, J., & Feak, C. (2012). *Academic writing for graduate students* (3rd ed.). Ann Arbor: The University of Michigan Press.

Vann, R., Lorenz, F., & Meyer, D. (1991). Error gravity: Response to errors in the written discourse of nonnative speakers of English. In L. Hamp-Lyons (Ed.), *Assessing second language writing* (pp. 181–196). Norwood, NJ: Ablex.

Vann, R., Meyer, D., & Lorenz, F. (1984). Error gravity: A study of faculty opinion of ESL errors. *TESOL Quarterly, 18,* 427–440.

Vaughan, C. (1991). Holistic assessment: What goes on in the raters' minds? In L. Hamp-Lyons (Ed.), *Assessing second language writing* (pp. 111–126). Norwood, NJ: Ablex.

Waring, R. (2002). *Why should we build up a start-up vocabulary quickly?* [On-line]. Retrieved from www.robwaring.org/vocab/principles/early.htm

Weigle, S. (2002). *Assessing writing.* Cambridge: Cambridge University Press.

West, M. (1953). *A general service list of English words.* London: Longman.

Zamel, V. (1982). Writing: The process of discovering meaning. *TESOL Quarterly, 16,* 195–210.

Zamel, V. (1987). Recent research on writing pedagogy. *TESOL Quarterly, 21,* 697–715.

Zamel, V. (1995). Strangers in academia: The experiences of faculty and ESL students across curriculum. *College Composition and Communication, 46,* 506–521.

PART II
Curriculum Design for L2 Writing and Language Building

5

HOW TO DESIGN EFFECTIVE CURRICULA FOR LANGUAGE AND WRITING COURSES

This chapter discusses:

- Curriculum nuts and bolts
- The first order of business: The learning objectives
- Material and unit sequencing
- The syllabus
- Assessment and grading
- Coordinating instruction
- The nitty-gritty of making lesson plans

Introduction

Curriculum designs, like all other practicalities and views on teaching and learning in education, follow the trends in developmental and cognitive psychology, the evolution and changes in social values associated with the expectations of learners' skills and knowledge, and the subject matter—or content—deemed important in the society and recommended by specialists (see chapter 1). Who is considered to be a specialist also crucially depends on contemporary views prevalent in the society: the faculty in teacher education programs, social and political leaders who hold positions in national and local governments, school consultants, or business leaders and major employers. Their views have an indelible impact on what is considered to be important in teaching and what is socially valued and expected in language learning.

Learning a language is different from learning and practicing concepts in math or physics, working on experiments in chemistry, or reading about and understanding historical events. A number of fundamental differences exist between learning academic subjects and learning another language. In practically all academic subjects where disciplinary knowledge is taught, learned, and applied, both teachers and students work with what is typically considered as knowledge accumulated in research and teaching in specific areas of study. That is, in the course of the development of human civilization, a large body of concepts, hypotheses, theories, and facts (i.e., academic and disciplinary knowledge) has been constructed and accumulated. It is typically passed on from generation to generation by means of teaching, reading, and school learning.

On the other hand, in the case of most language users, the knowledge of language is not something that is taught or learned as an academic subject (more on this below). Rather, a facility with language represents a range of demonstrable skills that are manifested in the form of language usage, for both first and second languages. Philosophical debates of what represents knowledge go back even further than Plato's definition of knowledge as "justified true belief." Even in Foreign Language (FL) teaching programs in high school or college, such as those in Chinese, French, or Farsi, teachers are not particularly concerned with the students' knowledge of facts, information, or theoretical or practical understanding of the "subject" that is language.[1] Rather, the purpose of all L2—but not necessarily FL—teaching pertains to enabling the language learners to use the language appropriately in any particular given context or setting in order to achieve their personal, social, professional, or vocational goals.

To this end, and due to the fact that all language usage is fundamentally intuitive and skill-based, rather than based on overt and demonstrable knowledge of facts, information, and theories, the effectiveness of language teaching and learning necessarily and inextricably takes into account a number of factors, such as learner-external factors (e.g., social variables, language exposure and experience, interactional constraints, and the like), learner-internal factors (e.g., cultural, cognitive, or language transfer-related), language aptitude, or learning motivation. It seems pretty clear that all these considerations cannot be taken into account in most curriculum models, but several factors are common to practically all curriculum designs.

Curriculum Nuts and Bolts

As was discussed in chapter 1, the common components of all school and academic curricula consist of several essential and foundational constituents, without which no course of study can materialize. These constituents include the scope of skills that are addressed in teaching and the order in which they are addressed, a course plan (one can think of it as a map of the road with turns and landmarks), and the appropriate materials selected to bring the learners closer to achieving their learning objectives.

COMPONENTS OF LANGUAGE TEACHING CURRICULUM

The What and in What Order: Curriculum and Instructional Time

- Scope (the what) and Sequence (the order) of language and writing skills development.
  - Curricular objectives of teaching and learning the skills, specific for each level (or school grade) of language and writing proficiency.
  - The sequence of teaching and learning writing and language skills (i.e., the progression, e.g., in, say, reading or writing) or sub-skills (such as note-taking).

The Course Plan

- The Plan (the syllabus) that outlines the incremental steps to meet the objectives (e.g., the rationale, language areas/topics to be covered (and assignments), and assessment/ evaluation criteria).
  - Language/content to meet the objectives.
  - Measurable and quantifiable language performance standards.

The How

- Teaching materials: textbooks, activities, workbooks, projects, and assessments/tests to guide instruction and skill evaluation.

Keeping an Eye on What Parallels and What Follows

This is the big picture of the entire language teaching and learning process.

- Coordinating the What and in What Order of skills and other courses that a student is required to complete at the same time or at the next level to achieve their writing and language learning objectives (e.g., reading and writing or speaking and listening).

Based on Posner (2004)

To simplify the somewhat complicated and reasonably comprehensive overview of what a curriculum is and what it is not (see chapter 1 for an earlier discussion), the following essential points apply to all cases of creating a curriculum in practically any language teaching context, from a short workshop to a multi-year major course of study.

The gist of curriculum building for language instruction can be summarized as:

Establish		Create		Designate		Identify
The What & in What Order	→	the Plan to achieve this	→	the How (materials, tasks, assessment)	→	What Accompanies/ Follows

> **Talking Shop**
>
> Typically, program administrators and curriculum developers comment that, in many classrooms, it is the textbook that determines the course curriculum, rather than the students' language learning goals. Why do you think this may be the case? Discuss your views with your colleagues.

The First Order of Business: The Learning (and Teaching) Objectives

The foundation of a curricular model begins with the essential "studies of the learners" (Tyler, 1949) and the learner language (see chapter 1). Such studies provide a broad perspective on the language and writing skills that practically all learners need to attain to develop facility in L2 academic abilities. In many contexts, a vast body of research can provide a basis for the initial step of identifying learners' skills and proficiencies that may be already in place or those that may require additional instruction. For example, even in the case of beginners or pre-literate learners, it is still essential to determine with what specific language skills instruction should commence (see chapters 3 and 4). The next essential move is to establish the scope of language learning objectives that in fact can be reasonably achieved during the specified instructional time, which can range from a few days to several years. Most typically, a curriculum is created for a school term.

Thus, at the outset, it is important to figure out the baseline of the learners' language skills, on which a curriculum can be built. In various programs, schools, or educational institutions, the initial estimations of learners' skills and proficiencies can come in the form of TOEFL (Test of English as a Foreign Language) or IELTS (International English Language Testing System) test scores, placement tests, or diagnostic essays.[2] That is, once the initial levels of learners' skills are identified, it is then possible to determine their learning objectives to be attained.

When a course curriculum is designed to meet the learning goals and objectives of specific groups of learners with similar characteristics and proficiencies and in similar contexts, then it can be easily modified (or only slightly adjusted) for other cohorts. On the other hand, if the types of learners and their characteristics and proficiencies change, then the course curriculum may need to be revisited and revised.

Learning Objectives, a definition: Objectives indicate what the teacher wants the students to learn. These are "explicit formulations of the ways in which students are expected to be changed by the educative process"(Anderson & Krathwohl, 2001, p. 3; Bloom, 1956, p. 26). In language learning, objectives specify the language features that students are expected to learn and how well these should be learned (more on this below).

Learning Outcomes, a definition: Learning outcomes describe what students should be able to do as a result of their educational experiences and how well they should be able to do it (Simpson, 1972).

A Bit of History

Since at least the 1950s (Bloom, 1956), a large number of volumes have been published on how to develop educational and learning objectives for a course of study (e.g., Anderson and Krathwohl (2001)). It is important to keep in mind, however, that most common statements found in the literature on developing educational objectives do not easily apply to language learning and teaching. The former are usually constructed for knowledge-based course work in the disciplines, such as history, economics, or sociology, rather than for skill-based learning, as is the case with language.

A majority of the contemporary taxonomies of educational objectives are rooted—or claim to be rooted—in the original Bloom's (1956) taxonomy (classification), which was created by a sizeable group of educational psychologists for general education and university courses. After more than four years of work, these specialists developed a theoretical framework for classifying desired learning outcomes for students with a goal of building a bank of interchangeable tests, test items, and ideas about testing among several universities. Because designing and refining reliable tests is expensive, laborious, and time-consuming, the renowned educational measurement experts had the goal of implementing an efficient exchange of tests or portions of tests by means of pooling their resources. Because clearly stated educational objectives can serve as a foundation for developing course curricula and tests, the group began their work by establishing a standard range of terminology that indicates what learning outcomes specific test items were intended to measure (Anderson & Krathwohl, 2001).

In many contemporary versions of the taxonomy, the learner outcomes are typically presented using **verbs** (as in *count, define, describe, draw, find, label, list, match, name, quote, recall, recite, sequence, tell, write*), rather than the nouns of the 1956 taxonomy, to indicate what learners should be able to do by the end of their courses. Currently, in an age when learner outcomes are expected to be defined and explicitly stated at practically all levels of education, with the possible exception of Kindergarten, there are probably hundreds (or more) of the various verb lists available for constructing learning objectives and outcome statements. Much like resume-writing resources provide lists of verbs to use or avoid, these learner outcome verb lists are expected to help teachers come up with the right objectives (and outcomes). It is typically believed that such "action words" (Anderson & Krathwohl, 2001, p. 5) are better suited to describe the cognitive processes and the knowledge "students are expected to acquire or construct" (p. 12).

In knowledge-based courses, the numerous current versions of objective taxonomies of educational objectives include lists of verbs that can be useful for constructing learning objectives, such as:

apply	*compute*	*prepare*	*show*
change	*identify*	*produce*	*transfer*
choose	*interview*	*select*	*use*

For example:

- *Identify the audience for a particular communication and tailor the communication for that audience.*
- *Demonstrate knowledge of the personal and social problems that put children and families at risk.*
- *Describe three major theories on the historical development of women's movements.*

Language Learning Objectives and Outcomes

For language learning and development, the usefulness of these and similar verbs may be somewhat constrained because, as with math, using a language is skill-based. By and large, in language skills, the usage of verbs may be limited to something along the lines of *identify, demonstrate, develop, use* or *be able to use, read, produce, comprehend, speak, communicate,* or *explain*. Furthermore, given a great range of language learning contexts and the enormous diversity of language learners and their learning goals, a limited number of verbs, such as those ubiquitously found in the literature on the taxonomies of educational objectives, may simply be applicable to different types of human abilities. Not to mention that at practically any level of language learning and proficiency, learners are likely to perform the tasks included in *identifying, demonstrating, developing, using, reading, producing, comprehending,* or *communicating*.

The abilities referred to by means of the classical learning objective verbs are common to the prototypical language teaching domains in the four traditional language skills (i.e., listening, speaking, reading, and writing) as well as their integrated varieties. For this reason, in constructing reasonable and reasoned language learning objectives, a better option is to employ both **verbs and nouns**, such as *learn and use* *phrasal verbs, construct complex sentences, memorize and use academic vocabulary in context, create and employ thesis statements,* or *identify a main idea in written or spoken texts.*

Action Point

If you are currently taking a course at an educational institution and if the course has explicitly stated learning objectives, can you identify the main objective(s) among others? In your view, is this course knowledge- or skill-based?

Make a list of the characteristics of the explicitly stated learning objectives that enable you to identify the most important differences between the two. Also make a list of verbs, nouns, and descriptors that you can identify in the objective statements. Compare your lists to those made by your colleagues and determine the reasons for various divergent interpretations of the objective statements.

Language learning objectives may not be the same as the objectives of teaching.

- Learning objectives seek to establish what learners should be able to do or what skills they can be expected to develop by the end of the instructional term.
- Teaching objectives specify what the teacher can or will be expected to do to help students to achieve their learning objectives.

In instructional settings and schools where subject matter content is taught and learned together with the language, both the learner and the teacher typically need to meet two sets of objectives: those in content learning and those in language learning. It goes without saying that achieving dual objectives during the same instructional time is far more complicated than attaining a single objective, be it in content or in language learning.

Talking Shop

Experienced language instructors know that in most classrooms or contexts of teaching, there is a difference between learning objectives and learning outcomes. Why do you think such differences occur in practically every instance of teaching? There are probably multiple reasons that have a role to play. Discuss this important point with your colleagues.

Typically, language learning objectives are constructed in terms of learner outcomes (Mager, 1997). When defining learning objectives, it is important to keep in mind that these should be **specific** in order to be useful and usable and **realistic**. Most importantly, learning objectives have to be **measurable** in some way. To put it another way, it may be impossible to measure *understanding, knowing, preparing, practicing,* or *transferring.*

On the other hand, constructing language learning objectives in terms of the following specific, quantifiable, and measurable descriptors can be very practical, for example:

- **Adverbs**—*correctly, accurately, appropriately, (mostly,* if defined) *error-free, free of specific types of errors*
- **Verbs**—*use, employ, apply, demonstrate (that students know or the knowledge of), display, show, exhibit, answer (questions or comprehension questions), respond (to a greeting, situation, or a teacher's comment/correction)*
- **Verbs and Quantifiables**—*produce 2–3 sentences or paragraphs (in writing), retell a one-page story, respond to 2–3–4 questions about a reading, lecture, assignment, or lab experiment*

A solid statement of learning objectives should include at least two parts:

- what learners should be able to do
- how well they should be able to do it (i.e., measurements of the performance quality or the standard that can be considered minimally acceptable)

Examples (1) and (2) demonstrate crucial differences between vague learning objectives that may not be very achievable or measurable, and ones that can in fact do the job.

Example (1)

- NOT—Students will understand the meanings and functions of the present progressive tense.
- BUT—Students will be able to recognize <u>correctly/accurately</u> occurrences of present progressive tense and identify their functions in spoken discourse (common) and in written prose (very rare).

Another example that deals with learning academic vocabulary in speaking, reading, and writing:

Example (2)
By the end of the term, students should be able to:

- NOT—gain facility with the meanings and uses of academic words/phrases (or, say, academic nouns that end in -*ion*, -*ness*, -*ment*, and -*ity*)
- BUT—learn and use correctly (a defined number, e.g., 100 or 200) academic words/phrases (or, say, academic nouns that end in -*ion*, -*ness*, -*ment*, and -*ity*)

> A crucial difference between well-written learning outcome statements and those that are less so is a means of effectively measuring whether the stated outcomes have been achieved. Vague and indefinable outcome statements can lead only to like outcomes.

In addition, when constructing learning objectives (not the same as outcomes), it is important to keep in mind that these need to be assessed and assessable in the progression of the course.

When constructing language learning objectives, it is always important to build in extra time for repeated reviews and practice (also called *spaced repetition*). As was mentioned in chapters 2 and 3, the fact that vocabulary, grammar constructions, or discourse properties are taught does not mean that they are learned. In the case of vocabulary teaching and learning, for example, adults may require some 12 to 15 exposures to words or phrases in order to retain them. Productive uses of language features in, say, speaking or writing may lag far behind receptive skills required for comprehension (Laufer & Nation, 1995; Nation, 1990).

> The fact that particular language features are taught does not mean that they are learned.

Action Point

Usually, when instructors set out to write learning objectives in language courses, they begin by determining what learners should be able to do (rather than "know" as in disciplinary courses) by the end of the instructional time.

Construct a rough draft of learning objective statements for a language area, such as, for example, common conversational devices (greetings, small talk about one's personal background and family life, or conversation closing), concrete vocabulary (e.g., furniture: *table, chair, desk*; or fruit: *apple, orange, melon*), or any other language unit that is close at hand.

Material and Unit Sequencing

As many teachers know from experience, a course can be organized in several ways, and each of these may work equally well. That is, there may be a number of "best" course sequences. A course can sequenced based on its learning objectives, its instructional time length, the learning needs of the students, or the instructor's professional experience, beliefs, or the extent of personal exposure to language learning. It is important to remember, however, that the outline and the order of learning objectives needs to reflect the material sequencing; that is, the order of the stated learning objectives has to correspond to the order of material in the teaching sequence. The context of teaching and the amount of instructional time and the number of class sessions may also play a fundamental role in how a course is structured. For example, if a course is taught in 4-hour weekly sessions, the material organization is likely to be different from that in a course that meets twice a week for 2 hours. L2 writing courses that include vocabulary or grammar components would probably progress and be structured differently than those that focus exclusively on constructing written academic prose. Thus, it is unusual for the outline of the objectives to be revised once the materials and contents are arranged in a particular order.

The Essentials of Material Sequencing

To provide learners opportunities to practice what they have already learned and to enable them to learn new material and develop new skills effectively, contents in a course, a unit, or a lesson need to adhere to the same consistent principle at all times: from simpler to more complex, and from more familiar to less familiar (e.g., Graves, 2000).

> The essential characteristics of material sequencing within large or small instructional units—from whole courses to individual lessons—apply to teaching any and all language skills:
>
> - From simpler to more complex
> - From less demanding to more demanding
> - From more controlled/teacher-guided to less controlled/teacher-guided
> - From more familiar and practiced to less familiar and practiced

In some pedagogical contexts, such as content-based instruction or theme-based teaching, materials and units are organized around topics, themes, or academic subjects (see Snow and Brinton, 1997) for an extensive overview of content-based instruction). The same essential characteristics of material sequencing apply to make learning effective and manageable for learners.

A clear and well-organized material sequence can make all the difference when it comes to more or less effective language learning (and teaching). In practically all language teaching, material organization needs to be substantiated and well justified. Careful content sequencing also plays a key role at assessment time (more on this below).

Action Point

L2 learners and textbook writers may have a different perspective on what is simpler and what is more complex than native speakers of English. For example, the present simple tense that refers to usual, habitual, and frequently repeated actions, as in *I go to school where I take violin lessons* is typically considered to be far more difficult for L2 learners to use correctly than the present progressive tense, as in *I am taking a violin lesson*, which refers to actions that take place at the present moment. Take a look at the table of contents and a couple of sample units (these are frequently available online) in any L2 grammar, vocabulary, or writing textbook.

What are a few identifying features of simpler or more complex grammar structures, vocabulary items, or writing tasks? How can one figure out what represents a less demanding or a more demanding grammar structure, set of vocabulary items, or writing activities? Construct a short list of guidelines to distinguish between simpler and less demanding items and those that are more complex and demanding.

Hint: For most people, concrete actions, words, moments in time, and the like are usually easier to learn and refer to than their abstract counterparts.

In general terms, pedagogical materials or language features belong to two large classes: those that need to proceed in a specific order and build on one another, and those that can be taught in any sort of arrangement at the appropriate level (Nation & Macalister, 2010).

Sequential Materials and Units

Numerous grammar constructions such as verb tenses or sentence structure have to be taught and learned based on their progression of complexity; for example, the present perfect tense (*have seen*) is considerably more complex than the present simple and the past simple tenses, and simple sentences are far less complex than compound sentences, or, as the name would imply, complex sentences. The same is true about vocabulary sets, or writing or listening comprehension tasks. When working with language features that require sequencing and progression, it is essential to allocate extra time for additional and iterative (repeated) practice and review within a larger unit or a lesson.

Non-Sequential Units

Other types of materials may be taught and learned in any order within a course or at a specific level of language proficiency. For instance, instructional units that are organized by topics or reading a few books, carefully selected and appropriate for the level, do not require sequencing. These can be selected depending on learners' interests, their goals for language learning (e.g., entering a university), and available materials (e.g., Snow & Brinton, 1997). However, in such cases, it is important that the level of materials be relatively consistent and suitable for learners' proficiency levels.

Sequencing and Reviewing for Language Building

Frequent opportunities for review (and more review) and additional practice represent one of the essential factors in skill learning and retention. Thus, the instructional material and incremental units should be staggered in partial overlaps from the old to the new, and then again from the earlier learned language features to the newer and, finally, to the newest. For instance, it may useful to present various—and new—functions of the previously taught grammar constructions or vocabulary sets, new contexts for their uses, or their uses across language skills to encourage repeated reviews and additional practice. For example, using particular grammar structures or vocabulary in reading, listening, or writing contexts can lead to expanding learners' language range, as well as ensure the necessary review and practice (Figure 5.1).

Novel applications of these structures and words can be also carried out in materials or texts for reading or writing, or on different topics (Nation & McAlister, 2010). Systematic variations in material reviews across language skills and in context can be added at the outset, while a course curriculum is still being designed. As the amount of material that needs to be reviewed continues to grow throughout the course progression, instructional time devoted to reviews also has to increase.

> Budgeting the time needed for the essential reviews is simply an integral part of any language curriculum design.

Periodically, say, once every few days, it may be very beneficial to include substantial review and practice sessions that can cover a length of material or several units in a summative or expanded sort of fashion (more on this below). Because the amount of instructional material and language should increase as the course

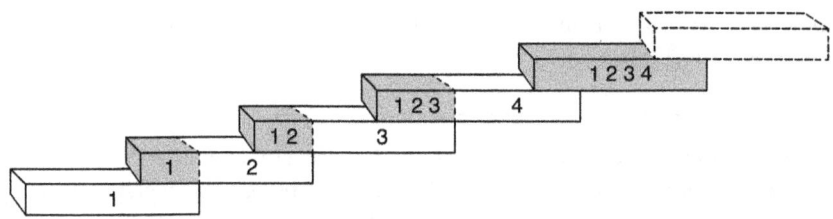

FIGURE 5.1 Building repeated material reviews into the curriculum to provide additional exposure, improve retention, and supplement practice.

progresses, it may be useful to have a range of practice types and exercises in stock to make such reviews more varied: maintaining learner interest can promote motivation for learning during the essential review sessions.

Figure 5.1 illustrates how to build the review opportunities into a course progression from one unit to the next and increase time for reviews of previously covered material as it continues to grow. Dedicated and substantial review sessions that cover a larger portion, an entire unit, or several units are invaluable as an iterative exposure to material and as supplementary practice.

> **Talking Shop**
>
> One of the least effective ways of teaching is to assume that once something is taught, it has been learned. Anyone who's ever tried to remember something (e.g., a phone number, a grocery list, a to-do list, or vocabulary in another language) knows only too well that such things have to be written down or remembered multiple times to make them available for retrieval from memory.
>
> Yet, many classroom teachers do not provide multiple opportunities for learners to review and practice language features—or provide insufficient opportunities. Why do you think this is the case? Please discuss your views with your colleagues and make a list of your observations that you can keep and think about.

When working with materials and units (also called modules) that are organized around topics or themes, by and large, the same principles of material reviews apply. The work on a topic- or theme-based module is usually divided into several lessons, and in this case, the review opportunities need to occur within the series of lessons (Ellis, 2003). Because topic modules often stand independently, the review of language features addressed in one unit may be harder to make cohesive with those in other units. One relatively certain way of ensuring that the requisite material review does in fact occur is to administer a small test or a quiz, or ask students to write a short in-class essay (more on this in the Syllabus and Learning Assessment section below).

> The very fact that tests, quizzes, or short essays are administered in class requires students to review the material in order to prepare. Such preparatory reviews are invaluable in language teaching to promote retention and supplement practice.
>
> **Administering tests and quizzes accomplishes the goal of getting learners to study and review the material before the test actually begins.**
>
> Short in-class tests or quizzes should be administered frequently—at least once a week—and at regular and predictable intervals, so that students can come to expect them, as the unit (or course) progresses. Not to mention that the material is likely to get more attention when tests or quizzes loom ahead. Recycled items on quizzes, e.g., repeated items from previous quizzes that students had difficulty with, further reinforces review.
>
> **Improved motivation for studying (not to be confused with learning) is guaranteed.**

A Special Note on Sequencing Vocabulary and Grammar Units

Vocabulary. As was stated in chapter 4, a great number of common L2 vocabulary items that occur in daily and conversational interactions do not need to be taught because learners almost always have plenty of exposure to high frequency words (West, 1953). That is, very common words are learned without special efforts and dedicated instructional time. As a point of reference, the 10 most common words in the English language are: *the, be, to, of, and, a, in, that, have,* and *I* (Leech, Rayson, & Wilson, 2001).

Currently, a great deal of research can be found on the usefulness of specific words for language learning. According to experts on vocabulary frequencies and occurrences, the most common 1,000 words account for 75% of the successive words in text and the second most frequent 1,000 words represent 5% of the successive words. However, only 570 academic words account for 10% of successive words in academic texts (Nation & Macalister, 2010).

Along these lines, rarely occurring and specialized L2 words are not worth the valuable—and often limited—instructional time because many learners simply do not encounter them or may not need to use them very often in their studies (Nation, 2008, 2009, 2013; Nation & Webb, 2011). Nor do academically bound learners need to learn a great number of interesting, but probably not very beneficial, words that find their way into many vocabulary textbooks on such topics as playing sports, attending weddings or funerals, climbing mountains, being a good neighbor, or going fishing. Although vocabulary sets associated with such enjoyable and fun topics are ubiquitous in L2 vocabulary textbooks, they represent lost opportunities for learning the vocabulary that is actually required of all academic learners (Hinkel, 2004a, 2011).

At present, the research on what vocabulary does need to be taught and learned for academically bound learners is a well-established and time-tested area. For this reason, in a vast body of publications and online, it is easy to identify what vocabulary needs to be included in the curriculum and what should not be.

> The most important objective for a teacher is to focus on strategies and techniques to teach learners to deal with vocabulary, learn it, and retain it (Nation & McAlister, 2010).

For academic L2 learners, the vocabulary sequence should focus first and foremost on words without which no student can survive at school and in college (e.g., *analysis, analyze, cycle, factor, predict, revolve*). Ideally, learning academic vocabulary should take place across the teaching of the essential language skills—namely, listening, speaking, reading, and writing (more on this below; see also chapters 3 and 4).

Grammar. The overviews of what is valued in school language and writing in chapter 2 and what is valued in college and university writing in chapter 3 show clearly that grammar constructions and units do not have an equal or even comparable importance for learning and teaching (Ur, 2011). That is, for example, without exception, all L2 learners and writers have to become highly proficient in the uses and functions of the present simple tense, which is probably the most common of all tenses in the academic prose.

Frequent occurrences of the present simple tense in sentences also necessitate intensive and extensive attention to subject-and-verb agreement. And teaching subject-and-verb agreement, in turn, requires a great deal of work on how to identify the sentence subject and the verb phrase correctly. These are essential—absolutely fundamental—components of grammar that have to be taught intensively and extensively at most, if not all, levels of instruction (Celce-Murcia, 1998, 2002).

On the other hand, in conversations, the present progressive and the past progressive occupy a significant place. Constructing grammatical sentences also calls for the presence of a subject (with the exceptions of commands, which seldom occur in school and academic prose) and a requisite—and correct—verb phrase.

Furthermore, the past simple and the present perfect (e.g., *have gone*) are also frequently found in academic language uses, but the past perfect (*had taught*), the past perfect progressive (*had been teaching*), and the future perfect progressive (*will have been learning*) are not. These structures have largely disappeared from use in many varieties of English (Hinkel, 2002a, 2004b). The uses and functions of gerunds and infinitives (*gathering information* or *to gather information*) are essential for learners to be able to employ correctly in any type of language, be it conversational or academic. However, a prototypical technique for teaching gerunds and infinitives in grammar courses addresses such gerund and infinitive constructions as *go camping/shopping/sightseeing/canoeing* or *forget to buy/offer to bring/decide to try*. These are usually taught in *verb + gerund* or *verb+ infinitive* combinations that do not serve a whole lot of purpose even in mundane conversations.

Unfortunately, the progression of grammar units in instruction almost always pivots on their order in any grammar textbook. This progression of English grammar units imitates that originally developed for teaching Latin to school children in the early 1800s (or maybe even earlier). The reasons that a number of outdated and less-than-productive features of language are incorporated in many grammar textbooks have to do with the prevailing beliefs of what a good grammar textbook should include. To put it simply, the typical presentation of grammar material in teaching has little to do with its value to the learners, for learning, or the frequency of its practical usage (Hinkel & Fotos, 2002).

Following the selection of grammar materials and their sequencing in textbooks has some value to the author or the publisher, but these may or may not match the learning objectives of specific learners. A majority of grammar courses incorporate a bit of a hodge-podge of material that contains very useful and productive constructions, as well as those that learners are likely to never encounter again (Celce-Murcia, 2002; Celce-Murcia & Olshtain, 2005).

The priorities for teaching and learning grammar features have long been established in research on spoken and written academic language, and some of these are highlighted in chapters 2–4.

The selection and progression of grammar features for teaching has to be driven primarily by their usefulness and frequency in academic language and writing.

Talking Shop

Currently, many teachers feel that they are not well prepared to teach L2 academic vocabulary and grammar. Yet, there are very few teacher-education programs in most English-speaking countries that offer courses on teaching both these language components.

In your experience, what are the reasons for the omission? What can teacher-education programs do to improve the quality of teacher preparation? What is the likelihood of the improvements taking place? Discuss your observations with your colleagues and see if it is possible to zero in on the prevailing social and cultural beliefs associated with vocabulary and grammar teaching at school.

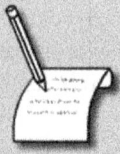

Action Point

A large number of studies on vocabulary and grammar frequencies have been published in the past half century. Their findings are easy to find online, e.g., searching for frequency counts of academic vocabulary or verb forms (or gerunds) is likely to bring up hundreds of thousands of hits.

Working alone or together with your colleagues, develop a list of top ten priorities for instruction in vocabulary sets or verb forms. There can probably be many reasonable and reasoned lists of "top ten priorities" for teaching a number of language features, but your list may simply be a good place to start.

The Syllabus

Once the course objectives are established, and the material sequences are identified and structured, writing a course syllabus is a relatively easy job. The foundational ground work goes first. When all the preliminaries are worked out carefully, reasonably, and appropriately, the syllabus is the presentation of the course outline to the students. Experience has shown that the syllabus does not have to be very detailed, and learners do not necessarily have to be familiar with all the nitty-gritty of the course development. On occasion, instructors construct syllabi that are several pages long, mostly for the purposes of their own course planning. When it comes to being presented with a language learning syllabus, there is definitely such a thing as too much information. Overwhelming students before the course actually gets started is not a great idea. If a detailed course plan is desired, it may take the form of a separate document that is not presented to students.

> The syllabus of the course is an outline. To be useful to students, it should be a clear, cohesive, and relatively short course plan.

Course Description

It is very important to explain the course rationale and the material sequencing to the students because their learning objectives and outcomes determine the direction of the course and the material coverage. Since the learning objectives drive the goals and means of teaching, the learners themselves represent the most important participants of the course.

The descriptions of courses (or classes) can be long or as short as one or two paragraphs. The main purpose of the course description is to give students an overview of what will be covered. The statement of learning objectives is probably the meatiest part of the syllabus, together with the course schedule, and it demonstrates the direction and progression of teaching and learning.

Typically, language courses have multiple learning objectives, and these need to have some sort of internal cohesion. Clarifying the major foci and the connections between them, as well as the usefulness and applicability of the course to meeting learning objectives, can also be accomplished at this point. Doing this is bound to raise the teacher's professional credibility.

> It is important for students to understand specifically what the direction of the course is and how it meets their learning objectives. The teacher and the students are in it together, and they seek to achieve the same learning objectives.

A course syllabus should include the following essential components:

- Basic information (e.g., the name of the course; a particular term and year, such as Fall 2018; meeting times; the instructor's name, email address, office location, and office hours)
- Course description and objectives
- Course progression, topics, and schedule
- Assessment and evaluation specifics (e.g., the types and formats of major assignments—papers and drafts, projects, presentations, tests, quizzes, and exams)
- Grading scales, rubrics, and policies, together with their weights in the course grade, including homework and participation
- Additional course policies (e.g., attendance, late submissions, deadline extensions, missed tests and exams and rescheduling, academic integrity and plagiarism)
- An obligatory note that the instructor reserves the right to make changes and adjustments throughout the term

The outline of course components can be flexible in their order of presentation, but by and large, most of them should be included in the syllabus. These are necessary for students to know: these ingredients do not merely provide the information, but they also describe the expectations of learning.

 **Action Point**

Students usually save the syllabi they receive in their courses. Please take a close look at several of the ones you have (or find online) and examine each one's presentation of the course outline, its essential components, and course description. What do some of these have in common? What is different? Evaluate the quality of these syllabi and determine which ones are better constructed—and which are not. What are the reasons that you consider some syllabi better than others?

As with everything else in teaching and learning, there can be a variety of opinions on what makes for a good syllabus and a sound course description. Working with your colleagues, compare their syllabus evaluations and identify the differences in your views on the syllabus quality. What features of the syllabi do your colleagues see as important? Which ones are less so? How do your evaluations differ from those of your colleagues? What can be the reasons for such differences?

The Course Progression, Topics, and Schedule

The course schedule takes into consideration how long the course lasts and how often it meets. The schedule can be based on the number of weeks or the instructional units. The most commonly found model of a course schedule usually sticks to a weekly progression (e.g., Week 1, Week 2, and Week 3). Announcing the course schedule at the outset has the advantage of allowing students to plan for tests, quizzes, and assignments. On the other hand, making a flexible schedule can account for learning and practicing demanding material and accounting for various eventualities that almost always arise in time—for example, the needed supplementary reviews, student absenteeism, or extensive class discussions (van Lier, 1996).

The authors of textbooks, workbooks, and other commercially available materials usually organize their unit contents to include a week's worth of material in each. However, not all unit subsections need to be taught, and occasionally some may turn out to be redundant (as in *ok, I get it already*) or less than relevant. Some language skills may be easier to learn than others (Graves, 2000). The teaching and learning of less demanding contents may take less than a week, but more demanding material may require supplemental work and extensive review and practice.

> Allowing for flexibility in the course schedule can in fact make a great deal of difference in achieving students' learning objectives. Flexible scheduling for learning and of the material progression can provide for the additional time to work on demanding contents and much needed review.

One of the famous issues often encountered by novice teachers or those who teach new skills in new contexts for the first time is that their course schedule progresses too fast (or sometimes too slowly).

An example of a flexible course schedule organized by contents and units of progression is presented in Figure 5.2. The schedule is developed for an advanced writing course for L2 undergraduate writers and is intended to prepare them for a general education course in composition for both native and non-native speakers of English.

When developing a course schedule, one common rookie faux pas (*bad step* or *misstep*) is to make a teaching and learning plan that is too dense or that moves along too quickly. Small-scale assessments, discussed below, will quickly help the teacher to identify this problem. Allowing ample time for review (and more review) also accounts for student absenteeism, in addition to providing excellent and necessary opportunities for learning and additional exposure to language (Hinkel, 2004a). Other important factors to keep in mind are how often the course meets, how long the class sessions are, assessment schedule (more on this in a subsequent section), holidays and student breaks, and other intervals when students may simply not be able to get as much studying done as at other times. For example, the day before a holiday or break is likely to be less advantageous for scheduling an intensive material review or a test than a couple of days earlier.

Course Concepts

The course will cover the following aspects of academic writing:

- Developing a thesis, presenting supporting details, drafting, and revising
- Summarizing and evaluating ideas in written sources, synthesizing information from several sources, citing sources, and paraphrasing
- Constructing academic argumentation and using persuasion devices, evaluating and comparing/contrasting information, and organizing ideas into a logical progression
- Identifying audience in writing, comparing reader- and writer-based texts, and adhering to academic text form and conventions
- Establishing and maintaining sentence and text coherence and cohesion

---

FIGURE 5.2 A Flexible Learning- and Unit-based Course Schedule. The course is planned to move in the progression of approximately 2 weeks per unit, for a total of 10 weeks. The progression of learning and material is structured to be flexible throughout the term.

Course Policies

Policies can be established by the academic institution, the department, and the instructor. Although course policies may differ depending on students' proficiencies, ages, learning goals, or levels of study, most instructors do not vary their expectations of students dramatically. In the long run, creating a bank of policy statements can save a great deal of time and work.

The policies typically noted on a syllabus deal with such matters as:

- Class attendance and absenteeism
- Plagiarism and academic integrity, and the rules for academic collaboration
- Missed or late assignments and tests/exams, and make-up work
- Expectations of classroom behavior (e.g., computer and cell phone use)
- Making changes in the syllabus or course policies

Other important matters that may be included in the policies are components and explanations of grading (see the next section), weighing of grades for assignments and tests (e.g., how many points each is worth), possible extra-credit work, and class participation credit. The statements of policy can be arranged in the order that is best suited for a specific course and the instructor (for example, as in the list above).

Assessment and Grading

Typically, many discussions of assessment begin with the assessment of learning needs. Currently, however, a great deal of data is available on the learning needs of various types of students with divergent learning goals and in a wide array of learning contexts. When undertaking an assessment of learning needs, this enormous body of research findings can be an excellent place to start. Assessments of learning needs entail complex, well-established, and laborious procedures that have been developed and refined for a broad range of contexts. Learning needs and learning contexts well covered in research can pertain to, for example, school-age youngsters or adults, new immigrants, professionals, university students, or academically bound language learners.

A large amount of research has been devoted to identifying the learning needs of these types of students, and at present, it is relatively easily accessible. For instance, chapters 2–4 review some of the important research findings that can help reduce the labor and time associated with assessing learning needs of many types of students.

Capitalizing on the recent findings of research and applying them to learning needs presents an excellent basis of constructing a language learning course (Adams & Artemeva, 2002; Hinkel, 2002b; ICAS, 2002; Rosenfeld, Courtney, &

Fowles, 2004). Additionally, the almost universally administered initial or placement assessments can afford opportunities for tailoring the course to the needs of a particular group of students or for a specific course progression, length, or instruction. In most contexts, initial assessments serve to ensure the course level of difficulty to make it a good fit. (A detailed set of rubrics of needs analyses in L2 writing, grammar, and/or vocabulary learning is included in Appendices A and B.)

For this reason, and in keeping with the research overviews in the earlier chapters, the remainder of this section will discuss the assessment of student learning and briefly touch on the assessment associated with the entire course as a whole.

Assessing Learning

As has been mentioned, for students, the main beneficial outcome of assessment is to provide learners reasons and opportunities for review, revision, and exposure to the features of language that the course is designed to address. Since time immemorial, regular assessments have been a routine part of most—if not all—language course curricula. The frequency and regularity of assessments is usually closely related to instruction in specific language skills; for example, vocabulary and grammar quizzes and tests usually take place more frequently than, for instance, assessments of speaking skills.

A question that often comes up in teachers' conversations has to do with differences between tests and assessments. Assessments are usually informal measures of learners' progress or achievement. Typically, assessments cover a shorter period of learning and a smaller range of material and contents than tests. In such contexts as supplementary language teaching or at beginning levels, for example, assessments can be carried out in the form of regular classroom activities (Brown, 1998), such as writing short reactions to readings, vocabulary practice, or grammar exercises. Assessment instruments, however, may be difficult to disguise when students know that their performance is being measured and when explicit performance criteria are provided (more on these below). On the other hand, tests may measure overall language proficiency, and a great deal can hinge on their outcomes (e.g., TOEFL is a high-stakes test of language proficiency).

> Regardless of their form, assessments of learning or achievement are planned activities that are designed to measure specific progress in students' language gains. Assessment instruments and grading/scoring criteria have to remain explicit and consistent throughout the course.

Small-Scale Assessments (Quizzes and Short Writing Tasks)

To create a course-intrinsic review (and review) structure, short (5, 10, or 15 minutes) quizzes and tests can take place daily, every other day, or weekly. Such small-scale and frequent assessments can be highly productive for a number of purposes: to identify language features or incremental skills that require further work, and to ascertain the effectiveness of a teaching activity or technique or the suitability of material sequencing or pacing (Nation, 2003, 2009; Nation & Newton, 2009).

> Small-scale assessments should be scheduled at regular intervals and be systematic in their timing and structure to allow students to prepare and understand learning expectations clearly.

Another advantage of small-scale assessments is that they make it easier to determine whether learning objectives are being achieved, based on the learners' incremental progress in the course sequence. Not to mention that the learning objectives for short periods of learning and teaching are relatively easy to construct and gauge.

> The importance of small-scale assessments for learners' motivation and a sense of progress cannot be emphasized enough. They provide valuable information for both students and teachers.

Looking at small-scale assessments from the teacher's perspective, grading and marking incremental pieces of student writing or short quizzes, for example, usually takes far less time than extensive written work or projects. Grading criteria for writing assignments and assessments, for instance, can be tied directly to the course learning objectives in a way that can take into consideration a range of the component skills required to produce a good quality piece of writing.

In the case of writing, for example, small-scale assessments should be accompanied by clearly stated—and scale-appropriate—learning objectives and evaluation criteria. These are intended to specify what should be learned at a particular point of course progression and how learning is assessed. It is very important that small-scale assessments be carried out based on the stated learning objectives and the criteria (measures or benchmarks) for the evaluation of the language features that are taught and learned (see Figure 5.3 for an example).

The learning and performance objectives and clearly stated expectations regarding language uses and writing quality can consist of the following component skills that do not need to be, in fact, collapsed into a single grade. In this way, what needs to be additionally taught and learned can come into focus and be specific for both the teacher and the learners. These components of a grade in small-scale writing assessments can—and probably should—remain incremental to provide

Grading Criteria for In-class Writing Assessments

The short in-class pieces of writing will be graded based on several important features:

- Clear structuring of ideas and discourse organization, including the clarity of the thesis (30 points)
- Accurate uses of the present simple tense and the past simple tense, complete sentences, and accurate subject-verb agreement (25 points)
- Appropriate and accurate uses of at least 15 (or 20) academic words from the vocabulary covered in the past two weeks (25 points)
- Appropriate/reasonable paragraphing, accurate capitalization, and punctuation of full sentences, both compound and complex (20 points)

FIGURE 5.3 Performance Objectives and Expectations of Component Skills with the Corresponding Number of Points. This breakdown can show clearly to both the teacher and the learner whether additional work is needed in any specific area. Small-scale writing assessments can be based on incremental grading to make the most of such highly useful feedback.

learners with highly useful feedback. An example of learning objectives, and assessment componential grading criteria, closely tied to specific learning objectives is presented in Figure 5.3.

As has been mentioned earlier, in order for the learning objectives and the criteria for small-scale assessments to be useful and goal-oriented in both teaching and learning, such measures have to be specific, quantifiable, and appropriate for a particular point in the course sequence.

> Frequent small-scale assessments, including those based on incremental components of grading provide numerous and clearly visible opportunities for course corrections in the progression of teaching and learning.

If an adjustment of the stated learning objectives for the entire course or its incremental components is needed, the feedback from small-scale assessments can lead to an overall improvement in student learning and the course curriculum. In this way, many facets of teaching and learning, material progression and sequencing, teaching techniques, and material coverage can be altered, adjusted, or completely revised at practically any juncture, without waiting until the completion of the course (see also Appendix A of this chapter for sample assessment criteria that can be used in part or in whole).

> **Talking Shop**
>
> In your view, what are the differences between the learning objectives for the whole course and for small-scale assessments? Can small-scale assessments be made cumulative, at least to some extent? What is the range of time and learning that small-scale assessments should cover? Can these ranges of time be doubled or even tripled?
>
> How would such a technique contribute to further learning and additional reviews of the material and contents? As with everything else in life, there are pros and cons to small-scale assessments. Discuss your views with your colleagues to determine if an optimal timing of small-scale assessments and the range of their coverage can be identified.

What Accompanies and What Follows: Coordinating Instruction

Coordinating instruction across levels and language skills affords several advantages. To begin with, teaching coordinated courses—for instance, in L2 reading and writing, listening and speaking, or listening and writing at the same level of learner proficiency—leads to cohesive instruction and learning. Furthermore, opportunities for learners' exposure to and practice in specific language components are thus increased. As has been noted throughout this book, multiple and repeated exposure to language elements, such as vocabulary or grammar, is required in order to retain and learn to use them (Hinkel, 2006, 2009a, 2009b).

On the other hand, coordinating teaching the skills calls for additional work, time, and adjustments, say, in sequencing and progression, from each instructor. In fact, this is one of the main reasons that coordinated teaching across language skills at the same level has not become a great deal more common than it currently is. That is, coordinating classroom teaching on a day-to-day or weekly basis sounds pedagogically astute but may be difficult to manage in reality. In light of the many constraints that typically accompany within-level coordination, the most reasonable and easiest way is to align day-to-day language and skill instruction and practice across courses taught by the same teacher.

Coordinating teaching within a level. The fact that coordinated teaching of incremental language components can be difficult to manage does not mean, however, that it is similarly challenging to coordinate within-level curricula. Undoubtedly, coordinating curricula across different courses can provide equally beneficial and requisite advantages in terms of repeated exposures to language, practice, and review. Coordinating curricula within levels of learners' proficiency and across two or more skills necessarily requires that instructional contents focus on the same or proximate language components at various phases of the course.

For example, the teaching of the past simple tense (*he/she/they went*) requires the learning of irregular verbs (*go—went—gone, buy—bought—bought, put—put—put*), as well as identifying the language contexts when the past tense uses are grammatically accurate. The reinforcement of the two skill elements (i.e., the verb forms and contextually appropriate tense usage; e.g., in conjunction with past-time adverbs and adverb phrases, such as *in 2013, last year,* and *ago*) can take place in the teaching of grammar, reading, and writing even when the exposure and practice do not occur simultaneously. In fact, the tried and true technique for language learning centers is **spaced** repetition that is planned for and takes place at intervals.

> The biggest advantage of coordinating curricula within a level is that the language components taught and practiced in one course are afforded additional exposures, uses, and applications in the context of another skill.

Coordinating teaching across levels. Repeated language practice and reviews can also be achieved in teaching at divergent proficiency levels. To follow on the example of the past tense for beginners, instruction at subsequent—for example, intermediate and high intermediate—levels can do very well to review and practice this language feature in context, such as reading and writing about past-time factual events that require uses of irregular verbs and adverbials. Not to mention that, additionally, such contexts can entail the learning and practice of relevant vocabulary in writing or speaking (e.g., *change/modify, point out/indicate,* or *examine/analyze;* see chapter 7 for important word lists).

> One of the greatest—if not the greatest—missteps in language teaching is to teach and practice language components for a period of time or in a localized segment of a curriculum only to abandon them later without subsequent review.

Teaching and practicing language features at one level crucially requires reintroducing, reviewing, and practicing them at subsequent levels, and usually more than one. In this light, coordinating teaching, learning, and review across levels are indispensable in a well-designed curriculum.

Talking Shop

Since the 1980s, a large body of research has demonstrated that coordinating language instruction within level is a double-edged sword.

> On the one hand, it can greatly benefit learners and lead to improved language usage and skills, thus aiding the achievement of learning objectives effectively. On the other, coordinated teaching is fraught with complications, some of which may not be easily overcome. Such limitations are probably true about numerous human undertakings that require working closely with other people or teams, as well as in situations when one's ability to do one's job depends on other people doing theirs.
>
> Based on your experience, what do you think the difficulties may be in coordinating within-level language teaching? Please consider a range of facets in such coordinated teaching, including financial, administrative, supervisory, teacher preparation and professional qualifications, and the like. What do your colleagues think? Have they been involved in within-level coordinated instruction? Do you think this type of teaching is popular? What are the reasons for its popularity or a lack of it?

Making a Lesson Plan

Definition: A lesson plan is a detailed and timed description of the course of instruction for one class. A lesson plan is constructed by the teacher to guide instruction and manage class time. A lesson plan has to include and be driven by the **learning objectives** of the lesson, the materials that are needed and used to achieve them, and the instructional activities that are used for this purpose.

The greatest benefit of constructing thoughtful and detailed lesson plans is that they help teachers be organized and prepared. Lesson plans that are oriented toward solid and clear learning objectives provide a structure to bring learners closer to attaining their goals. Furthermore, lesson plans can be recyclable in the future if they are adjusted for a new context or the next student cohort.

One foundational attribute of many lesson plans that is often overlooked is setting aside time for review. When writing lessons plans, it is essential to account for review and practice of the language features that students are required to learn to achieve their objectives. Instructional time has to be allowed for review, review, and more review.

> The first order of business in any lesson plan is to determine what language learning objectives the lesson instruction sets out to achieve. That is, the first priority is to figure out the final outcome.

Lesson plans do not have to—and probably should not—be prepared for only one class meeting, but they can be constructed for a sequential instructional unit that covers a number of class sessions. In progressive sequences, instructional and learning objectives may be easier to determine and develop with an eye on a bigger picture.

> Always, in all cases, and in any teaching context, lesson plans should be prepared for more instructional time rather than less. Overplanning is being well-prepared. It is always a great deal easier to drop portions of a plan or to chop it off than to come up short. The importance of planning too much instruction cannot be overemphasized.

Step 1: A lesson plan begins with the learning goals—or the achievable ends—of instruction. That is, it is important to identify what the students should learn in the lesson or over several lessons, as well as the measurable outcomes and standards that need to be met. Constructing the learning objectives should account for learning assessments and measures that are expected or required of students, as well as the students' own learning goals.

In the long run, creating a list of verbs and adverbs for writing learning objectives may prove to be very helpful (see the discussion earlier in this chapter). Such a list can be modified as needed in the context of teaching different language skills and learners with different proficiency levels. Another advantage of having the lists of verbs and adverbs is that they can become familiar to learners and become an additional opportunity for language exposure and practice.

For a lesson plan to be effective, it is important for the teacher to know—even if approximately—how much time work on the material, a classroom task, or activity can take.

> The second order of business is to determine how to divide the instructional time into realistic sections.

In any single lesson, it is important that students encounter varied types of language work, practice, and activities. These can consist of exposure to and production of language features. The types of language features that a lesson is devoted to does not have to vary greatly, but the types of activities entailed in classroom instruction need to be diverse.

> When constructing a lesson plan, a crucial consideration is that a class meeting should include more than one activity or section. Most learners tend to get bored or tired of performing the same task for longer than 20–30 minutes. Exposing learners to a variety of activities and divergent contexts of language uses has the added benefit of attendant language practice.

No matter how good a lesson plan is, it has to be flexible. Some groups of learners may find instructional material more difficult or less, some may require more detailed work with the material than others, some may take longer to process information, and at times, some may enjoy or be disinterested in various types of activities and practice. In short, it is important for both the teacher and the lesson plan to adjust accordingly.

> All lesson plans need to present students with a preview of the things to come. In the presentation, the lesson overview also needs to highlight the reasons that particular language features or material is taught in terms of learners' objectives and learners' own goals.

The purpose of the preview is to directly connect the instructional material and activities to learners' goals and objectives. For example, *Today, we will work on xxx and yyy because (a) xxx seems to be difficult for many, (b) yyy is essential for the production of academic writing and formal written prose in courses/disciplines such as zzz*. The preview is likely to be very short and take little time, but it is essential.

> All lessons need to incorporate a review of material covered earlier and at least the material covered in the previous lesson.

Talking Shop

The purpose of lesson previews is not very different from that of movie trailers or book summaries and previews on the back cover and cover flaps. Most people watch movie trailers in genres that interest them or read book summaries with interest. What are the purposes of allowing the audience to have previews? How are these similar to lesson previews?

If, for example, the teacher notices that the lesson preview does not seem interesting, relevant, or applicable to the learning objectives or students' learning goals, is it okay to change the content of the lesson on the spur of the moment? Or should the teacher stay the course, as is outlined in his or her original lesson plan?

Discuss your ideas with your colleagues and see what a variety of perspectives can surface when it comes to lesson previews, lesson plans, and on-the-fly, last-second changes.

Step 2: In order for the language work to move forward, the second step, which should take approximately 5–15 minutes, is the review of the materials covered in the previous lesson(s). The review can take any form that is best suited to meet the learning objectives—for example, various types of vocabulary or grammar games, such as round robin, spot checking, short quizzes, and the like.

Step 3: Work on the language components begins after the initial review. Ideally, in the instructional sequence, the language components and concepts in this central phase of the lesson should build on those that have been addressed in previous lessons or in the immediately preceding lesson. For example, if previously students worked on developing thesis statements, then an examination of excellent, passable, or faulty theses can take place; if students worked on compound sentences, then in progression, the punctuation of compound constructions can be beneficial; or, if previous vocabulary practice focused on phrasal verbs (e.g., *give in, give up, give off, turn on*), then collocations (words that usually co-occur together in discourse, e.g., *appropriate measures, make progress, advance the cause, keep control*) may also follow.

> In the central phase of the lesson, it is imperative to provide opportunities for production and practice with language components and concepts.

The language practice can take any productive form, such as working individually, in pairs, or groups and engaging in relevant and related language games, writing, or speaking. Students need to produce their own language material rather than, for instance, reading, listening, or watching a movie clip. Responding to questions orally or in writing; writing questions associated with reading, listening, or vocabulary; constructing sentences, stories, or skits; or responding to readings—all such activities require language production. This time can also incorporate clarifications of difficult or confusing language constructions and elements.

Step 4: The final lesson review can be relatively short and around 5 minutes. The purpose of the final review is to highlight the main aspects of the lesson, to check for learners' comprehension of the material and the homework assignment (if any), and to build in an opportunity of a very brief return to the language components covered in class.

A few notes on making a good lesson plan: In writing lesson plans made for one or several class meetings, it is wise in the long run to:

- Figure out—even if approximately—the amount of time each incremental portion of the lesson is expected to take. The timing may be adjusted as needed and with experience.
- Take notes about the reasons for making decisions associated with textbook modifications, supplementary materials, or sequence changes. With time,

many bases for decisions can be forgotten or overlooked, and in such situations, rereading old notes makes constructing a new lesson plan a great deal easier.
- Write down which sections or pages of the textbook material are covered in class and/or assigned as homework.
- List the language components, such as grammar structures or vocabulary.
- Write out detailed instructions to students and directions for the practice activities you plan to use. These will come in handy more than once.
- When working with beginners, it can be useful to write out the instructions on the board or provide a handout, sometimes at a step-by-step level of detail.
- If you plan to ask students comprehension questions on readings, or questions to elicit the uses of particular grammar constructions (e.g., the passive voice, as in *was made*; or the present simple tense, as in *goes to school*) or vocabulary items, write down the questions.
- In group activities, decide ahead of time how many students each group should include. Ideally, this number should not exceed 7 or 8, and not more than 10 in any case.
- If your lesson plan entails using teaching materials that are not in the textbook (e.g., postcards, movie clips, print advertisements, supplementary readings, family albums, audio recordings, or websites), prepare these ahead of time—this is important.

Caveats, Predictable Pitfalls, and Other Important Notes

Teaching different lessons and working with various teaching materials can result in greatly dissimilar lesson plans. In some situations, new materials, complex grammar constructions, difficult reading or listening selections, or an extensive writing practice can take up the entire time of the lesson, or even more than one lesson. In some cases, the production activity, such as role-plays, student skits or presentations, or in-class writing practice can take longer than expected. A good lesson plan should account for a range of language and practice complexity and varied lesson durations.

In various contexts or with different groups of students, even a tried-and-true activity may not work as well as intended. New class activities should be seen as experiments until proven successful both in teaching and learning. It is always wise to have a backup plan and/or another type of activity that is familiar. For example, if a lesson plan relies on the fact that students have done their homework, but about half of them did not, then the students may need to be divided into two groups and assigned different classroom tasks, with one group doing their homework after all, and the other being engaged in learning and working with new language features. An alternative lesson plan can focus on language practice and production in which both groups of learners can participate in class.

Action Point

When you attend several classes (4 or 5), observe and make notes of the lesson segments. Doing this might represent constructing a kind of a retrospective lesson plan. If possible, note the structure of the lessons taught by different instructors. Compare the elements and sequences in these retrospective lesson plans and identify their similarities and differences. Are some lessons more effective than others? What are the advantages and disadvantages of particular lesson plans? Can you guess the reasons for the differences in how lessons are sequenced and the order of their elements?

Some instructors teach without lesson plans. What do you think advantages and disadvantages are of teaching without a plan?

To obtain even a larger sample of retrospective plans, take a look at those collected by your colleagues, in addition to those in your sample. How are most plans similar and in what ways are they different? What does a broad-based picture of planning lessons show? Which lesson segments are requisite and which ones are optional? Discuss your findings with your colleagues.

The Actual Lesson Plan

When it comes to making lesson plans, the easiest way to proceed is to construct a template that is sufficiently flexible to allow for variations. There are always variations in lessons, and no two are ever the same. The following elements are important to consider, but in the end, each teacher eventually arrives at the template that works well for him or her. A workable lesson plan should:

- Be visible at a glance to keep track of material progression and timing of activities (it should fit on one sheet of paper)
- Be clear and easy to read and follow on one's feet and while teaching
- Establish direct and clear connections between the lesson in progress and earlier lesson(s)
- Have clear and direct applications to students' current work and projects
- Account for time and timing of activities—this is an essential attribute of all good lesson plans
- Provide for contingencies (overplan, overplan, and overplan!)

A couple of sample templates for lesson plans are presented below in Templates 1 and 2. They are relatively easy to make and modify (and modify) as needed.

Template 1

Learning Objective: By the end of the lesson, students should be able to write topic sentences in 3 paragraphs to prepare for their essays.

Reading/Writing _____   Level: Intermediate

Segment	What and How? (Activities)	Materials	Time
1. Short vocabulary and material review from previous lessons Previously learned words and a brief content overview at the start of the new lesson.	A mini-quiz: word dictation. Students provide definitions or clear examples.	Vocabulary lists from previous lessons	5–10 min.
2. Introduction of new material Focusing student attention on the new lesson: topic sentences, using examples from textbook readings (3–5) and visuals. Stating the lesson objective, connecting the objective to previous lessons/learning.	Examine paragraphs in textbook readings and identify main points and their placement in paragraphs	Textbook readings, overhead visually enhanced paragraphs with topic sentences highlighted	10 min.
3. Detailed presentation Examining the structure of paragraphs: topic sentences and their supporting points. Connections between topic sentences and paragraph points/supports. Check for student comprehension: students perform paragraph examination with guidance.	Analyze paragraph structure and supports: where is the main point? Where are the supporting points? Clearly identify connections.	Several paragraphs, visually enhanced paragraphs with topic sentences visually connected to supports	10–15 min.
4. Application and Practice New knowledge applied in context. Students write topic sentences—supporting sentences/points. Practice is guided through student production: work in pairs, small groups, or individually. Instructor circulates and guides as needed, monitors progress and provides feedback.	Students practice writing sentences: on the board and/or in their notebooks.		15 min.
5. Evaluation Each student is evaluated on achieving lesson objectives. Evaluation can be oral or written (complete paragraphs).	The teacher will check the notebook page.		
6. Application/Closure Homework: Write a short 3-paragraph essay: topic sentences and supports. (Practice that requires students to apply new knowledge to new contexts and work).		verbal	5 min.

(Format adapted from California Department of Education, California Professional Development Project)

Template 2

Date:
Unit: Paragraphs, topic sentences, short essays
Level: Intermediate Reading/Writing

Learning Goals and Objectives	Standards/Achievement of Objectives

Structure of Lesson:
    Review (including short quizzes)
    Activities
    Evaluation/Closing

Assessing Learning/Evaluation
State explicitly the **quantifiable** outcomes/evidence for the assessment of student work that specifies sufficient and successful progress toward learning standards/objectives.

Resources/Materials

Chapter Summary

The foundation of a curricular model begins with the essential "studies of the learners" (as noted in chapter 1) and the learner language (see chapter 4). The next essential move is to establish the **scope of language** learning objectives that in fact can be reasonably achieved during the specified instructional time.

Learning objectives seek to establish what learners should be able to do or what skills they can be expected to develop by the end of the instructional term. When defining learning objectives, it is important to keep in mind that these should be **specific** in order to be useful and usable and **realistic**. Most importantly, learning objectives have to be **measurable** in some way.

When the instructor is planning the **sequencing of materials and units**, it is important to remember that the order of the stated learning objectives has to correspond to the order of material in the teaching sequence. Coordinating sequencing of material in a class works most effectively by moving from simpler to more complex concepts and constructions. Coordinating sequencing of material over several courses has great pedagogical benefits, but sometimes equally great logistical challenges.

Once the course objectives are established, and the material sequences are identified and developed, writing a course syllabus is a relatively easy job. When all the preliminaries are worked out carefully, thoughtfully, and appropriately, the syllabus is in fact the presentation of the course outline to the students.

The importance of small-scale assessments for learners' motivation and a sense of progress cannot be emphasized enough. They provide valuable information for both students and teachers for course adjustments, refinement, and reformulation.

The greatest benefit of creating thoughtful and detailed **lesson plans** is that they help teachers be organized and prepared. Lesson plans that are driven by solid and clear learning objectives provide a structure to bring students closer to attaining their learning goals.

Notes

1 Typically, foreign language programs that teach another language as an academic subject in North America, for example, do not have the objective of preparing their students for the level of functionality expected of academically bound L2 learners, who are required to read and write full-fledged academic texts comparable to those read by peer native speakers.
2 In some cases, such as those in small and locally offered adult literacy classes, the learners' initial proficiency is not formally established, and few (if any) L2 literacy skills are often assumed.

Further Reading

Carson, J. G., Chase, N. D., Gibson, S. U., & Hargrove, M. F. (1992). Literacy demands of the undergraduate curriculum. *Reading Research and Instruction, 31,* 25–50.
Graves, K. (2000). *Designing language courses: A guide for teachers.* Boston: Heinle & Heinle.
Hinkel, E. (1997). Indirectness in L1 and L2 academic writing. *Journal of Pragmatics, 27,* 360–386.
Hinkel, E. (2005). Analyses of L2 text and what can be learned from them. In E. Hinkel (Ed.), *Handbook of research in second language teaching and learning* (pp. 615–628). Mahwah, NJ: Lawrence Erlbaum Associates.
Hinkel, E. (2011). *Handbook of research in second language teaching and learning* (Vol. 2). New York: Routledge.
Leki, I., & Carson, J. (1997). "Completely different worlds": EAP and the writing experiences of ESL students in university courses. *TESOL Quarterly, 31,* 39–70.

McCarthy, L. (1987). A stranger in strange lands: A college student writing across curriculum. *Research in the Teaching of English, 21*(3), 233–267.
Stern, H. H. (1983). *Fundamental concepts of language teaching*. Oxford: Oxford University Press.
Stern, H. H. (1992). *Issues and options in language teaching*. Oxford: Oxford University Press.

References

Adams, C., & Artemeva, N. (2002). Writing instruction in English for Academic Purposes (EAP) classes: Introducing second language learners to the academic community. In A. Johns (Ed.), *Genre in the classroom: Multiple perspectives* (pp. 179–196). Mahwah, NJ: Lawrence Erlbaum Associates.
Anderson, L., & Krathwohl, D. (Eds.). (2001). *A taxonomy for learning, teaching, and assessing: A revision of Bloom's taxonomy of educational objectives*. New York: Longman.
Bloom, B. (Ed.). (1956). *Taxonomy of educational objectives. Handbook 1: Cognitive domain*. New York: David McKay.
Brown, J. D. (Ed.). (1998). *New ways of classroom assessment*. Washington, DC: Teachers of English to Speakers of Other Languages.
Celce-Murcia, M. (1998). Discourse analysis and grammar instruction. In D. Oaks (Ed.), *Linguistics at work: A reader in applications*. (pp. 687–704). Fort Worth, TX: Harcourt Brace College Publishers.
Celce-Murcia, M. (2002). Why it makes sense to teach grammar in context and through discourse. In E. Hinkel & S. Fotos (Eds.), *New perspectives on grammar teaching in second language classrooms* (pp. 119–134). Mahwah, NJ: Lawrence Erlbaum Associates.
Celce-Murcia, M., & Olshtain, E. (2005). Discourse-based approaches: A new framework for second language teaching and learning. In E. Hinkel (Ed.), *Handbook of research in second language teaching and learning* (pp. 729–742). Mahwah, NJ: Laurence Erlbaum Associates.
Ellis, R. (2003). *Task-based language learning and teaching*. Oxford: Oxford University Press.
Graves, K. (2000). *Designing language courses: A guide for teachers*. Boston: Heinle & Heinle.
Hinkel, E. (2002a). *Second language writers' text*. Mahwah, NJ: Lawrence Erlbaum Associates.
Hinkel, E. (2002b). Teaching grammar in writing classes: Tenses and cohesion. In E. Hinkel & S. Fotos (Eds.), *New perspectives on grammar teaching in second language classrooms* (pp. 181–198). Mahwah, NJ: Lawrence Erlbaum Associates.
Hinkel, E. (2004a). *Teaching academic ESL writing: Practical techniques in vocabulary and grammar*. Mahwah, NJ: Lawrence Erlbaum Associates.
Hinkel, E. (2004b). Tense, aspect, and the passive voice in L1 and L2 writing. *Language Teaching Research, 8*, 5–29.
Hinkel, E. (2006). Current perspectives on teaching the four skills. *TESOL Quarterly, 40*(1), 109–131.
Hinkel, E. (2009a). Contrastive rhetoric. In U. Fix, A. Gardt, & J. Knape (Eds.), *International handbook of historical and systematic research in rhetoric and stylistics* (pp. 36–48). Berlin: Mouton de Gruyter.
Hinkel, E. (2009b). Integrating the four skills: Current and historical perspectives. In R. B. Kaplan (Ed.), *Oxford handbook in applied linguistics* (2nd ed., pp. 110–126). New York, NY: Oxford University Press.
Hinkel, E. (2011). What research on second language writing tells us and what it doesn't. In E. Hinkel (Ed.), *Handbook of research in second language teaching and Learning* (Vol. 2, pp. 523–538). New York: Routledge.

Hinkel, E., & Fotos, S. (Eds.). (2002). *New perspectives on grammar teaching in second language classrooms.* Mahwah, NJ: Lawrence Erlbaum Associates.
ICAS. (2002). *Academic literacy: A statement of competencies expected of students entering California's public colleges and universities.* Sacramento, CA: Intersegmental Committee of the Academic Senates of California Colleges and Universities.
Laufer, B., & Nation, P. (1995). Vocabulary size and use: Lexical richness in L2 written production. *Applied Linguistics, 16,* 307–322.
Leech, G., Rayson, P., & Wilson, A. (2001). *Word frequencies in written and spoken English.* London: Longman.
Mager, R. (1997). *Preparing instructional objectives* (3rd ed.). Atlanta: The Center for Effective Performance.
Nation, I. S. P. (1990). *Teaching and learning vocabulary.* New York: Newbury House.
Nation, I. S. P. (2003). Effective ways of building vocabulary knowledge. *ESL Magazine, 6*(4), 14–15.
Nation, I. S. P. (2008). *Teaching vocabulary.* Boston: Heinle & Heinle.
Nation, I. S. P. (2009). *Teaching ESL/EFL reading and writing.* New York: Routledge.
Nation, I. S. P. (2013). *Learning vocabulary in another language* (2nd ed.). Cambridge: Cambridge University Press.
Nation, I. S. P., & Macalister, J. (2010). *Language curriculum design.* New York: Routledge.
Nation, I. S. P., & Newton, J. (2009). *Teaching EFL/ESL listening and speaking.* New York: Routledge.
Nation, I. S. P., & Webb, S. (2011). Content-based instruction and vocabulary learning. In E. Hinkel (Ed.), *Handbook of research in second language teaching and learning* (Vol. 2, pp. 631–644). New York: Routledge.
Posner, G. (2004). *Analyzing the curriculum* (3rd ed.). New York: McGraw-Hill.
Rosenfeld, M., Courtney, R., & Fowles, M. (2004). *Identifying the writing tasks important for academic success at the undergraduate and graduate level.* Princeton, NJ: Educational Testing Service.
Simpson, E. J. (1972). *The classification of educational objectives in the psychomotor domain.* Washington, DC: Gryphon House.
Snow, M., & Brinton, D. (1997). *The content-based classroom: Perspectives on integrating language and content.* White Plains, NY: Addison-Wesley Longman.
Tyler, R. W. (1949). *Basic principles of curriculum and instruction.* Chicago: The University of Chicago Press.
Ur, P. (2011). Grammar teaching: Research, theory and practice. In E. Hinkel (Ed.), *Handbook of research in second language teaching and learning* (Vol. 2, pp. 507–522). New York: Routledge.
vanLier, L. (1996). *Interaction in the language curriculum: Awareness, autonomy, and authenticity.* London: Longman.
West, M. (1953). *A general service list of English words.* London: Longman.

APPENDIX A

Typical Rubrics and Needs Analysis Criteria for L2 Writing

Top-down Approach Based on L1 and L2 Writing Research and Discourse Analysis

Discourse (Global/Macro Organization)

Brief introduction of the topic
Main idea/thesis
Major supporting points/arguments
Types of thesis support:
    Facts/information from readings
    Explanations/illustrations
    Clear and logical examples
Progression/variation of ideas connected to the thesis
Acknowledging and responding to opposing points of view (in argumentative essays)
Brief ending/conclusion: brings together the major supporting points and connects them back to the thesis

Paragraph Division (one paragraph—one idea)

The topic sentence directly connected to the main idea/thesis
Minor supporting points for the topic sentence
Types of topic support
    One idea from readings
    Fact(s)
    Explanation/illustration
    One (expanded) example

Local (Micro) Text Construction

Unity (within and between paragraphs)
  Lexical cohesion/repeated meanings/synonymy
  Consistent tense
  Accurate pronoun reference
  Logical/sentence transitions
Progression of the idea/example within a paragraph

Register (can also be referred to as:)

Standard written English
Use of language appropriate to the task and intended audience
Word choice—vocabulary
Formal written expression

Grammar

Sentence structure/completeness
  Word order
  Run-ons
  Fragments
  Pronoun reference
Dependent clauses
  Word order
  Pronoun reference
Verb
  Tense and aspect
  Subject-verb agreement
  Active/passive
  Modals
  Irregular verbs
  Auxiliary verbs
Noun
  Number
  Quantifiers
  Articles

Vocabulary/Lexicon

Lexical accuracy and range
Correct morphological/word forms
Prepositions

Punctuation, capitalization, spelling

Paragraph Structure/Organization: Coherence/clarity

APPENDIX B

Analyzing Student Essays To Develop a Course Curriculum

Needs Analyses

The current research on macro and micro features of L2 writing and on specific areas of instruction is foundational in the teaching of L2 academic writing specifically. Thousands of research reports address discoursal, rhetorical, cohesive, syntactic, lexical, and other types of features common in L2 academic texts.

To develop a course curriculum, a needs analysis seeks to identify the types of L2 discourse and text features to become starting points for effective and efficient writing instruction. An analysis of samples of L2 academic prose serves as the basis of a tentative curriculum outline, depending based on the outcomes of needs analyses. When a general curriculum outline is in place, the final step is to determine which additional L2 text and/or discourse features should be included to match the learning needs of a specific group of learners.

Step 1

Based on testing/assessment criteria adopted locally and the findings of research on L2 writing and text, teachers can adapt the needs analysis and essay evaluation criteria below or work with the Sample Scoring/Evaluation Sheet (below) and make changes as necessary.

Step 2

A teacher or a group of teachers can analyze a representative sample of diagnostic student essays in their courses or program. Teachers can use the Scoring Sheet either for each essay singly or for the set of essays together. The analysis of single essays will need to be later consolidated into a Score Summary.

Conversely, the analysis can begin with a Score Summary and the essays together as a set. However, in this case, occasionally, it may be necessary to go back and take another look at some of the essays analyzed earlier. The Score Summary is the basis for (tentative) curriculum guidelines, which can be used for a variety of instructional purposes, including material writing or textbook selection.

Whether the analysis begins with each essay individually or as a set, the design of the initial Score Sheet may require adjustments to account for the learning needs of a particular group of students. In the final count, some of the discourse and text features in the initial Score Sheet may turn out to be less worthwhile, and others may need to be added, as the work with actual L2 writing curriculum evolves and progresses.

Step 3

When the Score Summary is completed, the curriculum development work is largely done. As the last step, curriculum guidelines should include records and notes on what the task of the curriculum development entailed to make subsequent adjustments and revisions easier, as needed. The entire set of curriculum development materials is likely to include the following:

- Based on the data in the final Score Summary, an outline for tentative curriculum guidelines for an L2 academic writing course.
- The reasons the initial (sample) Score Sheet warranted adjustments (if any) and the specific modifications that are needed to account for the language and discourse features identified (or not identified) in the student essays.
- The Score Summary with the overall results of essay analyses.

Sample Essay Score Sheet

_____Approx. # of words (fluency/development) (# of lines multiplied by # of words, 2nd or 3rd line)

Discourse Organization (From the beginning of the essay/Quick-scan as you read)

- ☐ Brief introduction
- ☐ Thesis
- ☐ Paragraph division
- ☐ Idea progression
- ☐ Conclusion/closing

Paragraph Structure/Essay Body (Essay overall/Quick scan)

_____ Approx. # of paragraphs

- ☐ Topic sentences in most paragraphs
- ☐ Support in most paragraphs for most main points (Example/Illustration or Factual)

_____ Approx. # of cohesion/lexical ties/synonyms (if any)

Error Analysis for Teaching and Editing Practice (Approx. numbers)

Sentence structure
- _____ Incomplete/too many elements _____ (Tally, if needed)
- _____ Subject-verb agreement _____ (Tally, if needed)
- _____ Run-ons _____ (Tally, if needed)
- _____ Word order _____ (Tally, if needed)

Noun ending errors
- _____ Singular/Plural _____ (Tally, if needed)
- _____ Other—suffixation _____ (Tally, if needed)

Verb errors
- _____ Tense _____ (Tally, if needed)
- _____ Form (irregular verbs) _____ (Tally, if needed)
- _____ Active/passive (form/meaning) _____ (Tally, if needed)
- _____ Modals _____ (Tally, if needed)

Other errors
- _____ Articles _____ (Tally, if needed)
- _____ Prepositions _____ (Tally, if needed)

Language Needs (Found or not found in student texts—approximate numbers)
Academic Vocabulary/Written Register
_____ Collocations
_____ Nominalizations
_____ Synonym clusters
  _____ Nouns
  _____ Verbs
  _____ Adjectives/Adverbs
_____ Catch-all (enumerative) nouns

  Hedges
  _____ Noun quantifiers
  _____ Frequency adverbs
  _____ Modal verbs

Grammar
_____ Compound sentences   _____ (Tally, if needed)
_____ Complex sentences   _____ (Tally, if needed)
  Subordinate clauses   _____ (Tally, if needed)
  _____ Adverb   _____ (Tally, if needed)
  _____ Adjective   _____ (Tally, if needed)
  _____ Noun   _____ (Tally, if needed)

Score Sheet Summary

Essay #	1	2	3	4	5	6	7	8
Approx. # of words								
Discourse Organization								
Brief introduction								
Thesis								
Paragraph division								
Idea progression								
Conclusion/closing								
Paragraph Structure/Essay Body								
Approx. # of paragraphs								
Topic sentences								
Support in most paragraphs								
Cohesion/lexical ties/synonyms								
Error Analysis for Teaching and Editing Practice								
Sentence structure								
Incomplete/too many elements								
Subject-verb agreement								
Run-ons								
Word order								
Noun ending errors								
Singular/Plural								
Other—suffixation								
Verb errors								
Tense								
Form (irregular verbs)								
Active/passive (form/meaning)								
Modals								
Other errors								
Articles								
Prepositions								

Language Needs							
Academic Vocabulary/Written Register							
Collocations							
Nominalizations							
Synonym clusters							
Nouns							
Verbs							
Adjectives/Adverbs							
Catch-all (enumerative) nouns							
Hedges							
Noun quantifiers							
Frequency adverbs							
Modal verbs							
Grammar							
Compound sentences							
Complex sentences							
Subordinate clauses							
Adverb							
Adjective							
Noun							

6
CHOOSING TEACHING MATERIALS AND ADAPTING TEXTBOOKS

This chapter discusses:

- Teaching materials and activities
- Adapting textbooks
- Textbooks that are too high for learners' proficiency levels
- Textbooks that are too low for learners' proficiency levels
- Supplementary reading materials
- Text features that may need to be altered in reading selections
- Personalizing irrelevant and poorly suited content
- Multi-use text modifications
- Teaching the students strategies for adapting reading
- Text features that may need to be altered in listening selections

Teaching Materials and Activities

The purpose of all teaching materials and activities is to address the learning objectives of the course and the curriculum of language study. Although some teachers undertake the development of instructional materials from start to finish, it is extremely laborious and time-consuming. For this reason, teachers rarely create materials for an entire course. In a vast majority of teaching contexts, some sort of commercially produced textbooks are adopted, including locally assembled sets of pre-selected materials (aka course packs).

In addition, in many contexts, learners expect a language course to have a textbook. Once a textbook is adopted, however, there is a degree of obligation for the teacher to use most of the material covered in the book. Otherwise, students may begrudge the cost of the book.[1] Thus, it is important that textbooks be carefully examined and chosen. As a general guideline, it may be easier to supplement textbook materials than to prepare the entire course from scratch.

In all cases and regardless of the type of textbook, selecting commercially produced textbooks and adapting them for a particular instructional context, proficiency level, or a group of students has to be driven by students' learning goals and objectives, rather than the other way round. Even in those cases when a course textbook and activities are selected by someone else and prescribed for teaching, it is still possible for classroom instructors to be selective and judicious in how learning objectives are addressed. In the end, it is the teacher who is responsible for making the ultimate decisions of what is taught, how well it is learned, and whether the objectives are achieved.

> Teaching materials and activities for learning have to stay focused on the learning goals and objectives throughout the course of instruction and during each lesson.

Pedagogically speaking, activities and textbook or workbook exercises are very similar in their learning goals and functions. Thus, both need to be selected with the same care and be directly applicable to learning goals and objectives (Celce-Murcia & Olshtain, 2005; Hinkel, 2002; Nation, 2003). What is taught has to lead to purposeful and engaged language uses and practice when learners are required to employ their language resources and be able to handle the level of language (Vale, Scarino, & McKay, 1991).

Small-scale assessments (see chapter 5) can demonstrate clearly and expediently whether specific materials and attendant activities are in fact effective and whether they lead to language learning and gains. If not, either materials or activities, or both, can be discarded or revised.

> In teaching, as with everything else in life, refining what is taught and how it is taught takes place over time and is probably based on more than one course (Nation & McAlister, 2010).

The foundational factors noted earlier on sequencing and the progression of instructional courses also have to apply to structuring each incremental unit of material: from simpler to more complex and from more familiar to less familiar (e.g., Graves, 2000). Ample opportunities for review and recycling practice are also of the essence.

> **The essential principle for selecting or creating materials and activities is:**
>
> **Teach the students and not the material.**

The biggest issues in selecting materials or textbooks for teaching is that they must "provide systematic coverage" of and practice in the important language features and skills that learners need to achieve their goals and objectives (Nation & McAlister, 2010, p. 163). For example, if a teacher adopts a textbook, chooses a reading book, or creates materials for a course, typically, each unit or text excerpt focuses on a different content or topic, with the vocabulary or grammar coverage specific to each unit. Opportunities for review and recycling of the language features may be difficult to find. In such cases, the language content of the course can appear to be disjointed and the teacher is faced with a need to develop supplementary materials and practice. A prototypical and highly ineffective technique for teaching reading and vocabulary, for example, is to select short and frequently simplified texts that are appropriate for learners' proficiencies. However, when the language content and topic of each text unit are different, reviewing and recycling of important vocabulary and language features is likely to be insufficient.

As many teachers know from experience, very few—if any—textbooks are suited for every group of learners. Thus, choosing, sequencing, and adapting teaching materials is something that most teachers do as a matter of routine. The most important factor in selecting and organizing suitable materials is to make them relevant directly and tangibly (really and definitively) applicable to students' learning goals and objectives. This is without a doubt a key consideration in what to teach and how to teach it.

For example, if students' goals and instructional objectives entail achieving proficiency in academic language, writing, and reading, then they probably should not spend instructional and study time on learning the language or reading and writing associated with such mainstay ESL topics as *holidays in my country, my pets,* or *my favorite teacher/best friend*. One of the major disadvantages of selecting materials that are poorly suited for learning and the learners is that it often results in a loss of motivation and interest.

To maintain learners' interest and involvement with what is taught, varying the types of materials and skills that are addressed can also be very helpful (e.g., reading a text can be supplemented by watching a movie clip or listening to a lecture) and making notes can be aided by reading and writing activities.

- Teaching materials and activities have to be selected based on relevance to and in keeping with the learning objectives and students' interests.
- To be relevant, materials and activities have to address the language skills that are directly applicable to learning goals.
- The easiest way to find out what types of materials and subject matter are of interest to learners is simply to ask them.

When learners are asked about their interests in the subject matter, it stands to reason that they expect their choices to count. If the teacher is not prepared to account for learners' stated interests in the course contents, then it may be best to skip this step. On the other hand, if the teacher chooses the contents without learners' input, dissatisfaction with the material coverage, subject matter, and topics is not uncommon. Usually, a good working solution is to incorporate the topics of high interest to students in combination with the material and activities that the teacher considers to be valuable and relevant for learning and meeting the objectives.

The relevance of materials and activities needs to be explained to learners systematically and consistently. Most students, because they are not trained in material design, cannot be expected to figure this out by themselves.

Action Point

Tables of contents in learner textbooks present a relatively clear picture of language components and topics that book authors or teachers may consider to be interesting and relevant for students. Please take a look at the table of contents in several systematically selected L2 books (as was mentioned earlier, these are frequently available online), such as those for intermediate reading, advanced writing, or beginning speaking courses. Assuming, for instance, that the book is to be adopted for adult and academically bound learners, what units and topics would be relevant? How many? In your view, what are the reasons that only a portion of any textbook is suitable for such a group of learners?

Additionally, if, say, a book is chosen for adult learners who set out to learn English to be able to travel abroad and interact with the locals for enjoyment, can you select one or two that are well suited? In this case, what types of materials and topics would be relevant? What is the proportion of the books that can be useful?

For either type of learners, what role would the students' interest play? How can one determine what material and activities are interesting and useful?

A word of caution: in the past two or three decades, selecting authentic (real and unsimplified) materials for L2 instruction has been all the rage. Unfortunately, using authentic English language texts to promote learners' reading or listening skills is fraught with complications. With the exception of advanced learners, authentic materials can simply be difficult for learners to understand and work with. That is, if such materials were accessible for comprehension, then the learners probably would not need language instruction or a teacher. For a vast majority of learners, level-appropriate and graded materials are far better suited

(Graves, 2000; Nation, 2013). However, it is essential for pedagogically prepared materials and activities to become progressively closer to authentic language uses; that is, the level of materials and activities has to "grow" together with learners' language gains throughout the course of instruction.

Adapting Textbooks

When working with a commercially published textbook, the first order of business is to determine whether the unit material, vocabulary, grammar, and subject matter meet the goals of a course curriculum and are suitable for the learners' proficiency levels. Textbook authors and publishers seek to make their books appealing to as many teachers and learners as possible, and this can result in a somewhat generic content and material coverage. For instance, controversial discussions are almost always avoided (this is also true about standardized L2 proficiency tests, such as the TOEFL), and the topics typically center on the life and concerns of the middle class; for example, there are very few poor, wealthy, unemployed, or heartbroken personages in language books. Many teachers and learners find commercially produced textbooks uninspired, boring, and constrained. Conversely, as was mentioned in chapter 5, authentic materials that can be interesting and useful to learners are almost always far too difficult for learners to make them beneficial and productive.

The fact is that there are very few textbooks that are a good match for all types of students and their varied proficiency levels. That is, there are probably no textbooks that require no adaptation in most language teaching contexts. For one thing, even highly generic content may not be appropriate for all learners, who can live in a broad range of cultures, be of very different ages, and are expected to participate in various types of learning activities. Most importantly, a book's language learning content, the extent of explanations or practice, and material sequencing, progression, and pace can be a mismatch with the course's learning goals and objectives.

On the other hand, in most teaching contexts, students expect that a language course includes a textbook, and the advantage for the teacher is that adopting one can save a great deal of work, provide for ready-to-use content and practice, and assure a degree of predictability and consistency.

Teachers who undertake to write their own teaching materials need to keep in mind that writing excellent texts and exercises requires a great deal of skill, experience, familiarity with current trends and ideas, and quality control. All commercially published books undergo many rounds of polishing, editing, review, revision, class testing, and refinement. In this light, adopting a textbook and adapting it is something that most teachers do as a matter of routine. Book and unit contents can be deleted, added, supplemented, reorganized, reordered, and modified in a number of ways.

> It is almost always easier and faster to adapt textbook materials and activities than to write them from scratch. Adapting books and units can save a great deal of work, effort, and refinement compared to producing original texts.

Textbooks that need to be adapted can be too high or too low for the learners' proficiency levels, present language content that is too broad or too narrow, provide insufficient or unsuitable activities and practice, or address irrelevant subject matter and language.

In language teaching, textbooks and authors are almost always influenced by contemporary teaching methods, views, and beliefs about how languages should be taught and how they are learned. Furthermore, particular beliefs and trends may prevail at various times and in various regions of the world. For example, in 1990s when the communicative method of teaching was all the rage, it was difficult to find textbooks that focused on academic vocabulary and grammar skills. Currently, however, textbooks that work with academic language and the skills that students need to learn are a great deal more popular.

In addition, trends and fashions in views of how language should be taught and how it is learned have an indelible impact on the instructional activities, topics, and contents of units and the types of practice that dominate the current methods of language instruction (e.g., Hinkel, 2011). Teachers, too, can be influenced by their training or by specific approaches to language teaching that may or may not be shared by textbook authors and publishers.

When adopting and adapting a textbook, teachers need to be aware of the various considerations that affect their own views on a textbook's usefulness to learners, as they work to achieve the learning objectives. To use another example, in several English-speaking countries, there are strong biases against vocabulary teaching and learning, and for this reason, most textbooks for developing academic writing skills do not include a vocabulary learning component even though developed L2 vocabulary is essential in academic writing. Thus, those teachers who believe that academic vocabulary can be taught and learned in the context of L2 writing instruction may be faced with the need to supplement textbooks and other teaching materials.

> In any textbook, there are probably as many ways to modify the language content, the subject matter and topics, and the sequencing of the material as there are teachers. By and large, it would be hard to find two teachers who would modify a textbook in similar ways.

> **Talking Shop**
>
> Based on a couple of chapters from any student textbook, can you determine the author's beliefs, preferred language teaching methodology, and specific views on how language should be taught and learned?
>
> Make a list of the clues that you detect in this relatively small sample and share them with your colleagues. As with textbook modifications, the list of methodological clues will surely differ from one teacher to the next.

A few general principles apply to practically all decisions in regard to changes in the book and unit contents:

- Practically all commercially published textbooks and authentic materials need to be adapted for practically any class or group of learners.
- Authentic language materials with content and subject matter suitable for adults or college-age students almost always contain language features (vocabulary and grammar) that are (far) too advanced for second language learners.
- Readings and language materials suitable for adults and college students in terms of both subject matter and language are very, very hard to find.
- There are, in fact, few types of subject matter that are suitable for all adults of all ages; genders; social classes; and educational, cultural, and occupational backgrounds.
- The subject matter and unit topics that are of high interest to textbook authors (or teachers), such as vegetarianism, alternative medicine, or presidential elections, may have little interest or relevance for students.

> The selection of texts or units for teaching and learning (i.e., the content, vocabulary, grammar, idioms and collocations, and discourse organization) is determined by whether they bring students closer to achieving their learning goals and objectives. The learning objectives, as they are defined in the curricular progression, are THE key consideration in adopting or skipping any and all textbook materials, activities, or topics.

> **Talking Shop**
>
> What are the reasons that textbooks have to be adapted in practically all cases? Why is it that textbook authors and publishers can't produce textbooks that can be used just as they are without adaptation? Discuss your views with your colleagues and see if it is possible to figure out these reasons.

> *Hint:* For publishers, the goal of publishing textbooks is to get them adopted in as many courses as possible.

Textbooks That Are Above Students' Levels of Proficiency (The Most Common Situation)

A general rule of thumb for determining whether students can comprehend the text and be able to learn from it effectively is as follows:

> Learners have to understand 95% of the words in written or spoken text in reading or listening in order to be able to work with it. The rate of unfamiliar words in text should not exceed 10%.

In their now-famous study, Hu and Nation (2000) found that none of the learners in their study could read adequately at 80% of coverage; some learners could at 90% and 95% coverage, but they were in the minority. Their conclusion was that 98% is the lexical coverage for adequate comprehension.

To figure out how many unfamiliar words a text contains, a very simple computation is sufficient. It won't be exact, but it will be close enough:

- On a page, or in a reading selection, or in a transcript of spoken text, count the number of words in the first or second line, across the page.
- Then count the number of lines in the text or on the page.
- Multiply the first number by the second, and this is the number of words on a page or in the text excerpt.

> For example, the number of words in the first line is 14, and the text is 24 lines long, thus, $14 \times 24 = 336$ words (approximately). The number of unfamiliar words should not exceed 34 ($336 \times 10\%$); between 17 (5%) and 25 unfamiliar words is probably much better.

Then the learners read or listen to the text. In reading, ask them to underline each word they do not understand, and in listening, the words can be simply counted as the selection continues. It goes without saying that the number of unfamiliar words can vary for different students, but it is simple enough to ask students to report their numbers. In this way, a clear picture can emerge in an instant: if only one or two students have a high number of unfamiliar words, then the text is probably appropriate for the class. If most students report that they are not familiar with a high number of words, then the text is probably not well suited. (Techniques on how to adapt the written or spoken text are discussed in the next section.)

Omitting, Adding, Changing, and Refocusing

In general terms, language content in student books are highly controlled in terms of vocabulary, idioms, grammar, topics, cultural aspects, and exercises and activities. Usually, but not always, such elements of textbooks are sequenced based on the progression of material difficulty; for example, more complex grammar components build on those that are seen to be less complex. However, the progression of material can be too fast or too slow for particular groups of learners, or the language contents can be relatively uniform throughout the textbook without a discernable progression. The textbook content may not address specific language skills or it may cover them insufficiently (e.g., a writing textbook may have grammar practice but not discourse structuring). Thus, the order of material or its progression may need to be rearranged or refocused.

Teaching activities that are suitable for one group of learners may not be very productive for another in terms of proficiency levels, age, gender, or cultural background. Teachers also have their preferred activities that they believe to be effective, but the textbook may not include them. Specific textbook activities may take more time than the teacher would like to spend on them. In short, the reasons for textbook modifications can be as numerous as their types (Nation & McAlister, 2010).

> Usually, it takes teaching the textbook more than once to determine all the needed modifications; as with everything else in life, some modifications may be more successful than others.
>
> It is important that modifications are made with the learners' needs and objectives in mind.

Action Point

Choose two or three units from a student textbook on, say, reading, writing, or listening, and identify various language content strands, such as vocabulary, grammar, writing, or cultural elements. Outline the sequence of these content components to see if the material is arranged in a progression.

In your view, does each language component receive an equal or disparate amount of attention and sufficient number of exercises and activities? Why do you think this is the case? If you were teaching this textbook, what would need to be altered, omitted, replaced, or supplemented? Make a list of the contents that you think should be modified and determine the types of the modifications needed. Discuss your possible alterations with your colleagues and find out about their rationale for thinking of modifications that are quite different from your own.

Common and prevalent text and unit modifications can be used with practically any textbook:

- Pre-teaching vocabulary items that are not familiar—no more than 10 to 12—that can be potentially useful
- Modifying and refocusing content/topics (e.g., by means of skipping portions of the text in a unit: *please skip paragraphs 2 and 3 on p. 80*).
- Omitting sections of units. Writing out which sections or pages are to be skipped when beginning work on a unit is always a good idea.
- Breaking up complex sentences with clauses or advanced phrases into two or more simple sentences. For example:

    Sponges are just barely animals, such a borderline case that until the 19th century they were called zoophytes, the animal-plants >>>>>>>
    Sponges are just barely animals. They are a borderline case. Until the 19th century, they were called the animal-plants.

- Adding or omitting content: In many cases, whole units may need to be substituted or omitted and sometimes replaced by different ones.
- Shortening the text (simply tell the students which portions of their readings to skip—selectively or wholly). Additionally, showing the students the portions to skip may prove to be highly helpful.
- Skipping the teaching of particular skills in textbooks that integrate the teaching of various skills, such as speaking, listening, and writing. For example, speaking activities can be omitted when the course curriculum does not deal with speaking (or sections on writing can be skipped in speaking/listening courses).
- Rearranging or re-sequencing the order of materials or activities.
- Skipping culturally irrelevant texts and segments. For example, outside the U.S. and Canada, readings on the Thanksgiving holiday require a great deal of cultural and lexical pre-teaching (e.g., *pilgrims, turkey, pumpkin pie*), but the topic and the attendant vocabulary are in fact irrelevant to many students' language learning objectives.
- Omitting low frequency vocabulary, advanced syntactic constructions (e.g., *having been there once before, he had no trouble finding the house*), infrequent or obscure idiomatic expressions (e.g., *that ship has sailed*).
- Glossing some of the advanced vocabulary by providing explanations (or definitions).

Modifying Activities and Adjusting the Expected Outcomes

Activities and exercises can also be modified similarly, and there are a number of easy techniques available for this purpose. They include:

- Reducing the number of activities, exercises, and tasks by dividing them into required or optional in the progression of a unit or several units.
- Shortening the length of activities, exercises, and tasks by skipping occasional steps and adjusting the expected outcomes.

When activities and classroom tasks in textbooks are modified, learners are expected to follow the steps and procedures that are different from those described or outlined in the book. That is, when a textbook activity or tasks is used as a spring-board, an alternative form of the classroom exercise or practice also requires an alteration of the steps that the learners are expected to perform to achieve the task or learning outcomes.

The classroom tasks and activities, as well as the steps entailed in completing them, undergo re-thinking and re-designing. These should be specified explicitly:

- The details or incremental steps of the procedures have to be supplied when students are expected to perform them to complete a task (e.g., Step 1 . . . Step 2 . . . Step 3 . . .).
- Examples of student tasks and the interim steps are almost always required.
- Extended time for the explanations of the incremental steps and procedures should be built into the task plan. Additional time should be allowed for student preparation and to give students time to practice the steps in class, with the teacher's supervision.

> Practically any element or segment in a textbook can be modified to suit learners' proficiency levels, learning objectives, and interests. Photocopies of pages or texts from the student textbook, scissors, and tape is all the equipment that may be necessary in most cases.

Supplementing and Adding

Because textbooks are written and published to make them marketable in a broad range of contexts, the unit subject matter is usually relatively bland, limited to topics of general interest. The learning objectives and learner interests must play a central role in selecting language contents and topics of the material. For this reason, frequently the textbook units and topics need to be supplemented. For example, a rather general and generic unit on environment and population can be supplemented by additional selections on the environment and the population growth and change locally to make the topic directly relevant and relatable. Virtually all general interest subject matter that is ubiquitous in textbooks can be made more interesting for teaching.

To determine whether the textbook material is interesting and relevant to learners, the easiest way is to simply ask them. One possibility may be to request that students fill out a short form with a few questions that require short but expanded answers (e.g., *in the textbook, what units are the most/least interesting? what topics would you like to read/write/listen about? what activities/exercises did you enjoy most/least and why?*). In addition to assisting the teacher in determining what topics and units should be supplemented, responses to such questions provide an additional language and writing practice. Constructing productive questions about textbooks may take more than one cycle, each accompanied by refinements, such as making questions broader or narrower. However, it is important for learners to have a say in the subject matter and the topics that the material covers. (Techniques for personalizing textbooks and the subject matter can be found below in this chapter.)

Action Point

Find a student textbook and examine the subject matter covered in several units. Decide whether it may be interesting to the learners in your region. Toward what age group and/or gender is the subject matter oriented? What language skills and language components is the subject matter intended to advance? Construct 5 or 6 questions that you may ask learners to respond to in regard to the topic of one unit and its activities and exercises. Present your questions to your colleagues to determine whether your questions elicit productive and useful responses that can help you to supplement the unit. Take a look at the questions constructed by your colleagues that can lead you to refine yours.

Textbooks That Are Below Students' Levels of Proficiency

Fortunately, adapting textbooks that are below students' proficiency levels is a great deal easier than working with those that are too high. Low-level materials can be easily supplemented with those that are more advanced.

A word of caution: Asking students to find supplementary materials on the topic(s) covered in a reading or listening unit often leads to much time and effort expended for little gain. Most students are not qualified to locate level-appropriate texts on specific topics and subject matter.

Thematically appropriate and cohesive materials are difficult to locate in newspapers or magazines that tend to cover a great range of unrelated contents. On the other hand, most specialist and thematic magazines and journals are far too advanced for ESL learners even at the highest proficiency levels.

Here are practical and relatively easy techniques for finding sources of supplementary materials on the subject matter and topics in student textbooks:

- Thematically related materials are much easier to locate in popular and level-appropriate books or textbooks on particular topic areas.
- A key consideration in this case is to locate books that include the level of language suitable for learners with particular levels of proficiency (see the list of suitable juvenile topic areas below).
- If a topic area of interest cannot be located among juvenile books written on topics appropriate for adults, then learners need to be taught strategies for adapting their readings to match their proficiency levels (also see below).

In each textbook unit, modifications can personalize bland or unsuitable subject matter when the level of language is below the learners' proficiency levels:

- Vocabulary or grammar may be supplemented by providing directly relevant word and grammar structure expansions. For example, a unit on environment can be supplemented by extended vocabulary, the uses of the present simple tense can be connected to the contextual occurrences and practice of the passive voice (*is caused* or *are affected*) the present perfect (*has created* or *has occurred*) or the past simple tenses.
- Exercises and activities can be added and/or extended if the amount of practice is insufficient (very common in commercial textbooks), and supplementary practice materials need to be added.

Supplementing vocabulary in a textbook unit on a great range of topics is relatively easy. For example, word meanings can be supplemented by close synonyms that can be usually found in a dictionary or by extending vocabulary to that found in closely associated topics. For instance, a unit on "Marriage, Family, and the Home" (Williams, Brown, Hood, & Seal, 2012) incorporates such words as *average, relative(-ly), rare, increasing(-ly), common, tremendous, significant, proportion, factor, estimate(-d),* and *affect.* These words are highly valuable to learners because they frequently occur in various genres (types) of written prose, from news media (newspapers and magazines) to academic textbooks (Hinkel, 2003, 2004, 2005; Nation, 1990, 2009, 2013). In the case of such requisite vocabulary, it is worth supplementing with additional words that can be near-synonyms.

To build a list of highly frequent academic vocabulary that can be used for supplementing textbook units on a large number of topics and subject matter, online dictionaries and thesauri can be very handy and fast (e.g., dictionary.com) where vocabulary sets can be constructed in a matter of minutes.

Here's an example of how to supplement vocabulary by adding close synonyms. A side note: Antonyms would not be very helpful in vocabulary supplementation because including them may lead to meaning confusions:

average ~~~ *typical, everyday, commonplace*
affect ~~~ *influence, impact*
estimate(-d) ~~~ *approximate, likely*
rare ~~~ *infrequent, uncommon, few*
significant ~~~ *important, prominent, substantial*

In any textbook unit, the number of words that can be supplemented can be large or small, depending on how much vocabulary expansion is needed. Supplementary vocabulary requires practice and review (and review) just as the rest of the vocabulary and grammar in textbook material.

Personalizing Irrelevant and Poorly Suited Contents and Topics

In many cases, textbook contents and topics are intended to be suitable for learners inside and outside English-speaking countries. These are typically oriented for young adults, but the topics may not easily translate from one teaching context to another (e.g., white-water rafting, rock climbing, skiing, air gliding, love and dating, parachuting, ghosts and ghost stories, being a vegetarian, health food, holistic and alternative medicines, or alternative life-styles, to name just a few).

In each unit, a few modifications can personalize such unsuitable content units:

- Begin with the book text as a springboard.
- Make a list of useful or high-frequency vocabulary and grammar structures covered/identified in the unit and present the list to the students.
- Ask students to write their own short stories that incorporate many or most of these vocabulary items and grammar constructions.
    For example, if the text covers the past simple tense (*climbed, reached*) or the present perfect tense (*has made, have decided*), then ask students to use the tense with other relevant verbs in their stories.
- If the book text is followed by comprehension questions, then ask students to write their own comprehension questions that apply specifically to their stories.
- Be sure to pre-teach question formation and grammar, and provide examples on the board or in a handout.
- Have students exchange their stories with their partners and write comprehension questions for their partners' stories.
- If working in small groups, students can switch the stories and the questions one more time and provide answers to the story follow-up questions. This can be a great way to practice and provide repeated exposure to vocabulary, selected grammar, interrogative (question) constructions, and (optional) full-sentence responses.

> **Talking Shop**
>
> One of the issues with writing assignments that are based on students' personal narratives or expositions of personal experiences is that such writing tasks do little to contribute to learners' exposure to new vocabulary and grammar constructions. That is, to accomplish these types of assignments, students rely on the language repertoire that they already have. How can personalization of poorly suited texts when students are assigned to write about their experiences lead to language development and learning? What can the teacher do to promote learners' work on new vocabulary and grammar constructions in the context of personalizing unsuitable contents and topics? Discuss your ideas with your colleagues and see if it is possible to come up with a range of classroom techniques for achieving learning objectives in such situations.

Multi-Use and Computer Scanning Text Modification Techniques

Several techniques for adapting texts, exercises, and activities within units can be useful—if the instructor plans to teach these adapted segments more than once. These techniques typically involve using computer scanners and technology. Given that scanning book text usually requires formatting and re-formatting the text, these text modifications may prove to be a little more time- and work-consuming. On the other hand, scanned text that is available for word-processing can permit additional text alterations, such as deleting low-frequency vocabulary items, simplifying grammar constructions, or adding vocabulary glosses.

> **Option 1**: Scanning portions of the text, exercise, or activity on the computer, re-typing, or re-writing some of the text and write-in glosses.
>
> **Option 2**: Instructing students to white-out, block out, or simply ignore vocabulary and grammar constructions that are too high for their proficiency levels, directly in their copies of the textbook.
>
> **Option 3**: Scanning the text and omitting low-frequency vocabulary and simplifying syntactic constructions (e.g., by means of deleting subordinate clauses, prepositional phrases, or whole sentences).

Choosing Supplementary Readings

In reading and writing courses, textbooks or units are frequently (if not always) supplemented by extra practice and sources of written prose. However, finding suitable and level-appropriate supplementary texts creates a dilemma: simplified and adapted materials are typically written for children or young teenagers, and in most cases, the subject matter and language variety are not likely to be suitable for adults or college-age readers. In books published for adults, the degree of language complexity (i.e., vocabulary, idioms, collocations, and grammar) is rarely appropriate for learners. As has been mentioned earlier, using authentic texts in language courses can present a number of problems.

A Commonplace Dilemma of Supplementary Reading

- In most simplified authentic texts that are written for juvenile native speakers, the subject matter and language are rarely suitable for adults and college-age learners.
- In most cases of subject matter and language suitable for adults and college-age learners, the language (i.e., vocabulary, idioms/collocations, and grammar) are far above L2 learners' proficiency levels.

Possible supplementary reading materials that may be suitable for adults/college-age learners with (somewhat) simplified language:

- Juvenile descriptions of scientific discoveries and historical events
- Juvenile biographies of famous scientists, historical and political figures, sports stars, or, in the case of younger learners, current pop-culture figures
- Juvenile books or magazine articles on
  - Natural history
  - Environment
  - Medical breakthroughs
  - Historical events
  - Scientific discoveries
- Teen/young adult/school-age magazine/Internet articles on current events and human interest stories

Supplementary readings cannot and should not replace essential instruction on reading and text processing, coping with the structure of discourse, and working with unfamiliar vocabulary.

For advanced learners, however, a number of sources and reading options can be available, but these choices often require learner strategy training (described below) to ensure that students can work with the text. A further advantage of employing reading strategies is that they can enable learners to read unsimplified authentic prose in their college and university studies, as well as in the professions and vocations.

> **Action Point**
>
> Visit a local library or a book store (or online bookseller) and investigate a good sample (20 or 30) of books written for school age learners or teenagers. Make a list of titles and jot down a few notes about the contents: a synopsis on the back cover or a publisher's description is probably sufficient. Different types of books are intended for a range of readers' ages and reading skills. Examining the types of vocabulary and grammar found on any or most pages may give relatively good clues about the text complexity and the necessary levels of language proficiency.
>
> Are any, some, or all books in your sample suitable for school age learners or adult learners? Who might be the learners for whom juvenile reading books published in English are likely to be suitable? If you did not find any suitable books for either school age or adult learners, then what could serve as a potential reading material for one of these groups?
>
> Based on your experience, develop set of criteria that can be given to learners to assist them in finding a suitable book. Discuss your criteria with your colleagues and see if they can benefit from your findings and you from theirs.

Teaching the Strategies for Adapting Readings

Strategy training for advanced learners represents one of the most valuable long-term benefits of language and reading education. Much experience has demonstrated that the strategies learned in the course of language study can provide important advantages and coping techniques that can last long after the language course is over (Hinkel, 2004).

Strategy 1

- While reading the text, learners skip the vocabulary items that they do not understand and that were not pre-taught.
- Having skipped a number of words, a student continues reading another 2–4 sentences—and not any longer.
- Then the reader needs to pause and check to see if, at that juncture, the text is understood—without the skipped/omitted vocabulary.

- If yes, then the student continues reading—until reaching a point when the text is no longer comprehensible.
- If, after the next 2–4 sentences learners do not comprehend their reading and are lost in the text, then it is now time to go back to the point in text where they stopped comprehending the material (a couple of sentences).
- At that juncture, learners need to look up in the dictionary the word or words that are essential for understanding the text.
- A student continues reading until the text becomes incomprehensible again, at a new juncture. Then re-trace the text a couple of sentences back, where understanding is lost, look up the essential word(s) in the dictionary, re-read the text. And so on.

Strategy 2

When learners are assigned readings in regular textbooks at school, supplementary materials, such as newspaper/magazine articles or media reports, unsimplified text can often be daunting—and extremely laborious and time-consuming. In this case, the entire text needs to be simplified, and not just its smaller increments.

Adapting large segments of readings, such as chapter sections or whole articles, is easier than it may seem. The technique described below is also very helpful in the teaching of writing:

- On, say, a page of a text/reading, students read only the topic sentences in each paragraph.
- When the end of the page is reached, a reader pauses to assess if the gist of the material is understood.
- If the text is comprehensible, the reader continues on to the next page or half a page, until the gist of the text is no longer comprehensible.
  - When the gist of the text becomes difficult to understand, students re-trace their steps back to the point in the text where the gist of the meaning is lost.
  - As the next step, learners read the entire paragraphs, and not just topic sentences, until the text becomes intelligible again.
- When the text is comprehensible again, students can revert to reading only topic sentences, until the gist of the text is lost again.
- Then the text is re-traced to the juncture where the meaning is lost.
- Students read entire paragraphs, and not just the topic sentence, until they regain their understanding of the text, and then reading only the topic sentences would do.

Students who learn to use the strategies for adapting extensive reading materials in unsimplified texts have an important advantage: in reading, the more, the more principle applies very strongly. That is, the learners who are able to read large amounts of text almost always become better at it, in addition to the fact that their vocabulary specifically and reading proficiency improve greatly (Nation, 2009). As Nation (2013, p. 155) points out, improving one's reading and vocabulary "is not an all-or-nothing piece of learning, but . . . it is a gradual process." Learners who are taught how to adapt the text in the process of reading are able to read large amounts of text necessarily to develop advanced language proficiency, but it won't happen overnight.

Action Point

Observe your own behavior when you read professional books or texts in another language. Make a detailed list of the tactics and strategies you employ while reading. What do you do when you read?

Do you preview and review the text? Know your purpose for reading? Do you anticipate and make predictions about the text as you go? Do you modify them when you come across new information?

What do you do when you find an unfamiliar word? Do you try to figure out its meaning or do you skip it whenever possible? Do you look it up in the dictionary or ask someone? How many words to you try to figure out, skip, or look up?

Are you aware of your text comprehension? Do you check to see if you comprehend the text? How do you know? Do you stop to think whether the reading makes sense as you are reading? What do you do when you stop understanding what you are reading? How much of the text do you expect to understand?

Do you re-read? How much of the text and how often? Do you skip portions of the text? At the end, can you identify the main points of the text? How much time and work do you spend on figures, table, maps, or graphs? Can you identify the differences between the author's position and facts?

In a nutshell, what reading strategies do you use? Are any of these usable in a language classroom and with language learners? Discuss your findings and your list of strategies with your colleagues and see if they can benefit from your findings and you from theirs.

Modifying Text in Listening Selections

In addition to the techniques for adapting the reading selections above, a few more steps may be needed for listening selections:

- Pre-teach—no more than 10 to 12 items—and pre-model vocabulary (by repeating it aloud) before listening.

- Chop the listening selection into manageable segments by stopping/pausing the flow of speech/tape/listening selection.
- Gloss and explain advanced vocabulary and grammar constructions during the pauses.
- Model or repeat slowly—probably more than once—small portions of the listening selection that can range from vocabulary to phrases to sentences.
- Play and model small segments of the text repeatedly.
- Gradually lengthen the repeated text segments (e.g., re-play phrases or sentences first, then re-play paragraphs/chunks, and finally re-play the entire selection several times).
- To reduce the difficulty of subsequent listening repetitions, make sure that between listenings, students have an opportunity to practice and use in context the vocabulary items that can be potentially useful.
- Re-focus the purpose of listening (e.g., listening for general gist can become listening for information or listening for idioms or particular grammar constructions, such as contractions or tenses or politeness forms).
- All these additional foci of listening can be used as features to build speaking activities in follow-up work.

Listening Follow-Up Tasks and Activities

As with other alterations of activities and classroom tasks, in the modified version, the steps for completing an activity are different from those described in the book, and the steps have to be clearly explained. With listening activities and tasks, the teacher should demonstrate and model unfamiliar vocabulary and complex procedures that learners are expected to perform. Again, as with reading and writing activities, extra time should be allowed for practicing various new steps and procedures. It goes without saying that the additional time and practice also provides increased opportunities for language usage and practice.

Chapter Summary

The fact is that there are very few textbooks that are a good match for all types of students and their varied proficiency levels, but it is almost always easier and faster to adapt textbook materials and activities than to write them from scratch. Usually, it takes teaching the textbook more than once to determine all the needed modifications.

Common and prevalent text and unit modifications that can be used with practically any textbook include techniques such as pre-teaching vocabulary, and rearranging or omitting sections as needed.

Textbooks that are above the students' level require more work from the teacher in terms of simplifying, omitting, and sometimes re-writing text. Strategy training for advanced learners represents one of the most valuable long-term benefits of language and reading education. Learners who are taught how to adapt the text in the process of reading are able to read large amounts of text necessarily to develop advanced language proficiency, but it won't happen overnight. Textbooks that are below the students' level usually require supplemental material.

Note

1 When a teacher needs to omit sections of a textbook, it is a good idea to explain to the students what is being skipped and why. Having clear learning objectives on the syllabus makes this discussion easy.

Further Reading

Carson, J. G., Chase, N. D., Gibson, S. U., & Hargrove, M. F. (1992). Literacy demands of the undergraduate curriculum. *Reading Research and Instruction, 31*, 25–50.

Howatt, A. P. R., & Widdowson, H. (2004). *A history of English language teaching* (2nd ed.). Oxford: Oxford University Press.

Mehan, H. (1979). *Learning lessons.* Cambridge, MA: Harvard University Press.

Soven, M. (1999). *Teaching writing in middle and secondary schools: Theory, research, and practice.* Boston: Allyn and Bacon.

Taba, H. (1966). *Teaching strategies and cognitive functioning in elementary school children.* San Francisco: San Francisco State College.

Widdowson, H. (1990). *Aspects of language teaching.* Oxford: Oxford University Press.

Widdowson, H. (2003). *Defining issues in English language teaching.* Oxford: Oxford University Press.

Wilkins, D. (1972). *Linguistics in language teaching.* London: Edward Arnold.

References

Celce-Murcia, M., & Olshtain, E. (2005). Discourse-based approaches: A new framework for second language teaching and learning. In E. Hinkel (Ed.), *Handbook of research in second language teaching and learning* (pp. 729–742). Mahwah, NJ: Laurence Erlbaum Associates.

Graves, K. (2000). *Designing language courses: A guide for teachers.* Boston: Heinle & Heinle.

Hinkel, E. (2002). Teaching grammar in writing classes: Tenses and cohesion. In E. Hinkel & S. Fotos (Eds.), *New perspectives on grammar teaching in second language classrooms* (pp. 181–198). Mahwah, NJ: Lawrence Erlbaum Associates.

Hinkel, E. (2003). Simplicity without elegance: Features of sentences in L2 and L1 academic texts. *TESOL Quarterly, 37,* 275–301.

Hinkel, E. (2004). *Teaching academic ESL writing: Practical techniques in vocabulary and grammar.* Mahwah, NJ: Lawrence Erlbaum Associates.

Hinkel, E. (2005). Analyses of L2 text and what can be learned from them. In E. Hinkel (Ed.), *Handbook of research in second language teaching and learning* (pp. 615–628). Mahwah, NJ: Lawrence Erlbaum Associates.

Hinkel, E. (2011). Teaching culture in second and foreign language classrooms. In *Interlingual communication and teaching culture proceedings, Sogang KLEC 20th Anniversary International Conference* (pp. 19–33). Seoul: Sogang.

Hu, M., & Nation, P. (2000). Unknown vocabulary density and reading comprehension. *Reading in a Foreign Language 13*(1), 403–430.

Nation, I. S. P. (1990). *Teaching and learning vocabulary*. New York: Newbury House.

Nation, I. S. P. (2003). Effective ways of building vocabulary knowledge. *ESL Magazine, 6*(4), 14–15.

Nation, I. S. P. (2009). *Teaching ESL/EFL reading and writing*. New York: Routledge.

Nation, I. S. P. (2013). *Learning vocabulary in another language* (2nd ed.). Cambridge: Cambridge University Press.

Nation, I. S. P., & Macalister, J. (2010). *Language curriculum design*. New York: Routledge.

Vale, D., Scarino, A., & McKay, P. (1991). *Pocket ALL: A user's guide to the teaching of languages and ESL*. Melbourne: Curriculum Corporation of Australia.

Williams, J., Brown, K., Hood, S., & Seal, B. (2012). *Academic encounters (level 3); Reading and writing: Life in society* (2nd ed.). New York: Cambridge University Press

PART III
Language-Focused Curriculum Elements

PART II

Language-Focused Curriculum Element

7
LANGUAGE FOCUS

Teaching Academic Vocabulary, Collocations, and Pre-Fabs

This chapter discusses:

- Academic vocabulary learning in every lesson
- The importance of vocabulary in writing and other skills
- Vocabulary learning and retention
- Cross-curricular strategies and techniques for vocabulary teaching and learning
- Techniques for building up learners' vocabulary base
- Teaching and learning dictionary uses

> The fact is that while without grammar very little can be conveyed, without vocabulary <u>*nothing*</u> can be conveyed.
>
> D.A. *Wilkins (1972, p. 111, emphasis in the original)*

Introduction: Academic Vocabulary Learning in Every Lesson

Teaching and learning in the academy is simply not possible without academic language and vocabulary. Academic language is the language that is spoken in education at every level. Conversational interactions and spoken social exchanges employ conversational discourse and vocabulary that are substantially different and much narrower than academic language. Much research has demonstrated that conversational vocabulary consists of approximately 2,000 frequent words, while academic vocabulary and the language of textbooks can be as large as 20,000 to 85,000 words (Nagy, 2005; Nagy & Anderson, 1984; Nation, 2013). Unfortunately, merely reading textbooks is not sufficient for learners to develop a substantial range of academic words. Research on vocabulary in L2 textbooks has demonstrated that they do not recycle vocabulary (varied and rich vocabulary is highly valued in English-language writing). Vocabulary recycling is left almost exclusively up to the teacher and classroom instruction.

Typically, learners from better educated L1 families have a greater exposure to academic language, reading, and vocabulary essential in schooling than those who live with L2 families or in L2 communities. L2 learners from all walks of life and different family backgrounds need to build up a vocabulary range to enable them to succeed in attaining their educational objectives.

Substantial and well-developed academic vocabulary is required for success in education and schooling, college and university studies, as well as for the work world and careers (Zwiers, 2014). Academic vocabulary shortfalls and limitations may lead to life-long consequences and unfortunate outcomes in terms of learners' academic success, opportunities, and potentials. In classroom instruction and throughout the curriculum, teaching academic vocabulary persistently and deliberately can make a great deal of difference for learners' vocabulary growth and the development of the foundational vocabulary base for reading and writing. In many cases, vocabulary can focus on general academic words and expressions and those that are specific to a discipline or subject area. An effective teaching of vocabulary entails a great deal of persistence and effort.

Important academic vocabulary and expressions for reading and writing need to be emphasized, repeated, and practiced, practiced, practiced in every lesson, even if for small amounts of class time, such as between 5 and 20 minutes (more on this later in the chapter). For example, academic vocabulary often refers to abstract and complex concepts that require explanations to be understood, e.g., *metaphor, proof, democracy*, or *monarchy*. While many L1 learners may already be familiar with some meanings of these words or the meanings of many abstract academic words, in the case of L2 learners, such concepts have to be explained, and the words learned with persistence and repetition. A broad and solid base in academic vocabulary is essential for learning math (e.g., *equation, proportion, percent, formula*), natural and social sciences (e.g., *weather, climate, society, government*), and for reading and writing (e.g., *thesis, topic, analogy, coherence*).

In the contexts of specific lessons, curriculum, and studies of the subject matter, teaching and learning of academic vocabulary can be accomplished with great success (Nation & Webb, 2011; Zwiers, 2008). A substantial range of academic vocabulary can be attained by identifying, teaching, and explaining subject-specific vocabulary and by providing students plentiful opportunities for understanding, learning, and using it in subject-specific and more general academic contexts (Ferris & Roberts, 2001).

Vocabulary growth and gains plateau over time unless teachers and/or learners themselves actively and persistently work to increase the vocabulary range (Laufer, 1998; Laufer & Paribakht, 1998; Schmitt & Meara, 1997).

Academic vocabulary teaching and learning throughout topics, lessons, and as much curriculum as possible can provide students opportunities for much needed exposure, regular practice, repetition, and more practice. For instance, unfamiliar and abstract words, such as *measure, influence,* or *significance,* can be presented and discussed prior to the teaching of the actual contexts and materials in which they occur. With additional and multiple exposures, students can practice academic vocabulary when it is encountered in content and become familiar over time (Rott, 1999).

The remainder of this chapter is devoted to a number of academic vocabulary teaching strategies and techniques. These can take various forms in the classroom with great effect and in the contexts of instruction in practically any subject: in the teaching of any language skill or academic content. The strategies and techniques discussed here can, for example, be presented in the form of typical academic writing tasks, short reviews, or smaller pieces of reading and writing that students have to perform in the classroom or outside it. Writing activities are invaluable when it comes to learning new academic words and expressions. Short quizzes, academic papers, and exercises, all can serve the same purpose throughout each lesson and the curriculum for teaching.

The Importance of Vocabulary in Writing (and Other Language Skills)

A large number of investigations carried out on the essential skills needed to produce school and academic writing have been based on large and small data sets. By and large, these consist of studies with foci on the vocabulary found in practically all types of academic prose and thus typically also expected in student writing, as well (Hinkel, 2003).

Many analyses of school and academic writing at various levels of instruction have demonstrated that student prose is expected to adhere to fairly regular conventions in the uses of vocabulary and collocations (words that often co-occur together in discourse as in *strong tea* or *a bar of soap,* but not *a piece of soap*) (Coxhead, 2008; Hinkel, 2011, 2014; Laufer & Waldman, 2011). Additional studies have also shown that instruction in the vocabulary of academic prose leads to substantial improvements in the quality of student text (Graves, August, & Mancilla-Martinez, 2012; Johnson, Acevedo, & Mercado, 2013; Laufer & Nation, 1995). For instance, Keith Folse's (2004) overview of vocabulary teaching in conjunction with all language skills, including writing, emphasizes that L2 production requires extensive and intensive vocabulary teaching. In other publications, the positive effect of the increased vocabulary range on L2 writing is also well documented (Folse, 2006; Laufer & Nation, 1999; Lee & Muncie, 2006).

Along these lines, other studies have also elucidated the value for the uses of formulaic expressions in L2 writing (e.g., *the author states that, this paper discusses and analyzes xxx, on the whole, generally speaking*). Although such investigations have been comparatively fewer than the studies of vocabulary, researchers and methodologists have found that these can be very useful and productive in L2 academic writing (Cowie, 1992; Howarth, 1998; Lewis, 2000; Read, 2000; Wray, 2002, 2004). Research on academic text and discourse has established clearly that large portions of academic prose consists of prefabricated constructions, many of which can operate according to the slot-and-filler principle (which assigns a lexical string appropriate in a grammatical construction) (Jones & Haywood, 2004; Nattinger & DeCarrico, 1992), as long as the resulting construction is comprehensible and relatively free of errors. L2 writing quality can benefit greatly by the usage of both preconstructed expressions (also called prefabs), such as those above, and discrete words and phrases in their texts.

The findings of the research on the amount of vocabulary accessible to native and nonnative speakers are presented in Table 7.1 as a point of reference. The importance of a solid base in academic vocabulary in production of L2 writing is also discussed in detail in chapters 3 and 4.

The data in Table 7.1 demonstrate unambiguously that academic L2 vocabulary has to be taught and learned, and there is not a moment to lose. That is, the vocabulary range of junior high school students may be similar to that of highly educated nonnative speakers of English, such as post-doctoral students in English-speaking countries (Nation & Waring, 1997; Waring & Nation, 2004). It seems clear, though, that the types of accessible word families of school-age learners is not likely to be the same as that of post-doctoral non-native speakers. In general terms, the vocabulary needed for teaching adults—and particularly so for teaching academic L2 writing—is not similar to that suited for teaching school age learners.

TABLE 7.1 Vocabulary Sizes*

Native Speakers of English	Number of Word Families
Average native speaker	17,000
First-year college students	16,679
Older adults	21,252
Educated native speakers	30,000 (approximately)
Junior high school students	9,684
An average novel for teenager	5,000 words (not word families) approximately

Non-Native Speakers of English	
Graduate/post-doctoral nonnative students (receptive vocabulary only)	8,000–9,000 (approximately)

*Based on the data provided in the following publications: D'Anna, Zechmeister, and Hall, (1991), Nation (2006), Goulden, Nation, and Read (1990), Zechmeister, D'Anna, Hall, Paus, and Smith (1993), and Zechmeister, Chronis, Cull, D'Anna, and Healy (1995).

Action Point

Make a trip to a local public library or a large bookstore and locate the section with books for junior high students (sometimes called "juvenile books" or "juvenile literature"). What topics do these books address?

Choose, say, 5 or 6 books on such academic topics as scientific explorations, biographies of scientists or famous authors, or nature. How is the text written? How long are the chapters? What is the size of the font? In short, note the physical characteristics and the content presentation in these books.

If you were teaching a vocabulary or a reading course for L2 university students or scholars, would these books be appropriate? In what ways would they be and in what ways wouldn't they? Can these books or reading materials be modified to make them more suitable? How would you go about identifying suitable reading materials for academically bound adult learners with limited vocabulary ranges?

A vast body of published research on learning vocabulary and collocations and its connections to the quality of L2 writing as demonstrated on writing tests and assessments can be summarized simply.

- High and significant correlations have been repeatedly established between vocabulary size and practically all rater assessments of writing quality, writing performance in college/university courses, and with general language proficiency scores (Bachman & Palmer, 1996; Bors & Stokes, 1999; Laufer & Nation, 1995).
- Raters of writing are consistently influenced by the lexical range and richness even when they are not expected or instructed to focus on vocabulary (Educational Testing Service, 2004).

One of the fundamentals of all teaching is that when vocabulary is taught, it does not mean that it is learned.

With vocabulary teaching, it is also important to remember that, in many cases, word complexity and the complexity of its meaning do not necessarily follow the progression from easy to learn to difficult to learn. The reasons may simply lie in the fact that the teacher has a somewhat limited impact on student vocabulary learning.

When a lesson is completed, words can be forgotten, confused with other words, or their meanings can become conflated with meanings of other words. When a vocabulary unit or set is finished, it does not mean that students have learned all the words that it includes or that they have become proficient vocabulary users (Waring and Nation, 2004).

The Teacher's Job

When it comes to vocabulary teaching, the teachers' job consists of the following six components:

- Determining the most effective and efficient ways of vocabulary teaching and learning, based on the learning objectives and learners' goals (see chapter 5)
- Identifying vocabulary and collocations that are most needed in language building and learning, as well as in writing
- Planning the progression and sequencing of instructional materials, that is, vocabulary and collocations to increase vocabulary range and promote retention
- Teaching learners how to learn vocabulary effectively and efficiently. A word needs to be encountered between 10 and 16 times in order for it to be learned (more on this below)
- Providing opportunities for contextualized vocabulary uses and increasing writing (and reading) fluency
- Assessing learners' progress and adjusting instruction and sequencing as needed, that is, refining and modifying teaching to best meet learners' needs

Vocabulary Learning and Retention

In learning another language, a development of a solid vocabulary base cannot be overestimated. Learning vocabulary can take place in the context of attaining practically any L2 skill, from listening and speaking to reading and writing. In learning to write in L2, the range of vocabulary plays a crucial role: ideas cannot be expressed without the means to express them.

In many cases of vocabulary teaching, a word or a phrase are introduced in the classroom, their meanings and contextual uses are explained with a little bit of practice, and then these items can be relegated to further activities and assignments. Frequently, in subsequent vocabulary work, these new items are not revisited or revisited insufficiently, and then they are often abandoned. Much research on vocabulary learning has demonstrated, however, that anywhere between 10 and 16 exposures to a new word can produce a significant gain in vocabulary growth (Laufer 1997, 1998; Nation, 1990, 2008, 2013; Schmitt 2004). In fact, the more exposures, the better.

> The key to vocabulary learning is not actually learning words and word families. The key to expanding one's vocabulary range is vocabulary retention.

💬 Talking Shop

Some world-renowned authorities on L2 vocabulary teaching, such as Paul Nation (2008), say that teaching incremental vocabulary items and collocations in the classroom is a waste of time. In fact, one of the most important of the teachers' jobs is to teach students strategies for learning vocabulary and collocations effectively. Experience has shown, however, that teachers usually do not subscribe to this position, despite a great number of research findings.

What do you think the reasons may be for Nation's standpoint? Do you agree with his outlook? Discuss your views with your colleagues and see what their experiences and opinions are.

As was mentioned in chapter 6, to understand spoken or written texts, most learners need to comprehend 95% of the running words, and no less than 90%. Vocabulary retention requires intensive and extensive practice. In the early stages, vocabulary learning is easy because early learning includes highly frequent words, but less frequent words (e.g., academic vocabulary) are harder to learn, and they need to be purposefully taught and learned. Initial vocabulary learning often leads to increases in receptive vocabulary (words and phrases are recognized and understood in reading and listening), but not necessarily in productive vocabulary and active usage in writing or speaking (Lee, 2003).

To begin with, vocabulary learning can include such basic practice as pronouncing the words, reading aloud, word and sentence dictation, and spelling (Nation, 2013). Spelling exercises and practice can be particularly valuable for learners whose L1 alphabets and orthography are derived from the writing systems other than those adopted in English or many other European languages (Birch, 2011, 2013).

> A large **receptive** vocabulary does not necessarily result in a better free active vocabulary in writing. The growth of productive vocabulary in writing occurs slowly and in the process of writing practice.

>  **Action Point**
>
> Take a look at any standardized test or test preparation materials and books for academic language (e.g., the TOEFL, SAT, ACT, or GRE). These are easy to locate in any bookstore or language teaching program. The importance of vocabulary teaching and learning—at least for the purposes of tests and assessments—becomes very clear.
>
> Write down around 60–70 words and expressions that are tested in these materials even if for preparation and practice. Then count those that have concrete meaning or abstract meanings. Which words and expressions are tested more often? Why do you think one type of vocabulary is found more frequently in the tests of academic language? What goals do these tests set out to meet?
>
> And now the million-dollar question: do standardized tests or test preparation materials actually address learners' receptive or productive vocabulary? How can you tell?

Cross-Curricular Strategies and Techniques for Vocabulary Teaching and Learning

In general terms, the purpose of vocabulary learning strategies is to enable learners to complete a range of language learning steps and tasks and achieve their learning objectives. Effective and ineffective learning strategies are of particular importance when learners work with large amounts of vocabulary. The vocabulary learning strategies and techniques discussed here are not only applicable to learning specific types or sets of words and expressions, but they represent generally productive or less productive components of vocabulary learning. Although in many cases learners are able to figure out which learning technique is more effective than the other, they often do not have sufficient training to understand the reasons, revise a learning strategy, or to select another that is more effective.

> In general terms, the purpose of teaching the distinctions between more or less effective and efficient vocabulary learning strategies and techniques is to enable learners to become autonomous in their language learning.

Despite the fact that a great deal of research has been carried out on efficient and inefficient vocabulary learning strategies, a few of those that work less than well have endured. Since language learners rarely, if ever, undertake to familiarize themselves with research, one of the most important teachers' tasks is to help students to become more effective in their vocabulary learning. As has been noted, vocabulary teaching and learning can take place in the context of any class, course, or curriculum.

The most important factor in building up a substantial vocabulary base that is essential for producing reasonably competent L2 academic writing is consistency and persistence in effective studies. It is also important to keep in mind that, like most academic undertakings, effective vocabulary learning and deploying of efficient strategies and techniques takes time and practice (and practice). Vocabulary learning and using is a language skill, and most advanced skill development is a deliberate process that requires setting incremental goals and focused attention.

> **Talking Shop**
>
> In the traditional teaching of L2 and FL, curricula and instruction are separated into incremental language skills, such as speaking, reading, or writing. The reasons for this approach to teaching are primarily historical, but they have endured also due to the perceived expedience (good value for the time) of separate lessons and courses. It is clear that, in this chapter and throughout this book, the perspective on language teaching curriculum and the gradual process of language learning differs from the traditional one (a secret note: the author of this book is a nonnative user of English).
>
> What do you think the advantages and disadvantages may be for separating language curriculum and teaching by skill or intertwining various language skills in instruction? In your own experience as a language learner or teacher, which approach can lead to greater and more efficient language gains? What possible difference might emerge between learners' or teachers' views? Discuss your perspective with your colleagues and see what their experiences are.

Ineffective Vocabulary Learning Techniques

Some of the common, but less than useful, strategies are discussed below simply because these are ubiquitous in various locations and among various types of learners. For example, students who are particularly diligent and motivated may choose unsimplified L2 texts when they believe that, over time, this technique can bring them closer to achieving their goal of reading complex prose.

A large number of studies have been demonstrated that the vocabulary threshold, that is, the lowest vocabulary range that is needed for reasonable comprehension, is one of the crucial aspects in L2 vocabulary learning (and reading).

This is particularly relevant in curriculum and course design, as well as in establishing students' learning objectives (discussed in chapter 6). Some research reports have identified the vocabulary threshold needed for comprehension (but not necessarily written production) of authentic academic texts as around 7,000 word families (Hu & Nation, 2000; Laufer & Ravenhorst-Kalovski, 2010). That is, by the end of their preparatory studies, L2 learners should attempt to achieve this overall vocabulary learning objective.

However, vocabulary learning is an incremental and iterative (repeated) process, and learners' threshold of comprehension, for example, at the beginning or intermediate levels can be expected to differ considerably. For instance, as noted earlier, Hu and Nation (2000) state that no comprehension takes place when learners understand only 80% of the text and that some a small number of learners may need only 90% to 95%. The majority, however, require even higher vocabulary ranges, where the number of familiar words in a passage is close to 98% (Nation, 2013). The essential vocabulary sizes that differ from level to level are known as vocabulary thresholds.

The two most common ineffective vocabulary learning techniques:

- Reading or listening (both are receptive skills) above "the threshold level" of comprehension is the most common of all poor strategies.
- Guessing the meaning of words from context where the number of familiar words is smaller than 4 out every 5. This is the second most common poor strategy. Some researchers have shown that successful text comprehension is possible in contexts with 19 known words out of every 20 (Laufer, 1989; Nation & Waring, 1997).

The idea that guessing the meaning of words from context has arisen from a body of research on children who are learning to read in L1 English in English-speaking environments. By far, the vast majority of words in reading in one's native language is learned in extensive reading (or reading for enjoyment) and numerous and repeated exposures to vocabulary in the course of education and schooling, rather than by means of direct and explicit teaching. However, in the 1990s, some researchers extrapolated these findings on children learning to read in their L1 to L2 learners and L2 vocabulary learning (Coady, 1997). Because of its intuitive attractiveness to teachers who are native speakers of English or other languages and who themselves acquired large vocabularies in this way, the myth on how L2 vocabulary can be learned has failed to disappear.

A very large number of investigations on the effectiveness of guessing unknown L2 vocabulary in context have demonstrated repeatedly that accurate or even proximate guessing of meaning in reading is hardly ever possible (Laufer, 1997; Laufer & Ravenhorst-Kalovski, 2010; Hu & Nation, 2000; Nation, 1990, 2013). The reasons lie in the fact that most L2 learners may not know not just one or two words in the context of several dozen or hundreds; they probably do not know too many words in any context. Thus, with so many unfamiliar words, accurate or proximate guessing of word meaning can be very difficult (Birch, 2013). In fact, as various studies noted here have demonstrated, expecting learners to make successful guesses may be simply unrealistic.

Action Point

The Guessing Game: Four short sentences are presented below. The words in these sentences that are likely to be unfamiliar to most learners have been omitted. Take a few guesses and see if you can fill in the gaps relatively accurately:

The xxxx xxxxxxx in Los Angeles promises xxxxx xxxxxxxx xxxxxxxxxx the year. A xxxxxxxxxxxxxxxx in the weather of the xxxxxx is the xxxx-xxxxxxxxx high xxxxxxxx area of the north xxxxxxx Ocean. This xxxxxxxx center moves xxxxxxxxx in summer, holding xxxxxxxxxxx well to the north, and as a result the xxxx receives little xxxxxxxxxxxxx during that period. Winter xxxxxx bring xxxxxxxxxx, xxxxxxxxxxxxxxxxxxxxx. (Retrieved and adapted from www.wrcc.dri.edu/narratives/CALIFORNIA.htm, on March 15, 2014)

You are likely to guess that the text is about the weather in Los Angeles because of the words *weather* and *Los Angeles* and summer and winter. However, it is not possible to guess from the text what it actually says about the summer and the winter weather.

Turn the page to see the complete text with gaps filled in. How many words were you able, in fact, to guess correctly? How many did you miss? What do you think about the efficiency and effectiveness of learning L2 vocabulary in context? What do your colleagues think?

Effective Teaching Techniques

In course curriculum and instruction, there is a distinction between receptive vocabulary that is needed for listening and reading comprehension and productive vocabulary that learners can employ in producing language, that is, speaking and writing. Productive language and vocabulary usage is much more difficult to attain because all facets of word knowledge have to be deployed: recall, orthography and spelling or sounds, word form(s), structural variables (e.g., affixes or prepositions), and appropriate meanings in context. On the other hand, receptive word knowledge can be a great deal less demanding when only a recognition of the form and its attendant meanings are relevant and salient (Nation, 2008, 2013).

As most teachers and learners know from experience, in L2 learning, receptive language and vocabulary are more developed and practiced in virtually all cases.

Another important consideration is that L2 receptive vocabulary almost always remains larger than the productive, and special efforts are often needed to "push" receptive word knowledge into productive uses. Such additional efforts can take the form of more frequent repetition and exposure, and explicitly requiring learners to use vocabulary in writing (and speaking), which Swain (1995, 2005) calls comprehensible output. A good deal of work and pre-teaching is almost always needed for productive language tasks, such as writing.

Receptive vocabulary can be successfully "pushed" into written production in limited and purposeful sets that are well thought-out. For example, vocabulary associated with a particular topic, such as weather, climate, finance, a historical event, or Harry Potter's magic, can be pushed in producing writing.

- To increase the range of vocabulary in writing (productive), explicitly and directly activating receptive vocabulary is requisite.
- Focusing on (and rewarding!) word uses in written production and vocabulary richness are essential to expanding productive vocabulary size.
- Language production (speaking and writing), as opposed to reception, leads to better vocabulary learning over time (Laufer & Nation, 1995, 1999).

> In teaching and learning, it important to remember that it can be work- and time-consuming to push vocabulary uses from receptive to productive. Motivating learners in this rather difficult practice is of the essence.

A course curriculum and lesson plans need to incorporate a number of components that can lead to persistent, consistent, and deliberate vocabulary learning. Writing practice provides one of the best techniques for activating receptive vocabulary in productive usage. In learning EFL, where opportunities for language production occur almost exclusively in the classroom, "pushing" vocabulary from receptive to productive is bound to be more difficult than in ESL/L2 contexts.

> Answer to the Guessing Game on p. xxx:
> The arid climate in Los Angeles promises scant humidity throughout the year. A dominating factor in the weather of the region is the semi-permanent high pressure area of the north Pacific Ocean. This pressure center moves northward in summer, holding storm tracks well to the north, and as a result the area receives little precipitation during that period. Winter storms bring widespread, moderate precipitation.

Techniques for Building Up Learners' Vocabulary Base

The basic steps in any and all vocabulary teaching:

1. Identifying the words students need to know (e.g., University Word List or Academic Word List—numerous websites on the Internet contain the two lists)
2. Helping students memorize and retain these words (e.g., teaching vocabulary learning strategies).
3. Practicing words (and subsequently word families) in different and meaningful ways.

As has been mentioned, one of the teacher's tasks is to select vocabulary for student learning. It seems clear at the outset that beginning learners should not start with complex or difficult words, but simple ones that are highly useful and frequent.

- Vocabulary teaching begins with the most frequent words and moves to those that are less frequent.
    Students should be able to make lists of valuable, frequent, and productive words and put them on flash cards. Examples with these words, phrases, and synonyms can be added to the lists and flash cards (a Note on Flash Cards is included at the end of this chapter).
- Spaced repetition is the mother of all remembering/vocabulary retention. Review, review, review the words learned. For example, effective vocabulary reviews can take place at regular intervals, such as one, two, three, and seven days apart. Vocabulary practice and review is the essential foundation of vocabulary learning and remembering.

> **Spaced repetition is the single most important technique in all vocabulary teaching.**

- Words with concrete meanings are easier to learn than abstract concepts. For this reason, words with concrete meanings are easier to teach.
    Academic vocabulary is largely abstract and polysemous (words with multiple meanings), and it often refers to complex concepts. Another constraint is that abstract words can have more culturally bound meanings than those that refer to concrete objects. For example, such words as *homework, chapter,* or *income* can be demonstrated or explained relatively easily. On the other hand, the words *evidence, factor,* or *method* would require learners to have a bit of language proficiency to understand the explanations and use the words appropriately in context.
- Online and electronic dictionaries are easy ways to access a dictionary or a thesaurus. Many online dictionaries are available on the Internet, and looking

up a word online takes a fraction of the time of doing it the old-fashioned way by looking up words in large dictionary volumes.

To provide learners opportunities for reviewing high-frequency vocabulary and spaced repetition, several productive and simple techniques can be highly useful. A few suggestions and examples of easily implemented and simple practice opportunities:

- A spelling quiz or a short dictation (5–10 minutes) of words or phrases learned a few days ago or yesterday
- Writing a short definition of or giving a couple of sentence examples with a word or phrase
- Short oral questions with a word that require oral responses
- Pair work that requires learners to exchange their flash cards and test one another
- Identifying parts of words and constructing new words with prefixes and suffixes. In the long run, this is probably one of the most useful exercises and practice opportunities because it requires learners to review the meanings of a number of word parts. An example can be found in the "Action Point" below.

> The key consideration in learning practice is to give learners an opportunity to encounter and use the vocabulary that they would not otherwise have in their spoken casual and informal interactions.

Action Point

A sample of student activity on new word-building, prefixes, suffixes, and derivations is found below. A headword (or a prefix or a suffix) is presented to students, and then they have a few minutes to make a list of simple or derived words with the headword or affix. Students can compete to see who comes up with the longest list and work in small groups of 2–4.

For example:

VARY (the headword)	
invariable	invariably
variability	variable
variables	variably
variance	variant
variants	variation
variations	varied
varies	varying

> What factor(s) do you think make the headword *vary* productive and useful for learners? Can you come up with additional words that can have numerous, practical, and commonly used derivatives? A few additional possibilities: *analysis, create, self, head, formula.* Prepare a list of headwords that can useful to you in your own teaching and for your students.

Additional important areas in teaching students how to expand their vocabulary deal with collocations and lexical (set and relatively inflexible) phrases, small clusters of academic nouns and verbs with similar meanings, high-frequency academic (and largely Greco-Latin) prefixes, and dictionary strategies. These will be presented in turn.

Teaching Collocations and Lexical Phrases

Collocations (and lexical phrases) are combinations of two or more words that tend to be found together in text and discourse (e.g., *hard rain, pouring rain, heavy rain,* but not *big rain* or *strong rain*).

In academic language building, learning frequent collocations, such as those in the earlier examples, is of the essence. Numerous studies have demonstrated conclusively that even in the cases of learners with a substantial vocabulary base, L2 writing may appear inaccurate and unidiomatic when collocations are inappropriately or infrequently employed (Hinkel, 2002a, 2002b; Howarth, 1998; Lewis, 2000; Pawley & Syder, 1983; Peters, 1983).

Collocations can include words in combinations with any types of other words (e.g., nouns, verbs, prepositions, and prepositional phrases). A few examples can be found with the noun *cause* and the verb *cause*, for instance.

> *Cause* (noun)—*an underlying cause, a root cause, (for/with) a good cause, a cause for concern, a common cause,* or *a lost cause*
> *Cause* (verb)—*cause problems, cause inconvenience*

Typically, collocations consist of two elements: a pivot word which is the main/focal word in the collocation and its accompanying word(s) (one or more; e.g., *change jobs, change direction, change course,* or *change gears*) (Shin & Nation, 2008). Collocations can be lexical (those that deal with meaning), as in the above examples, or grammatical.

Most lexical collocations fall in the following types of word combinations:

- verbs and nouns (e.g., *change the subject, change sides, change one's mind*)
- adjectives and nouns (e.g., *heavy traffic, strong influence, severe shortage, mild weather*)
- nouns and nouns (sometimes conjoined by a preposition) (e.g., *building design, trade agreement, guest of honor, bar of soap*)

- verb and adverb/preposition (e.g., *vaguely remember, strongly advocate, add significantly, greatly appreciate, accurately assess*)

Collocations and lexical phrases cannot be assembled from their component words: they have evolved in the language historically and are somewhat arbitrary. All language users, L1 and L2 alike, have to learn them, instead of being able to derive them.

Many learners are simply unaware that collocations and lexical phrases are highly prevalent in many languages, including English. For this reason, collocations are often glossed over and remain unnoticed. Thus, the first step in teaching these language features is to increase students' awareness and bring their attention to such phrases. Unfortunately, in much language and vocabulary teaching, collocations are not strongly emphasized.

> For many learners, it is easier to work with collocations as whole phrases (as in, for example, one long word) rather than trying to assemble phrases from their component parts.

An effective technique for teaching learners to notice collocations is bring their attention to phrases and sets of words that occur frequently in reading. Collocations are so numerous that it is probably impossible to address all of them, but learners need to know that a book's worth page of text can include approximately between 20 and 50 of these.

To train students to notice collocations, the teacher can start by bringing learners' attention to pivot words and those that accompany (go with) them. Explicitly teaching and noting the most frequent phrases, such as *for example, on the other hand*, or *for this reason* may save a bit of time and effort in the long run.

As the next step, demonstrating typical combinations of pivot words and their accompaniments, using columns, tables, and appropriate substitutions can further highlight collocation frequency and provide models for students to use in their own vocabulary notebooks (an example can be found in the "Action Point" below). Quizzes on collocations can be simple and easy. Students are presented with a pivot word and are asked to supply collocates (accompanying words); these can be fruitful and highly productive.

Action Point

An example of student practice or a quiz on collocations is presented below. A pivot word is presented in the left column, and students have to come up with as many collocates (accompanying words) as they can during a particular amount of time, say, 5–10 minutes. Students can compete to see who comes up with the longest list and work in small groups of 2–4.

The pivot words can be as basic as *make, do, have, give,* or *take* for beginners, and more advanced, such as *assume, assign, achieve, conclude, consist, consult, define, denote, increase, decrease, presume, verify* (from the University Word List), for more proficient learners.

For example:

make (pivot word)	possible collocates: an appointment, an argument, an arrangement, an attempt, a cake, an excuse, a friend or friends, a joke, a phone call, a prediction, a speech, a suggestion
take (pivot word)	possible collocates: action, advantage (of), a bath, a break, care (of), a chance or chances, charge, a class, an exam, (a lot of) effort, heart, the lead, note, notes, an opportunity, a phone call, someone's suggestion(s)
achieve (pivot word)	possible collocates: goal, objective, result, success, aim, ambition, target, standards, level, (one's) potential, success, recognition, greatness, be difficult to, be easy to, be impossible to, be possible to

Construct your own practice activities for students and do them for the experience. Keep in mind that collocates can come before and after the pivot words. Productive pivots words can be found in any collocation dictionary. Some examples: *advice, fight, influence, issue, plan, relate, relationship,* or *role.* Can you come up with additional common pivot words? Prepare a list of pivot words that can useful to you in your own teaching and for your students.

A few suggestions for collocation practice and activities can be:

- News reports and restatement of information from the Business section of a newspaper (e.g., "And now we bring you the latest from the stock market")
- Business plans or presentations to "the board of directors" or a company president
- Poster sessions with formal explanations for fellow professionals, "stock holders," or potential "investors"

Useful collocation dictionaries that can provide comprehensive collections of pivot words and collocates:

- McIntosh, C., Francis, B., & Poole, R. (Eds.). (2009). *Oxford collocations dictionary for students of English* (2nd ed.). Oxford, UK: Oxford University Press.
- Rundell, M., & Fox, G. (Eds.). (2010). *Macmillan collocations dictionary for learners of English*. Oxford: Macmillan.
- Lea, D. (2002). *Oxford collocations dictionary for students of English*. Oxford: Oxford University Press.
- Benson, M., Benson, E., & Ilson, R. (2010). *The BBI combinatory dictionary of English: A guide to word combinations* (3rd ed.). Amsterdam: John Benjamins.
- *Longman Collocations Dictionary and Thesaurus*. (2010). Edinburgh: Pearson Education.

Talking Shop

J. R. Firth is often quoted having said "you know a word by the company it keeps" (Firth, 1957, p. 179). However, more recently, a number of researchers have noted that one of the reasons that students may not be aware of collocations is that many of their teachers may not be. That is, instructors typically focus much of their attention on word-based vocabulary or grammatical constructions, but far less so on collocations.

Do you agree that the teaching of collocations is often neglected because teachers are not aware of their importance in language usage? Why or why not? What do you think the reasons may be for the slight of collocations in teaching? Discuss your views with your colleagues and see what their experiences and opinions are.

Vocabulary Substitution Clusters for Academic Writing

Many studies have reported that the language employed to construct academic writing is highly formulaic (Cowie, 1992; Schmitt, 2004; Wray, 2002). By and large, formulaic constructions are not assembled from their component parts—that is, they are not compositional (see the discussion on collocations earlier in this chapter), but in most cases, they are idiomatic. Proficient writers, L1 and L2 alike, learn the formulaic language that dominates in formal academic prose through repeated uses (see the section on spaced repetition above) (Pawley & Syder, 1983; Wray, 1999).

From the perspective of language teaching, this provides additional support and evidence that collocations and other types of language elements used repeatedly can be easier and more fruitfully learned as whole units. Harold E. Palmer, a

British linguist and pioneer in the field of English language learning and teaching, originally made this observation in 1933 (as it applied to collocations):

> "successions of words which (for various reasons) . . . must or should be learnt, or is best, or most conveniently learnt as an integral whole or independent entity, rather than by the process of placing together their component parts"
>
> (Palmer, 1933, p.8).

In the context of teaching academic writing, it is important for learners to know well a number of common formulaic expressions that can ease the task of producing formal academic text (a more extensive discussion of this follows in chapter 8).

For example, the following formulaic expressions for constructing thesis and topic statements can make writing one up a relatively uncomplicated job:

> *The purpose of this essay/paper/analysis/overview is to xxx*
> (e.g., *take a look at/examine/discuss yyy.*)
> *The main emphasis/focus/goal/purpose of the/this*
> *essay/paper/project is to xxx*
> (e.g., *analyze/provide an overview/discussion of xxx.*)
> *This paper discusses/examines/investigates xxx.*
> *This paper claims/shows that xxx is / is not yyy.*

Thus, it stands to reason that learning a few additional academic nouns and verbs to use as substitutions in such formulaic expressions can greatly increase the range of options available to any L2 writer. For example, as substitutes for the nouns used in the earlier set of possible thesis statements, *essay, paper, analysis,* and *overview*—additional nouns that are similar in meaning can be learned and used as needed: *article, discussion,* or *exposition.* Such academic reporting verbs as *discusses, examines,* or *investigates* can find additional replacements: *argues, demonstrates, explains, reviews,* or *addresses.*

Learning a small number of close synonyms is the father of vocabulary growth and academic text construction in practically all cases of formal and academic L2 writing.

Additional benefits of learning close synonyms in vocabulary clusters is that they can make L2 writers' vocabulary ranges appear larger and more academic than they actually are. They can also provide learners with tools needed for constructing lexically cohesive text. It is not possible to establish lexical cohesion in one's prose without having lexical substitutions available to be deployed as needed (Hinkel, 2001).

- <u>Close</u> synonyms (it is important for the synonyms to be close) are also the easiest way to recycle and review vocabulary in writing and to develop a cohesive text (for example: *business—enterprise—company—corporation* or *result in—bring about—create—lead to*).
- As much as possible, vocabulary should be taught in <u>small</u> groups of near-synonyms (not more than 3–5 at a time; e.g., <u>*growth*</u>*—increase, gain, advancement* or <u>*factor*</u>*—aspect, facet, consideration*). The reason that the number of near synonyms has to be relatively small is to avoid words, their forms, and meanings interfering with one another and becoming confusing (Nation, 2008).

> **Talking Shop**
>
> When you write formal or academic text, do you make a special effort to vary your vocabulary and make sure that you avoid repeating words? Do you try to impress the reader by means of using varied and rich vocabulary? Do you believe that other writers also try to vary their vocabulary in formal prose? Why do you think this is?
>
> What could be cultural or social reasons that vocabulary is expected to be varied in such texts as literature, news media, or academic prose? What are the social values associated with extensive vocabulary ranges and usage?

Teaching and Learning a Few Essential Prefixes and Suffixes

The greatest difference between prefixes and suffixes is that prefixes appear before a word (or root/stem) and change its meaning (e.g., *pre-position* or *in-convenient*). Suffixes that are added to the end of an existing word (or root/stem) can form a new word (e.g., *help-ful* or *help-less*) or change the inflection (e.g., singular or plural).

Much research has been devoted to whether prefixes and suffixes are worth learning in light of how numerous they are in English and how constrained (inconsistent, lexicalized, and idiomatic) their applications may be to deriving and learning vocabulary. Since at least the 1920s, vocabulary researchers and teaching methodologists undertook a large body of studies to determine which prefixes and suffixes are more productive and efficient for learning and which are less so (Corson, 1985; Nagy & Anderson, 1984; Nation, 1990).

TABLE 7.2 Most Frequent and Highly Productive Prefixes and Suffixes (in declining order)

Prefix	Meaning	Suffix	Meaning
un-	not	-able	able (to be)
re-	again	-ation, -tion, -ion	state or quality
in-, im-, il-, ir-	not	-er	one who (nouns only)
dis-	away, from	-ish	relating to, characteristic
en-, em-	in	-less	without, not
non-	not	-ness	state, quality, condition
over-	above	-ful	full of
mis-	not	-ism	state or quality
sub-	under	-ist	one who performs an action
pre-	before	-age	action or process

(Based on Nation [1990, 2013] and White, Sowell, and Yanagihara [1989])

To make the job of learning prefixes and suffixes easier and more beneficial, the best strategy is to teach those that occur in high frequencies. To this end, teaching and helping students remember the meaning of the practically countless Greco-Latinate words in academic language is to focus on the most frequent and useful 15–20 English prefixes and suffixes. The list of 10 most frequent prefixes and 10 most frequent suffixes that have distinct meanings is presented in Table 7.2.

As with all vocabulary teaching, the task of learning the essential prefixes and suffixes falls to the learners themselves. The most efficient way to learn them is to put these on flash cards together with a few words in which these affixes can be found. For example, pairs or small groups of students receive (or make) about 30 or 40 small cards, with a prefix, a word, or a suffix. An additional twist can be added when the students are asked to make as many words as they can by combining the affixes and new words that are not found on the cards.

Action Point

For as long as second language researchers have tried to identify productive and unproductive prefixes and suffixes, they have debated the advantages and disadvantages of undertaking a big and somewhat tedious job of leaning them from the point of view of a cost and benefit analysis. The amount of work entailed in memorizing, identifying in context, and using word parts is substantial.

As a short exercise (no more than 5 minutes), try your hand in reversing this process and locating as many parts in the following academic words as you can (in random order):

> *unconstitutional, conceptualization, environmentalist, reformulation, misinterpretation, reinvention, inappropriately, institutionalizing, abnormal, normalization, demonstrative, reconstitutive, unparalleled, disproportionately, hypothetically, implementation, predictability, probability, statistician*
>
> Compare your word parsing and analysis with those of your colleagues. Can you figure out the meaning of each word from the meanings of its parts? What do you think makes the meanings of complex words more or less easy to figure out from the meanings of the parts?

Teaching and Learning Dictionary Uses

For most L2 learners and writers, dictionaries are absolutely essential. One of the common misconceptions is that bilingual dictionaries are inherently inferior to monolingual (English-English) dictionaries that are prepared for L1 users or highly advanced L2 learners. However, in order to use monolingual dictionaries successfully, learners already have to have a substantial vocabulary base to understand word definitions and usage examples. For most beginning or intermediate learners, monolingual dictionaries may not be very useful for this very reason (Nation, 2008).

In this case, using a bilingual dictionary is likely to be more effective, provided that it is well prepared and contains accurate definitions and examples. For high-intermediate learners, looking up words in both bilingual and monolingual dictionaries may also be beneficial because the latter contain valuable information about grammar and collocations that the former do not (Laufer & Hadar, 1997; Laufer & Kimmel, 1997).

In good quality dictionaries, the examples—even when they are inauthentic—are chosen or constructed with deliberation and care to demonstrate contextual meanings of the word and its grammatical forms. Examples of authentic texts and uses supplied in corpus-based dictionaries can be confusing and linguistically complex for most learners to analyze and use productively as models in their own writing.

> When used to understand a reading, monolingual dictionaries can be very fruitful for advanced learners because this can lead to additional exposures to vocabulary and learning. When a dictionary is needed for speaking or writing, bilingual dictionaries are likely to be more productive because they require less guessing of word definitions.

One of the important characteristics of a good dictionary is that it provides such essential information as pronunciation, word part structure, grammatical attributes of a word, numerous examples, derived forms (e.g., *short—shortly—shortage—shortness*), pointers to other related words, and collocations. Derived forms and related words is helpful for learning to identify frequent prefixes and suffixes without going too far afield. In general, few learners' dictionaries include information on word origins (etymology), but online dictionaries usually do.

To show learners how to use an English-English dictionary to their best advantage, a copy of a dictionary entry can be enlarged to make it easier to notice details. An example of the entry for the verb *occur* can be profitable to present and explain because it is frequently found in academic and news media language (adapted from *Webster's New World College Dictionary* (2014)). Such a demonstration can be turned into a lesson to benefit other aspects of the curriculum.

Useful instructional information that learners need to notice and use to their best advantage can be found in square brackets. A couple of examples are illustrated below in Examples (1) and (2). Both verbs, *define* and *establish*, appear on the University Word List (see above).

Example (1):

---

de-fine /pronunciation symbols/ [dih-fahyn] Show IPA
verb (used with object) [very important grammar information for writing]
de-fined, de-fin-ing

1. [the first and most frequent meaning] to state or <u>set</u> forth the meaning of (a <u>word</u>, phrase, etc.) [these can be used as replacements/synonyms]: *They disagreed on how to define "liberal."* [The teacher or students can provide additional examples of phrases and sentences with this meaning (e.g., *Now we need to define a triangle/the course/the issue*).]
2. [the second most common meaning] to explain or identify the nature or essential qualities of; <u>describe</u> [an important synonym] [possible replacements for the second meaning]: *to define judicial functions*
3. to fix or lay down clearly and <u>definitely</u>; specify distinctly: *to define one's responsibilities.* **Synonyms**: state, <u>name</u>, <u>describe, detail</u> [the latter two words are important synonyms that can be used as replacements], enumerate

[The next two and infrequent meanings are not particularly valuable for learners. It is not worth spending a great deal of time on these.]

4. to determine or fix the boundaries or extent of: *to define property with stakes*
5. to make clear the outline or form of: *The roof was boldly defined against the sky.*
   verb (used without object), de-fined, de-fin-ing [a rare form that is probably not worth the time]
6. to set forth the meaning of a word, phrase, etc.; construct a <u>definition</u> [a derived noun form *defin(e) + ition*]

Related forms: [Examples of phrases and sentences for these derived words and forms can be provided and discussed. Discussions and examples of related and derived word forms can be very useful and productive for learners in practically all types of instruction, **provided that the related words are frequent**.]

de·fin·a·ble, *adjective*
de·fin·a·bil·i·ty, *noun*
de·fin·a·bly, *adverb*
de·fine·ment, *noun*
de·fin·er, *noun*

Example (2):

es-tab-lish /pronunciation symbols/ [ih-stab-lish] Show IPA
verb (used with object) [very important grammar information for writing]

1. [the first and most frequent meaning—several excellent substitutions can be found here] to found, institute, build, or bring into being on a firm or stable basis: *to establish a university; to establish a medical practice*
2. [the second most common meaning; however, in this case, it is not as valuable as the first] to install or settle in a position, place, business, etc.: *to establish one's child in business*

[The next three meanings are context-specific, and the teacher may need to explain these judiciously, if at all.]

3. to show to be valid or true; prove: *to establish the facts of the matter*
4. to cause to be accepted or recognized: *to establish a custom; She established herself as a leading surgeon*
5. to bring about permanently: *to establish order*

Related forms: [These derived forms are mostly rare, and learners are not likely to encounter or use them in L2 writing. For this reason, they are not particularly valuable for learning.]

es·tab·lish·a·ble, *adjective*
es·tab·lish·er, *noun*
re·es·tab·lish, verb *(used with object)*
su·per·es·tab·lish, verb *(used with object)*

Synonyms
1. form, organize. See **fix**. 3. verify, substantiate. 6. decree.

Antonyms [Research has demonstrated that antonyms can be very confusing for learners and focusing on them is probably counter-productive.]
1. abolish. 3. disprove.

When working to construct vocabulary clusters for contextual substitutions and replacements (see an earlier section on Vocabulary Clusters), learners need to keep in mind the following rule typically adopted in dictionary-making:

> Within a dictionary entry, the closer a definition word with a similar meaning is located to the main word (as in meaning (1)), the closer the meanings of the two words usually are.

This is an important consideration in building up vocabulary clusters for substitutions/replacements. When a substitution word is not very similar to the meaning of the main word, unsuitable substitutions and replacements can make the text virtually incomprehensible. For example, the meaning of *occur* is closer to that of (1) *happen* than (2) *to be met with or found*, or (3) *to suggest itself in thought*, which has a narrow meaning that is largely idiomatic.

Vocabulary Teaching Techniques in Contexts of Other Language Skills

A very useful technique is pre-teaching the most valuable and/or high frequency words in a reading or listening selection or for a specific writing task, context, or topic. Important considerations when pre-teaching words that occur in text and context:

- Limit the number of words to be pre-taught to about 10. Pre-teaching too many words often results in form and meaning confusions.
- Pre-teaching creates an opportunity for encountering these words more frequently.

Short and frequent writing practice is probably one of the best ways to learn vocabulary and review it. As has been noted, producing short pieces of writing on a regular schedule can be a great way to recycle and review vocabulary learned in the past month, the past week, and the past two days.

- Writing practice and exercises need to focus on a specific topic, context, or theme that allows students as much practice as possible with targeted, specific, and topic-centered vocabulary. For example, when the topic of reading and vocabulary learning is *pets*, *global warming*, or *the story of my city*, the writing practice should address these topics, as well.
- Daily or weekly reading logs are the easiest way of practicing in writing the academic vocabulary learned in reading. Reading logs do not need to be graded, and checking them may be sufficient.

A Note on Flash Cards

L2 vocabulary teaching and learning represent probably one of the oldest human undertakings. Travelers, merchants, job seekers, professionals, tradesmen, students, soldiers, sailors, marriage partners, family relations, missionaries, writers, painters, adventurers, retirees, and many other various types of individuals have undertaken to identify and implement the most effective and efficient means of learning vocabulary in a language other than their mother tongue.

Learning vocabulary in another language has been a human activity probably for a few thousand years. For this reason, the amount of work, published or unpublished, on learning L2 vocabulary is truly vast. Since L2 vocabulary—that is, words and expressions—is discrete and can be learned piecemeal, the collective and experiential knowledge on the best ways of learning vocabulary is far more established and developed than on learning, for example, how to read, write, or be polite in another language. In contemporary times, when various technological and electronic means of L2 vocabulary learning have proliferated, one most important technique has endured through the recent decades: flash cards.

> Research has demonstrated that flash cards represent the single most efficient way of increasing vocabulary range.

Here are a few reasons that flash cards have remained the mainstay of learning words and expressions in another language:

- Flash cards are easy to carry around, use for review, mix, and supplement.
- Polysemous words that have many meanings can be easy to account for when using flash cards: e.g., *reflect*—1. *to cast back (heat, light)*; 2. *ponder, think*; 3. *show*
- The use of flash cards also leads to independent learning and promotes learner autonomy.
- Since all the words the students have to know cannot be taught, students have to be taught how to become independent learners and be held accountable for their own learning.

More recently, research has demonstrated that using with flash cards can lead to effective L2 vocabulary learning, improvements in visual word recognition and orthography, and increases in reading speed (Culyer, 1988; Schmitt & Schmitt, 1995; Tan & Nicholson, 1997). Additional uses of flash cards can be found in learning basic sentence constructions, prepositions, and relatively inflexible expressions, such as phrasal verbs (e.g., *give up, give in, look up to, look for*).

Another important advantage of working with flash cards is that learners can develop their own customized progressions of word difficulty within flash card sets. That is, due to the great flexibility of using flash cards, the decisions of which vocabulary items are more or less difficult is left exclusively to the learner, and the progression of word and meaning complexity can be highly adaptable and customizable for the individual.

Chapter Summary

Teaching and learning in the academy is simply not possible without academic language and vocabulary, but, unfortunately, merely reading textbooks is not sufficient for learners to develop a substantial range of academic words. Vocabulary has to be extensively and intensively taught, and it has to be a prominent part of a language curriculum. A course curriculum and lesson plans need to incorporate a number of components that can lead to persistent, consistent, and deliberate vocabulary learning. Spaced repetition is the single most important technique in all vocabulary teaching and writing practice provides one of the best techniques for activating receptive vocabulary in productive usage.

Numerous studies have demonstrated conclusively that even in the cases of learners with a substantial vocabulary base, L2 writing may appear inaccurate and unidiomatic when collocations are inappropriately or infrequently employed. The first step in teaching these language features is to increase students' awareness and bring their attention to such phrases. Learning a variety of close synonyms also makes vocabulary learning more efficient and has the additional benefit of making L2 writers' vocabulary ranges appear larger and more academic than they actually are. Close synonyms can also provide learners with tools needed for constructing lexically cohesive text. In addition to teaching collocations and close synonyms, teachers can help students by teaching high frequency prefixes and suffixes, as well as techniques for using the dictionary and flash cards. Research has demonstrated that flash cards represent the single most efficient way of increasing vocabulary range.

Further Reading

Folse, K. (2004). *Vocabulary myths: Applying second language research to classroom teaching*. Ann Arbor, MI: University of Michigan Press.

Folse, K. (2006). The effect of written exercise on L2 vocabulary retention. *TESOL Quarterly, 40*(2), 273–293.

Hinkel, E. (2002). *Second language writers' text*. Mahwah, NJ: Lawrence Erlbaum Associates.

Hinkel, E. (2011). What research on second language writing tells us and what it doesn't. In E. Hinkel (Ed.), *Handbook of research in second language teaching and learning* (Vol. 2, pp. 523–538). New York: Routledge.

Nagy, W. (2005). Why vocabulary instruction needs to be long-term and comprehensive. In E. Hiebert & M. Kamil (Ed.), *Teaching and learning vocabulary: Bringing research to practice* (pp. 27–44). Mahwah, NJ: Lawrence Erlbaum Associates.

Nation, I. S. P. (2005). Ten best ideas for teaching vocabulary. *The Language Teacher, 29*(7), 11–14.

Nation, I. S. P. (2011). Research into practice: Vocabulary. *Language Teaching, 44*, 529–539.

Nation, I. S. P. (2013). *Learning vocabulary in another language* (2nd ed.). Cambridge: Cambridge University Press.

Nation, I. S. P., & Webb, S. (2011). Content-based instruction and vocabulary learning. In E. Hinkel (Ed.), *Handbook of research in second language teaching and learning* (Vol. 2, pp. 631–644). New York: Routledge.

Schmitt, N. (2000). *Vocabulary in language teaching*. Cambridge: Cambridge University Press.

Schmitt, N. (2008). Instructed second language vocabulary learning. *Language Teaching Research, 12*(3), 329–363.

Webb, S. (2007). The effects of repetition on vocabulary knowledge. *Applied Linguistics, 28*(1), 46–65.

References

Bachman, L., & Palmer, A. (1996). *Language testing in practice*. Oxford: Oxford University Press.

Birch, B. (2011). Out of my orthographic depth: Second language reading. In E. Hinkel (Ed.), *Handbook of research in second language teaching and learning* (Vol. 2, pp. 488–506). New York: Routledge.

Birch, B. (2013). *English L2 reading: Getting to the bottom* (3rd ed.). New York: Routledge.

Bors, D., & Stokes, T. (1999). *The effects of first language on performance on a short form of Raven's Advanced Progressive Matrices*. Paper presented at the Annual Meeting of the Canadian Society for Brain Behavior and Cognitive Science, London, Ontario.

Coady, J. (1997). L2 vocabulary acquisition: A synthesis of the research. In J. Coady & T. Huckin (Eds.), *Second language vocabulary acquisition* (pp. 273–290). Cambridge: Cambridge University Press.

Corson, D. (1985). *The lexical bar*. Oxford: Pergamon Press.

Cowie, A. P. (1992). Multiword lexical units and communicative language teaching. In P. Arnaud & H. Bejoint (Eds.), *Vocabulary and applied linguistics* (pp. 1–12). London: Macmillan.

Coxhead, A. (2008). Phraseology and English for academic purposes. In F. Meunier & S. Granger (Eds.), *Phraseology in language learning and teaching* (pp. 149–161). Amsterdam: John Benjamins.

Culyer, R. (1988). Using single concept cards and sentences for affective and effective reading. *Intervention in School and Clinic, 24*, 143–152.

D'Anna, C., Zechmeister, E., & Hall, J. (1991). Toward a meaningful definition of vocabulary size. *Journal of Reading Behavior, 23*, 109–122.

Educational Testing Service. (2004). *Test of written English guide* (5th ed.). Princeton, NJ: Author.

Ferris, D., & Roberts, B. (2001). Error feedback in L2 writing classes: How explicit does it need to be? *Journal of Second Language Writing, 10*, 161–184.

Firth, J. R. (1957). *Papers in Linguistics*. Oxford: Oxford University Press.

Folse, K. (2004). *Vocabulary myths: Applying second language research to classroom teaching*. Ann Arbor, MI: University of Michigan Press.

Folse, K. (2006). The effect of written exercise on L2 vocabulary retention. *TESOL Quarterly, 40*(2), 273–293.

Goulden, R., Nation, P., & Read, J. (1990). How large can a receptive vocabulary be? *Applied Linguistics, 11*(2), 341–363.

Graves, M., August, D., & Mancilla-Martinez, J. (2012). *Teaching vocabulary to English-language learners*. New York: Teachers College Press.

Hinkel, E. (2001). Matters of cohesion in L1 and L2 academic texts. *Applied Language Learning, 12*, 111–132.

Hinkel, E. (2002a). Expressing L1 literacy in L2 writing. In D. S. Li (Ed.), *Discourses in search of members: Festschrift in honor of Ronald Scollon's 60th birthday* (pp. 465–482). Greenwood, CT: Ablex.

Hinkel, E. (2002b). *Second language writers' text*. Mahwah, NJ: Lawrence Erlbaum Associates.

Hinkel, E. (2003). Simplicity without elegance: Features of sentences in L2 and L1 academic texts. *TESOL Quarterly, 37*, 275–301.

Howarth, P. (1998). The phraseology of learners' academic writing. In A. P. Cowie (Ed.), *Phraseology: Theory, analysis, and applications* (pp. 161–186). Oxford: Oxford University Press.

Hu, M., & Nation, P. (2000). Unknown vocabulary density and reading comprehension. *Reading in a Foreign Language, 13*(1), 403–430.

Johnson, M. D., Acevedo, A., & Mercado, L. (2013). We know we should teach vocabulary, but what vocabulary should we teach? Using lexical frequency profiles to expand L2 writers' vocabulary. *Writing and Pedagogy, 5*(1), 83–103.

Jones, M. & Haywood, S. (2004). Facilitating the acquisition of formulaic sequences: An exploratory study in an EAP context. In N. Schmitt (Ed.), *Formulaic sequences* (pp. 269–300). Amsterdam: John Benjamins.

Laufer, B. (1989). A factor of difficulty in vocabulary learning: Deceptive transparency. *AILA Review, 6*, 10–20.

Laufer, B. (1997). The lexical plight in second language reading. Words you don't know, words you think you know, and words you can't guess. In J. Coady & T. Huckin (Eds.), *Second language vocabulary acquisition: A rationale for pedagogy* (pp. 20–34). Cambridge: Cambridge University Press.

Laufer, B. (1998). The development of passive and active vocabulary in a second language: Same or different? *Applied Linguistics, 19*, 255–271.

Laufer, B., & Hadar, L. (1997). Assessing the effectiveness of monolingual, bilingual, and "bilingualised" dictionaries in the comprehension and production of new words. *The Modern Language Journal, 81*, 189–196.

Laufer, B., & Kimmel, M. (1997). Bilingualised dictionaries: How learners really use them. *System, 25*, 361–369.

Laufer, B., & Nation, P. (1995). Vocabulary size and use: Lexical richness in L2 written production. *Applied Linguistics, 16*, 307–322.

Laufer, B., & Nation, P. (1999). A vocabulary size test of controlled productive ability. *Language Testing, 16*(1), 33–51.

Laufer, B., & Paribakht, T. (1998). The relationship between passive and active vocabularies: Effects of language learning context. *Language Learning, 48*, 365–391.

Laufer, B., & Ravenhorst-Kalovski, G. (2010). Lexical threshold revisited: Lexical text coverage, learners' vocabulary size and reading comprehension. *Reading in a Foreign Language, 22*(1), 15–30.

Laufer, B., & Waldman, T. (2011). Verb-noun collocations in second language writing: A corpus analysis of learners' English. *Language Learning, 61*(2), 647–672.

Lee, S. (2003). ESL learners' vocabulary use in writing and the effects of explicit vocabulary instruction. *System, 31*(4), 537–561.

Lee, S., & Muncie, J. (2006). From receptive to productive: Improving ESL learners' use of vocabulary in a postreading composition task. *TESOL Quarterly, 40*(2), 295–320.

Lewis, M. (2000). *Teaching collocation: Further developments in the lexical approach*. London: Language Teaching Publications.

Nagy, W. (2005). Why vocabulary instruction needs to be long-term and comprehensive. In E. Hiebert & M. Kamil (Ed.), *Teaching and learning vocabulary: Bringing research to practice* (pp. 27–44). Mahwah, NJ: Lawrence Erlbaum Associates.

Nagy, W., & Anderson, R. (1984). How many words are there in printed school English? *Reading Research Quarterly, 19*, 304–330.

Nation, I. S. P. (1990). *Teaching and learning vocabulary.* New York: Newbury House.
Nation, I. S. P. (2006). How large a vocabulary is needed for reading and listening? *The Canadian Modern Language Review, 63,* 59–82.
Nation, I. S. P. (2008). *Teaching vocabulary.* Boston: Heinle & Heinle.
Nation, I. S. P. (2013). *Learning vocabulary in another language* (2nd ed.). Cambridge: Cambridge University Press.
Nation, I. S. P., & Webb, S. (2011). Content-based instruction and vocabulary learning. In E. Hinkel (Ed.), *Handbook of research in second language teaching and learning* (Vol. 2, pp. 631–644). New York: Routledge.
Nation, P., & Waring, R. (1997). Vocabulary size, text coverage, and word lists. In N. Schmitt & M. McCarthy (Eds.), *Vocabulary: Description, acquisition, and pedagogy* (pp. 6–20). Cambridge: Cambridge University Press.
Nattinger, J., & DeCarrico, J. (1992). *Lexical phrases and language teaching.* Oxford: Oxford University Press.
Palmer, H. E. (1933). *Second interim report on English collocations.* Tokyo: Kaitakusha.
Pawley, A., & Syder, F. (1983). Two puzzles for linguistic theory: Nativelike selection and nativelike fluency. In J. Richards & R. Schmidt, (Ed.), *Language and Communication* (pp. 191–225). London: Longman.
Peters, A. (1983). *The units of language acquisition.* Cambridge: Cambridge University Press.
Read, J. (2000). *Assessing vocabulary.* Cambridge: Cambridge University Press.
Rott, S. (1999). The effect of exposure frequency on intermediate language learners' incidental vocabulary acquisition and retention through reading. *Studies in Second Language Acquisition, 21,* 589–619.
Schmitt, N. (2004). *Formulaic sequences: Acquisition, processing and use.* Amsterdam: John Benjamins.
Schmitt, N., & Meara, P. (1997). Researching vocabulary through a word knowledge framework. *Studies in Second Language Acquisition, 19,* 17–36.
Schmitt, N., & Schmitt, D. (1995). Vocabulary notebooks: Theoretical underpinnings and practical suggestions. *ELT Journal, 49*(2), 133–143.
Shin, D., & Nation, P. (2008). Beyond single words: The most frequent collocations in spoken English. *ELT Journal, 62*(4), 339–348.
Swain, M. (1995). Three functions of output in second language learning. In G. Cook & B. Seidlhofer (Eds.), *Principles and practice in applied linguistics* (pp. 125–144). Oxford: Oxford University Press.
Swain, M. (2005). The output hypothesis: Theory and research. In E. Hinkel (Ed.), *Handbook of research in second language teaching and learning* (pp. 471–483). New York: Routledge.
Tan, A. & Nicholson, T. (1997). Flash cards revisited: Training poor readers to read words faster improves their comprehension of text. *Journal of Educational Psychology, 89*(2), 276–288.
Waring, R., & Nation, P. (2004). Second language reading and incidental vocabulary learning. *Angles on the English Speaking World, 4,* 11–23.
White, T., Sowell, J., & Yanagihara, A. (1989). Teaching elementary students to use word part clues. *The Reading Teacher, 42,* 302–308.
Wilkins, D. (1972). *Linguistics in language teaching.* London: Edward Arnold.
Wray, A. (1999). Formulaic sequences in learners and native speakers. *Language Teaching, 32,* 213–231.

Wray, A. (2002). *Formulaic language and the lexicon.* Cambridge: Cambridge University Press.

Wray, A. (2004). 'Here's one I prepared earlier': Formulaic language learning on television. In N. Schmitt (Ed.), *Formulaic sequences* (pp. 249–268). Amsterdam: John Benjamins.

Zechmeister, E., Chronis, A., Cull, W., D'Anna, C., & Healy, N. (1995). Growth of a functionally important lexicon. *Journal of Reading Behavior, 27*(2), 201–212.

Zechmeister, E., D'Anna, C., Hall, J., Paus, C., & Smith, J. (1993). Metacognitive and other knowledge about the mental lexicon: Do we know how many words we know? *Applied Linguistics, 14*(1), 188–206.

Zwiers, J. (2008). *Building academic language: Essential practices for content classrooms.* San Francisco: Jossey-Bass.

Zwiers, J. (2014). *Building academic language: Meeting Common Core Standards across disciplines, Grades 5–12* (2nd ed.). San Francisco: Jossey-Bass.

8
LANGUAGE FOCUS
Teaching Academic Grammar for Writing

This chapter discusses:

- Construction grammar and its efficiency and practicality for L2 writing
- Language teaching and construction grammar
- Teaching academic language with pre-fabs
- Noticing in academic reading and practicing in writing
- Error correction and teaching editing

Grammar is an essential tool for producing at minimum comprehensible sentences that can become a part of coherent text. Although in theory the value of explicit grammar instruction has been debated by researchers and methodologists alike, the basic fact is that "without grammar very little can be conveyed" Wilkins (1972, p. 111), as noted in chapter 7. While numerous and raucous debates continue, grammar is the tool without which phrases, sentences, and text—spoken or written—cannot be produced. In grammar instruction, just as with vocabulary teaching, the first order of priority is to determine the teaching and learning objectives: what learners need to know and should be able to do.

Currently, a great deal is known about essential grammar constructions for producing L2 academic writing. Similarly, much is known about how to teach various grammar elements and components, and a large amount of grammar-teaching materials for both teachers and students is published every year. There is no doubt that these materials are highly useful to advance learners' language proficiency, and by extension, L2 writing skills. In fact, the language teaching world would probably not be the same without thorough, well-prepared, carefully thought-out, and systematically structured publications.

The purpose of this chapter in fact is not to attempt to condense the vast knowledge and practice materials for students into a small (miniature?) grammar manual. In fact, the goal of this chapter is to provide efficient tools for teachers and learners by means of presenting and illustrating a few short-cuts. These research-based and time-tested principles and techniques can enable students to develop facility with the grammar of academic prose expeditiously.

In recent years and in the context of applications of construction grammar to teaching L2 academic writing, research has shown that making use of formulaic expressions and memorizing long chunks of text (and making substitutions within them) is far more efficient and effective than learning to assemble new linguistic strings in the process of language production.

As Wilkins (1972, p. 102) comments, learning an L2 in vocabulary and grammatical units (chunks), instead of discrete words or word elements, can often "cover in half the time what is . . . expected from a whole year of language learning." It is important to note, however, that despite the cognitive, linguistic, and psycholinguistic evidence that memorizing language chunks represents an effective and unrestrictive means of expanding learners' vocabulary and grammatical ranges, a cultural and pedagogical bias exists against the idea of memorization of long chunks of text (Hinkel, 2002a, 2009; Nation, 2013; Peters, 1983).

For the purpose of academic writing, a grammar curriculum and classroom teaching at any proficiency level, beginning with the intermediate, needs to include ongoing and persistent noticing activities, such as examinations and analyses of constructions and grammar features in formal writing, including textbooks, academic readings, or even science or business media reports. Analyses of grammar structures and their uses in academic text can serve as the basis and evidence for the application of construction grammar principles and techniques to teaching L2 academic writing. In addition, learners who are familiar with grammar rules, as they are traditionally taught, but have trouble with their usage in L2 writing contexts can see how traditional grammar is deployed in text.

Along these lines, noticing and awareness of collocations and constructions encountered in academic texts play a particularly important role in developing accuracy in uses of structures and noticing errors. When learners notice correct uses of grammar construction structures, they can then compare them to those they themselves produce and have an opportunity to self-correct.

Self-correction or editing are activities that focus on an analysis of errors, and this process begins with noticing (James, 1998; Schmidt, 2001). Both noticing of accurate constructions in text and self-correction have a place in practically every L2 writing class. These valuable teaching and learning activities need to be built into the curriculum at the outset because, by their very nature, they are effective if they are recursive, systematic, and purposeful. An additional consideration is that almost all learners and L2 writers expect and can greatly profit from instruction on how to make their language production more accurate.

In practically all cases, teachers have the ultimate responsibility for effective curricular and instructional decisions that can have a profound effect on students' learning. Classroom instructors are the ones who are best suited to implement appropriate, relevant, and effective instruction. They are the best judges of the applicability of particular curricular models that can be combined with other approaches to provide the greatest benefit for their students.

Language Teaching and Construction Grammar

The theoretical and practical foundations for the construction grammar approach to L2 teaching and learning lie in cognitive linguistics and construction grammar. Construction grammar is an approach to analyzing and teaching language that emerged primarily due to wide-spread disenchantment with the neglect of the quality of production in communicative teaching (see, for example, Hinkel [2003, 2006] and Widdowson [2003]).

In construction grammar, the main unit of language, both in speaking and writing, is the grammatical construction, and not incremental grammar and vocabulary elements that require rules to combine them into phrases and sentences (see chapter 7 for a discussion of collocations). Construction grammar in language teaching and learning presents "a whole unit" approach to all kinds of formulaic and conventionalized form-meaning combinations (or pairings). That is, the grammar of English is made up of various construction sets that dominate in formal academic prose—for example, phrasal verbs (e.g., *give up, give in, give out*), prepositional phrases (e.g., *in the morning, on Monday, at noon*), and collocations, which can be taught and learned as pre-fabricated expressions (e.g., Nattinger & DeCarrico, 1992; Wray, 2002; Wray & Perkins, 2000). The greatest benefit of construction grammar is that it allows language teachers to work with more efficient pathways in practical language teaching (Hinkel, 2009, 2013).

Grammar instruction that has the goal of preparing students for professional activities and academic studies in English-speaking countries needs to be designed to develop learners' practical and useful skills, directly relevant to producing written and academic text. Teaching grammar for L2 writing cannot take place in isolation from the vocabulary and discourse features of text; for example, the verb tenses in academic prose are determined by the type of context in which they are used: the present tense is useful in citations of sources but less so in descriptions of case studies (Hinkel, 2002b).

Most importantly, grammar instruction has to take place in tandem with instruction on vocabulary and academic collocations. A great deal of research has been carried out on the effectiveness of learning grammar in contextual multiword constructions (Lewis, 1993, 1997; Liu, 2011, 2012; Nattinger & DeCarrico, 1992). The goal of practice (and practice, and practice) with grammar constructions is to help learners develop **productive** fluency in academic writing and, to some degree, automaticity in generating academic prose.

In the 1980s, Cowie (1988, p. 131) analyzed a large body of authentic English data. He found that thousands of multi-word units of language (also called chunks) remain stable in form across much of their range of occurrence and that thousands of others "tolerate only minor variations," which are themselves regular and predictable in their uses (see the Appendix A of this chapter for a sample of sentence and phrase stems).

To date, a large body of research has established the fact that effective L2 writing and usage in academic and other contexts demands relatively advanced language proficiency. For this reason, applications of construction grammar models to L2 pedagogy do not need to conflict with those that have proven to be fruitful and expedient in any setting where L2 is taught and learned.

> **Talking Shop**
>
> In the past, grammar occupied a central place in language instruction, in part driven by such teaching methods as Grammar-Translation, which dominated language teaching in the 1950s and 1960s. Currently, there are relatively few teachers who are well versed in grammar teaching. Some say that many teachers cannot explain the difference between a noun and a verb (and, no, a noun is not a person, place, or thing because place (as in *here, there,* and *everywhere* can be an adverb, e.g. *in the garden, on the table*).
>
> What do you think the reasons for this development are? Do you think that practicing teachers need to have a solid grounding in grammar? Discuss your views with your colleagues and see what their experiences and opinions are.

In virtually all academic and learning contexts, however, producing reasonably fluent and accurate spoken and written L2 text requires students to attain a relatively advanced range of vocabulary and grammar features. As every L2 user knows from experience, attaining a necessary level of proficiency takes focused instruction and concerted effort from both teachers and learners. And expediting this process at least to some extent definitely couldn't hurt. Construction grammar is another tool, highly effective and efficient in many settings, that teachers can use to help students get to where they want and need to be in their language proficiency.

Construction Grammar: Foundations and Assumptions

Construction grammar is based on research in language cognition and linguistics:

- Cognitive linguistics establishes connections between sets of constructions—in the form of word and phrase strings—and thus enables a greater control of learner grammar in speech and writing. That is, when working with whole constructions, both form and function are essential—that is, morphosyntactic features of language (word forms), as well as meaning and pragmatic functions. For example, *the author of the book states that . . .* vs. *this guy in the book is talking about . . .*

- The language system and everyday language usage do not entail assembling (or building) structures, based on a myriad of rules, in the process of communication. To use an example, many tiny and medium-sized pieces of language need to be assembled in an introductory sentence string such as:

    The increasing interest in xxx has heightened the need for . . . /to . . .

    In this example, the following opportunities for language errors arise immediately. These can be errors with articles, active/passive forms of adjectives, prepositions, tenses and verb forms, noun and verb form confusion, and other errors of all sorts:

    The increasing interest in xxx has heightened the need for [noun] *. . . /to* [verb] *. . .*

    All of these opportunities for errors can be eliminated by means of an approach adopted in construction grammar (more on this below).

- Instead of assembling a great number of constructions while producing spoken or written text, construction grammar instead relies on "storing" them, as prototypical constructions (i.e., word and phrase strings with substitutable parts and deploying them as needed in context). For example:

    The author/book/article ~~ states/comments/notes/continues/observes/ points out/indicates that

- These constructions range from the highly regular and systematic to the almost completely idiomatic (e.g., collocations). For example, the uses of *little/a little, few/a few,* or *some/several* are far more regular than *an interest has arisen* or *many educators/scientists/analysts have recently turned to,* which are (almost) collocations. (These cannot be grammatically assembled from their constituent elements.)
- In construction grammar, there is no clear-cut division between regular and collocational/idiomatic expressions. That is, such thorny issues as regular, irregular, and collocational constructions can be simply taught and learned as whole units, thus skipping the entire difficult and error-prone process required for assembling them.
- Constructions can be deployed in writing, for example, as written genres require. For example, *Hey dude* vs. *Dear Dean Powells* or *the guy in the book is saying* vs. *the author states that* can be appropriate and requisite in various genres and registers (language features that impart levels formality suitable in the context) of writing, but confusing the two may not be the best way to proceed.

- Instruction in construction grammar actually teaches the forms and associated principles based on which both native and nonnative speakers can control contextually appropriate language production. That is, novice academic writers, L1 and L2 alike, have to learn these, too, in high school or college (N. Ellis, 1997).

According to Wray and Perkins (2000) and Wray (2002), in L2 teaching prefabricated chunks can and should be treated as various types of "word strings" that are to be stored and retrieved whole from memory. Many adults can recite L1 or L2 poems or texts that they learned several decades earlier, and there is little reason to doubt that L2 learners are quite capable of similar feats in their L2 production.

Action Point

As noted earlier, Nick Ellis emphasizes that novice academic writers, regardless of their first language, have to learn how to use academic grammar and language in the course of their schooling and education.

How did you learn to write formal academic prose? When did instruction in formal writing begin in your background? Was it in elementary school? In middle school? When was your first book report assigned, for example? At the university level, when does instruction in formal academic writing take place? For how long? How long might it take an L2 learner to learn to produce formal prose? What are the reasons for a dramatic disparity between the academic proficiency of L1 and L2 writers, given that both types have to learn to write formal prose?

Survey your colleagues, who may be L1 or L2 academic writers, and see if their experience with learning how to write formal academic prose is similar to yours. What are the most prominent differences between L1 and L2 writers when they are learning to produce formal prose required at the college/university level, based on the responses?

What? Memorize?

According to N. Ellis (1997, p. 129–130), pre-fab and collocational chunks can consist of entire memorized sentences or phrases that include from four to ten words, and these can allow learners to create new constructions to add to their stock of expressions. In this sense, for learners, grammatical constructions, such as commonly occurring sentences, clauses, and phrases, can be "viewed as big words" and memorized as lexicalized stems that are (almost) idiomatic (see an earlier discussion in chapter 7). Many of these pre-constructed sentences and phrases are "institutionalized" because they occur more frequently in certain types of discourse than in others (Hinkel, 2009, 2011, 2013; Nation, 2009, 2013; Pawley & Syder, 1983).

The number of such memorizable constructions and sentences is limited only by one's available time and diligence. Research has also demonstrated that memorizing long chunks of text "is at its simplest the equivalent of memorizing so many long 'words,' but only if no grammatical analysis (e.g., segmentation) is ever performed on these items, a virtual impossibility in the contexts of creative second language learning" (N. Ellis, 1997, pp. 129–130).

> **Talking Shop**
>
> Anne Peters (1983, p. 109) points out that despite the abundant linguistic and psycholinguistic evidence that memorizing language chunks represents an effective and unrestrictive means of expanding learners' vocabulary and grammatical ranges, a cultural and "pedagogical bias" exists against the idea of memorization of long chunks of text. She underscores that making substitutions within formulaic expressions is objected to "on the grounds that they are so mindless that they are ineffective in promoting second language learning."
>
> What are your views on memorization and why? What is the evidence to support them? Do you think that Peters is correct in calling out a cultural and "pedagogical bias" that typically dominates almost exclusively in English-speaking countries? In your opinion, how does "pedagogical bias" arise? Does it benefit language learners?

Key Advantages

In light of the fact that language instruction almost always takes place under great time constraints for many teachers and learners, it is important to maximize language gains and make learning as efficient as possible.

- Using language chunks in instruction and learning to write in L2 is likely to be one of the few available expedient routes to relative L2 accuracy and fluency that leads to production and subsequent automatization (Hinkel, 2004a).
- For language learners, a tremendous advantage in construction grammar lies in expedited learning and reduced work load. For example, high-frequency constructions, collocations, phrases, and expressions can be learned as whole

units, instead of just their elements that have to be further assembled during the process of language production (Hinkel, 2011, 2013).
- Differences and similarities between constructions allow learners to create new construction units in various combinations or to modify those that are already "stored away."
- For L2 learners and academic writers, common or frequently repeated problem areas, say, with articles and prepositional phrases, or sentence fragments (incomplete sentences), can also be relatively easily avoided, if these are dealt with as whole constructions, instead of being incrementally assembled.
- In language teaching, a very efficient perspective is to look at grammar and vocabulary as a continuum of constructions, from the highly systematic and regular (e.g., 3rd person singular verbs or subject-verb agreement) to the much more fixed, such as collocations or idioms (e.g., *change is in the air*, or *this evidence sheds a great deal of light on current technological advancements*).

The construction grammar approach to language teaching can be used with language elements of all shapes and sizes, from tiny bits, such as word prefixes and suffixes, to phrases to whole sentences or even sets of sentences, including the perennial areas of difficulty, such as metaphors and idioms.

Action Point

Recently, L1 student writing manuals that work exclusively with sentence and phrase templates have become extraordinarily popular (e.g., *They Say, I Say: The Moves That Matter in Academic Writing,* by Graff and Birkenstein (2014) is now in its third edition).

Do you have a mental or mnemonic list (or several lists) of words, phrases, and expressions that you use regularly in your own academic writing? When you are writing an academic paper, do you focus specifically on using academic words and expressions? Make a list of these and then organize it to classify these expressions based on some sort of principle. What principled classification do you choose for your list? By function (e.g., this expression is useful in introductions)? By parts of speech (e.g., nouns go here, and verbs go there)? What is the principle that organizes your own personal list of academic writing expressions?

Where did these lists come from? Where did you learn them? If most L1 academic writers and teachers have such lists in their minds, should L2 learners be also have them to use in learning to write in another language?

Teaching Academic Language with Prefabs

To some extent, the uses of specific language features may depend on the discipline and context in which spoken or written text is produced. Predictably, for example, business case studies, reports in biology or chemistry, or descriptions of experiments in psychology may contain a higher number of past tense verbs than a paper that discusses generally applicable observations. For example, most introductory textbooks in philosophy, sociology, economics, or biology include high numbers of present tense verbs (Hinkel, 2004b, 2011; Nation, 2013). (A relatively thorough list of prefabs for various text and discourse moves within an academic essay/paper can be found in Appendices A–F at the end of this chapter.)

Despite some amount of variation that can be identified in the linguistic features of texts across disciplines and particular academic subgenres, many researchers have identified what some call recurring features of L2 and academic register and text (Nation, 2008; Nation & Webb, 2011). Other studies of L2 and academic text have identified a range of vocabulary and grammar features that require focused instruction and concerted effort from both teachers and learners (Nation, 2009, 2013; Widdowson, 2003).

Among the most urgent language features that require persistent and intensive instruction, the following occupy a top priority. All these can be taught and learned in conjunction with the phrases and sentence stems (see Appendices A–F) where they tend to occur. These language elements include:

- The sentence structure and sentence constructing skills, and the phrase structure (Appendix A)
- Subordinate clauses for background information (e.g., *Although xxx, yyy*)
- Functions and uses of verb tenses in context and discourse (e.g., the citational present, as in *Smith (1979) stateS/findS/noteS*)
- Functions and uses of passive phrases in academic text (e.g., *this issue has been examined*) (Appendix B)
- Functions of adverbs to mark the information flow in discourse (e.g., *in addition, as a result, for this reason*)
- Functions and uses of hedging devices in academic prose (e.g., *usually/ typically, occasionally/in some cases*) (Appendix F)

(Based on Hinkel, 2002a)

Although at first glance teaching the features of academic discourse and text may seem difficult and somewhat overwhelming, the greatest advantage of such an approach is that written and academic discourse is highly formulaic and conventionalized. With the ground work in prefabs and follow-up practice, producing academic prose in both speech and writing is actually relatively easy.

 **Action Point**

When you read formal texts, such as textbooks, academic articles, or news media reports, do you notice various types of pre-fab constructions (e.g., *to be concerned about, look forward to, play an important/prominent role in, to be in the red/black,* or *more or less*) that seem to occur in practically all types of written prose? How do you know when you encounter a pre-fab? How can you tell the difference between pre-fabs and non-pre-fabs?

Locate four or five newspaper articles—these can be easily found online. Make a list of pre-fabs and count how many you can find. Is it possible to organize them in some sort of a classification by type or meaning or based on some other principle? Do you think that is possible for learners to notice and recognize pre-fabs in texts? Why or why not?

A great deal of research carried out on the effectiveness of learning grammar in contextual lexicalized chunks and sentence stems (i.e., whole sentences and phrases, and recurrent patterned expressions) has shown that these are fundamental to both L1 and L2 learning and use (Nattinger & DeCarrico, 1992). Stock grammatical and lexical chunks can become an efficient means of expanding L2 learners' language range, particularly when they are also taught how to substitute discrete elements appropriately and in practical ways. For example, the fact that the function of noun clauses is similar to that of simple nouns can be addressed by means of substitutions in patterned expressions common in academic prose:

> The experiment/data/study shows that xxx increases (with yyy)/an increase of xxx/the growth/rise of xxx.

Heightening learners' awareness of the structure of complete sentences in academic prose (as opposed to fragments), as well as important distinctions between conversational and casual register and academic (formal) written register, should represent ongoing instructional objectives at all levels of proficiency. In grammar learning, becoming aware of how structures are used, combined with explicit teaching, can provide an additional benefit because learners can notice structures that otherwise they may simply miss.

For a vast majority of L2 learners, the task of becoming proficient users of L2 academic vocabulary may not be attainable within the time commonly considered reasonable for the completion of their academic preparatory studies. A more reasonable and attainable goal in increasing the vocabulary range in students' L2 writing is to work with vocabulary substitutions (discussed in chapter 7) that learners can use in constructing texts in most writing tasks across all disciplines.

For example, the number of reporting verbs that can be employed to mark paraphrases is around a dozen, and they can be learned with relative ease while working on a writing assignment (e.g., *the author says, states, indicates, comments, notes, observes, believes, points out, emphasizes, advocates, reports, concludes, underscores, mentions, finds*, not to mention phrases with similar textual functions, such as *according to the author, as the author states/indicates, in the author's view/opinion/understanding*, or *as noted/stated/mentioned*).

> **Talking Shop**
>
> A considerable language proficiency is required to produce competent L2 academic writing. Learning another language for many years represents a virtually universal characteristic of schooling and education in most countries around the world. Yet, upon completion of their language learning programs, comparatively few individuals actually attain the language proficiency and language skills needed to produce an academic essay or paper in their L2s. Why do you think this is?
>
> What is your L2? Can you engage in an L2 conversation on the street or with your neighbor? Read and understand an L2 newspaper or a textbook? Write a letter? Can you write an L2 academic assignment? What are the differences in language proficiency and skills required to accomplish these tasks? Discuss your views with your colleagues and see what their experiences and opinions are.

Noticing and Analyzing Academic Texts

One of the greatest advantages of teaching learners to notice and analyze grammar constructions and collocations as they occur in academic texts is that these instructional activities are very flexible and customizable. The analysis of grammar structures in texts focuses on <u>form-meaning-function</u> connections in written prose and the writer's reasons for using particular constructions. The teacher can select specific texts assigned for analysis and examine the types of structures, phrases, and systems that are prevalent and those that can be fruitful for learners (Frodesen, 2014). In this way, students can be made responsible for their own learning, and this is also an ongoing curriculum objective.

> The curricular objective of noticing instruction and text examinations, as well as purposeful, focused, and recursive explanations and real text illustrations, is to develop learners' essential awareness of common grammatical features.

The complexity of constructions for analysis can vary depending on learners' proficiency levels and the degree of structure difficulty. For example, for intermediate learners, noticing how simple and compound sentences are constructed is a suitable practice, and for advanced learners, noticing the construction of subordinate clauses can prove to be helpful in the long run.

In addition to the variations in the degree of difficulty of constructions and phrases, the complexity, levels, and subject matter of texts selected for analysis can also play an important role in tailoring instruction depending on learning objectives and learners' proficiency. For instance, authentic academic texts may not be appropriate for beginning or intermediate students, but could be a good fit for those at advanced levels.

An excellent venue for such analytical activities at any proficiency level may be to collect scaled and graded assignments produced by real students (authors' permissions must be obtained in advance) to demonstrate and analyze. In selecting the text for noticing and text-analysis activities, it is important for the teacher to work with the examples of writing that are typically expected of the learners and to take into account the grammar features that are specific to these types of writing.

For example, the teacher explains that single-word modifiers, such as nouns or adjectives precede the noun that they modify (describe) even when several are listed in a succession (e.g., *a small animal, a large human population, summer annual plant*). However, modifying phrases follow the noun or the noun phrase that they modify (e.g., *Rice is an annual plant usually cultivated in flooded and irrigated fields*).

Action Point

Most L2 writers, including advanced writers, continue to have problems with quantifiers, such as *little/a little, few/a few, much/many, some/several,* or *amount/number* that hinge on whether they are used with count or uncountable nouns (*book—books, computer—computers* vs. *rice, knowledge, information*). There are a number of highly frequent and seemingly simple structures that continue to be problematic for a majority of L2 users and writers at all levels of proficiency.

Your task is to make a noticing lesson that is based on text analysis to explain and illustrate the accurate usage of quantifiers (or any other similar structures) that require a great deal of repeated teaching and learning. To accomplish this task, select a set of text examples for each quantifier and prepare an explanation of how and when these are used and what the distinctions between them are. Text-based examples of these structures are easy to locate online because they are extraordinarily frequent and occur in all manner of formal written prose, such as news media reports, blogs, or articles.

Your examples and explanations have to be as clear and comprehensible as possible. They also have to be thoroughly and carefully illustrated to make the distinctions between these constructions unambiguous.

There are many other, similarly problematic, constructions:

- Nouns as modifiers of other nouns (also called compound nouns), e.g., *rice field, vegetable soup, university instructor,* or *vocabulary list* where the first noun modifies the second one, but definitely not **nation flag, *wood pencil, *culture norm, *economy data, *three-credits-hour course,* a **20-years-old student.*
- Many academic countable nouns, such as *business, development, difficulty, failure, industry, injustice, structure, technology, truth,* have different meanings in singular or plural forms. When used in the singular, they refer to concepts or whole notions; when used in the plural, they refer to specific instances, types, kinds, and occurrences of these notions. The singular form *technology* refers to all types of *technology* as a concept, but the plural *technologies* to various types/subsets of *technology,* such as computer, automotive, or telecommunication.

Teaching and Learning How to Notice and Analyze Grammar Features

Noticing and text-based instructional activities can be profitable for learners even at the middle school level of instruction. The possibilities are endless, including:

- Grammar features characteristic of simplified or authentic academic texts
- The text and grammatical features of model paragraphs and whole essays
- Grammar structures in the written assignments of beginners or advanced students
- Grammar elements typical of student assignments in language classes or in the disciplines, such as the humanities, business, or social sciences
- Specific kinds of more or less grave errors (more on this below)
- Examples of consistent and ubiquitous grammar (or discourse) problems in L2 writing

Text analysis activities and practice can focus on one or two constructions at a time. In the course of learning, the range and type of such language examinations can result in a substantial exposure to academic grammar constructions and collocations and thus help achieve teaching and learning objectives. Systematic noticing and text-based practice can also allow learners build up their own lists of common and useful constructions, sentence stems, phrases, and idiomatic expressions.

The following factors should be taken into account when the teacher chooses the structures for noticing and classroom text analysis (Frodesen, 2014):

- The level of structure difficulty needs to be suitable for the students' language proficiency; for example, advanced structures, say, noun clauses or complex passives, are not a good fit for beginners or low-intermediate learners.
- Grammar structures should be selected to be relevant to students' actual writing tasks and based on real language needs for academic writing; that is, the connections between noticing and text analysis instruction have to be direct and clear.
- Students should have immediate and numerous opportunities to practice the structures in their writing.
- Text analysis and examinations should be as clear, concise, and self-evident, as much as possible.
- Modifying text by means of a variety of fonts and font sizes, underlining, and using other means of making the grammar point easy to grasp is of the essence.

When students read, they can be assigned to notice and write down the structures of the types that are analyzed in class ongoing throughout the course. Over time, the range and type of the structures on their noticing agenda will continue to grow. A sample of such a cumulative list can include, for example, quantifiers with adjective and noun modifiers, the order of adjectives in an adjective phrase, sentence constructions, as well as the uses of modal verbs and hedging devices.

For example, at the high intermediate and/or advanced levels, grammar teaching can focus on constructions typically found in introductory academic textbooks (e.g., history texts heavily rely on the use of the past tense, and economics and sociology books can be practical in instruction on the present tense and uses of the passive voice). At higher proficiency levels, noticing and text-based instruction can also highlight the effects of grammatical features on discourse and text (e.g., tense uses in generalizations and contextual tense shifts). In addition, the discourse functions of referential pronouns (*this, that,* and *the other*) and impersonal pronouns (*it is clear/evident/seems that/stands to reason*), the hedging functions of modal verbs (*it might be possible/the price of dollar may rise/economists can adjust the rates*), and parallel phrase constructions (*the author and the reader*), found in abundance in practically all academic prose, can be noticed, analyzed, and practiced (notice that this sentence also contains a parallel structure).

Contextual tense and time shifts represent an excellent example of noticing and analyzing how various English tenses are used in real life and in constructing academic prose. Many L2 writers have trouble figuring out the connections between tenses and time, and when tense shifts occur or do not occur in context. In written text in English, the uses of the present tense or the past tense (and the tense system in general) provide an important means of textual cohesion.

The uses of the present and the past tenses in academic writing are highly conventionalized. However, fortunately, it is relatively easy to teach students to avoid and correct them. In L2 academic writing, tenses are often employed inconsistently based on L2 writers' logical analyses of the organization of events along the time continuum instead of following the conventions of tense use. For example, the past tense may be used in contexts specifically marked by past-time adverbs or references (e.g., *during the previous year, last quarter,* or *in 2014*).

In contexts that are not overtly marked for the past, the uses of the "academic" present tense can be appropriate and even advisable. For example, Smith and Robinson (1995) and Peterson (1996) <u>remind</u> us that the role of the individual in society <u>continues</u> to change over time. They <u>argue</u> that historical events <u>are grounded</u> in how members of the society <u>value</u> their contribution to social processes.

Once the reasons for contextual tense shifts and overtly marked time frames are identified, the learners can begin the analysis. Initially, they can examine a text passage with the verbs marked (or underlined) and explain why a particular tense is used (e.g., to refer to concepts that are generally true).

The uses of time adverbs and other contextual time markers can also be noted because these language elements determine the contextual time frame. Subsequently, learners can practice with texts and in contexts in which verb tenses are unmarked, or they can write short assignments to practice the uses of the "academic" present (or specific examples from the past, such as case studies or historical events).

Action Point

McCarthy and Carter (1994, p. 100) refer to what they call "the historical present," which is very common in academic texts and discourse. The uses of the historical present tense are considered to be practical and appropriate in a range of contexts, such as introductions and citations from sources, to indicate "the 'now-relevance'" (p. 102) of research and information.

Take a brief look at any academic text (e.g., a textbook or an article). Which tense dominates in this small sample of academic prose? What are the contexts in which the present tense or the past tense verbs can be found? How are these tenses marked? Make a quick list of such contexts. In your view, would similar text analyses be helpful for teaching? Would such practice lead to improved noticing skills?

Recognizing grammatical and lexical (vocabulary and meaning) __cohesive links and ties__ is another type of very useful and productive text practice. Students can be assigned to read texts of various lengths from published sources. These can be as short as one or two paragraphs or as long as several pages. (Longer texts and cohesive tie assignments can be done outside of class as homework.)

The texts can be selected from newspapers for intermediate level students, Internet news reports or society/human interest stories, or introductory university-level textbooks. Examinations of cohesive chains can focus on easily accessible language features such as personal pronouns, demonstrative pronouns (*this, that, these, those*), sentence transitions/connectors, and lexical cohesion.

The analysis of text begins with identifying and marking as many cohesive and lexical ties (as well as lexical substitutions, discussed in chapter 7) as possible. In addition, examinations of texts can also address grammar constructions that have similar meanings or locate the structures that link known/old and new information. Following the teacher-guided early practice, L2 writers can analyze texts independently.

This type of practice focuses students' attention to how text cohesion is established and maintained by means of pronouns, phrase and meaning repetition, or the uses of the passive voice. In practically all texts, several cohesive ties and chains are at play at the same time, and learners can use a numbering system to mark them. The following example illustrates this type of text analysis and noticing practice.

In this excerpt, the cohesive chain is relatively easy to identify, and several cohesive chains are developed simultaneously without interfering with one another. Cohesive Chain [1] connects the occurrences of *market(s)*. Buyers, buy, and *buying* are linked by chain [2]. Cohesive connection [3] begins with *sellers* and moves to sales. Line [4] connects *prices*. Chain [5] joins the words and phrases associated with times and places of buying and selling.

> Markets[1] can take many forms. Some markets[1] are highly organized, such as the markets[1] for agricultural commodities. In these markets[1], buyers[2] and sellers[3] meet at a *specific time and* place[5], where prices[4] are set and sales[3] are arranged.
>
> More often, markets[1] are less organized, for example, an ice cream market[1] in a small town. Buyers[2] of ice cream do not *meet together*[5] at any particular time. Sellers[3] of ice-cream are in *different locations*[5] and offer somewhat different products. The prices[4] of ice cream are not set and sales[3] are not arranged. Each seller[3] posts a price[4] for an ice cream cone, and each buyer[2] decides how much ice cream to buy[2] at each store[5]. (Based on Mankiw, 2014).

An analysis of texts from introductory textbooks, such as the one above, can become an excellent means of focusing on how cohesive ties and chains are created in academic prose for L2 writers at intermediate or higher levels of proficiency. Repetition and lexical (vocabulary and meaning) ties are relatively easy to notice and identify.

The greatest benefit of analyzing texts and teaching learners to notice the cohesive elements lies in the importance of making vocabulary and grammatical choices in context. For instance, in practically all academic writing, as in the example above, the known/old information is placed at the beginning of the sentence, and the new information closer to the end. It is important for L2 writers to notice and recognize that constructing academic texts in this way is likely to result in more cohesive and coherent prose overall.

> **Talking Shop**
>
> In general, text analysis and noticing practice have taken a back seat to other types of instruction on L2 writing. Despite the fact that numerous researchers and methodologists (e.g., Marianne Celce-Murcia, Rod Ellis, Nick Ellis, Richard Schmidt, and Sandra Fotos) have strongly advocated in favor of text-based and context-based teaching of L2 writing for many decades, it has not been implemented to its full potential.
>
> What do you think the reasons may be for the fact that text and discourse analyses are not as common as they should be? Discuss your views with your colleagues and see what their experiences and opinions are.

A Few Considerations for Teaching Noticing and Text Analysis

Effective noticing is of the essence of when learning to write formal academic prose. To learn different meanings that words and constructions may have in different contexts, learners need to pay attention to textual features as they read or write.

The greatest issue with learning to notice words and grammar in context is that, first, learners need to know what specific text features they should notice and, second, they must consider what about these features requires attention.

The teacher's job is to guide learners and point out the important and necessary vocabulary and grammar constructions and then to discuss their uses and meanings in the academic text. Nation (2013) comments that a discussion of vocabulary items subsequent to noticing represents a highly productive way to learn new words in reading.

Noticing forms of words and structures can take place while students listen and read, participate in activities, or even look for synonyms. To notice uses, meanings, and functions of words and grammar constructions, learners need to be aware of language as a complex system. Noticing and identifying the functions of words and structures is a slow and laborious process that affects a student's reading and writing speed. In the case of reading, analyzing the text and its features takes away some of the enjoyment of reading because it removes attention from the context and ideas to focus it on language elements.

In grammar learning, becoming aware of how structures are used, combined with explicit teaching, can provide an additional benefit because learners can notice structures that otherwise they may simply miss (R. Ellis, 1997). According to R. Ellis (1990), noticing and awareness play a particularly prominent role in developing accuracy in uses of structures and noticing errors. If learners notice correct uses of structures, they can then compare them to those they themselves produce and self-correct. Self-correction or editing are activities that undertake an analysis of errors that begin with noticing (James, 1998). It may be unreasonable to expect that L2 learners will be able to figure out the systematic intricacies that govern, for example, subject-verb agreement on their own; however, noticing combined with an explanation consistently helps L2 writers improve their skills.

> **Talking Shop**
>
> Research has demonstrated convincingly that success in academic vocabulary learning crucially depends on exposure to appropriate-level academic texts with conscious noticing of how various words are used (e.g., such nouns as *triangle, traffic, tradition,* and *topic* can be accessible even to beginners). Nonetheless, many teachers believe that noticing instruction and text analysis are less effective than they actually are.
>
> What do you think the reasons may be for such a disparity between research findings and teachers' beliefs? What are your views on the effectiveness of teaching noticing and text analysis in L2 writing instruction? Discuss your views with your colleagues and see what their experiences and opinions are.

Initially, with the teacher's guidance, learners need to be engaged in active noticing, developing noticing skills, and learning. In noticing instruction, explicit teaching of vocabulary and grammar plays a crucial role. In addition to tense shifts and cohesive ties, grammar constructions that are essential in L2 academic writing relatively easily lend themselves to text analysis and examination. This type of practice promotes learning in context and noticing, and it can include a large number of features, such as, for example:

- Complex noun phrases (*the farm production market, buyers' and sellers tax burden, miraculous health benefits of milk, a compensating differential for the cost of becoming educated*)
- Hedging and hedges (*in general, usually, somewhat, in this regard, a great deal, some number, on occasion, once in a while*)
- Parallel structures (*skilled and unskilled labor, a beach-badge checker and a garbage collector, highly educated workers and less educated workers*)
- Punctuation (xxx and yyy, as in *this, that, the other, and everything else*)
- Sentence combining (*We discussed this in an earlier chapter. The word "capital" refers to the economy's stock of equipment and structures → As we discussed in an earlier chapter, the word "capital" refers to . . .*)
- Giving examples (*when the price of milk rises, some farmers may switch to milk from other products, for example*)

All these are required for building academic prose, and it may be difficult, if not impossible, for L2 writers to notice, identify, and analyze these on their own.

Error Correction and Teaching Editing

Grammar errors are a fact of life in any L2 course, and a great deal of literature published in the past half century has dealt with research on the effectiveness—or a lack of it—of grammar correction. According to Leki, Cumming, and Silva (2008), by the mid-2000s, 68 research reports had been published on a large number of error properties in L2 writing.

 **Talking Shop**

In your view, what could be the reasons for a proliferation of research reports on errors in L2 writing? Do you think it is possible to determine that some construction is used incorrectly in all cases?

What could be the difference between what is sometimes called an "awkward" and an erroneous construction? How can a researcher be certain that he or she identifies "an error" appropriately? What could some safeguards be to make certain that a construction is erroneous, rather than "awkward"?

Currently the facts and findings of various research reports on which errors to correct, how to correct them, when, and with what frequency have led to conclusions that are somewhat mixed. Nonetheless, studies of L2 writers and learners have indicated clearly that students expect, value, and can benefit from work on improving grammatical accuracy in their writing.

> One of the most important facets of effective and productive error correction is that it has to be directly relevant, timely, and applicable to students' own writing.

As was discussed in chapter 4, not all L2 writing errors are created equal. They vary greatly in terms of their gravity, frequency, type, context, or effects on text intelligibility or the reader. However, at present, much is known about the common and recurrent types of grammatical problems that can benefit from attention and persistent instruction.

Generally speaking, a curricular view of work on L2 grammar errors can be two-fold (Frodesen, 2014):

- Correcting and responding to errors that are encountered in writing—a reactive focus
- Research-based targeting of common errors that are typical of much L2 writing—a proactive focus

Typically, a combination of both is most effective and productive from a curricular standpoint.

The most serious grammar errors are ubiquitous in L2 writing. These should be included as curricular foci in teaching reactively and proactively in most instruction and throughout the course (Frodesen, 2014; Hinkel, 2005, 2013):

- Verb tenses
- Word order
- Word morphology (word form)
- *It*-deletion in cleft constructions
- Relative (adjective) clauses
- Subject-verb agreement (including noun number and countability)

Teaching L2 writers how to pay attention to errors, along with self-editing and self-correction strategies, are valuable components of a curriculum that can serve L2 writers well in the long run. Expectations of grammatical accuracy in writing represent an indelible part of schooling and education at practically all levels, as well as a necessary quality of effective written communication.

However, as every L2 writer knows from experience, learning to edit one's own text and identify mistakes is notoriously difficult. For this reason, instruction in self-correction and editing has to be deliberate, careful, systematic, and judicious (Ferris, 2003, 2004; Ferris & Hedgcock, 2005).

> The curricular objective of error correction and teaching self-editing is to enable L2 learners become independent writers.

In practically all cases of editing instruction, students' proficiency levels and curricular objectives determine the types of errors to select for ongoing attention, work, and teaching activities.

> Explanations of how particular structures can be used correctly in context and typical errors that occur with these structures may need to be persistent and iterative (repeated) to be effective.

As was noted in chapter 7, the fact that something is taught does not mean that it is learned.

Action Point

Locate, identify, and classify by type all the errors you can in the following excerpt from a student assignment.

***Nowaday, there're many developments day by day. And news spread all over the world even in less time than 24 hours because of the convenient of Internet. So when some one makes a invention or discovering something new, everyone should consider him as the first and refer to him while use his result after that. Especially in science and engineering fields, many people tries to deal similar problems at the same time. When one of them make a progress and declear that again. This consider as a kind of competition.

In order to prevent plagiarism ideas from occuring, we should protect one's work in law. In this way, people will be encourage to do something new and be the first. In the past, academic paper and work might not be spread as easy as it is today. I find it hard to look for some papers before 1990. More people in the world can access the Internet than before. Many people can check their email and search the informations they want to know due to the information technology. Furthermore, many people believe they the easy access to the Internet can reduce the information gap among people.

Discuss your findings with your colleagues and see whether their findings and classifications are similar.

Teaching learners to self-edit is a gradual process that proceeds in stages that build on one another.

1. To begin, students should be taught to notice common and serious errors. Text analysis activities, similar to those discussed earlier in this chapter, can lead to L2 writers' error awareness. Initial editing practice can take the form of modified learners' texts that contain limited and controlled types of errors that are not the students' own.
2. A reasonable and manageable initial stage of self-editing training should focus on two to three types of errors, depending on their complexity. For example, these can be countable and uncountable nouns, singular and plural noun choices, simple present and simple past tenses, or stative verbs (those that are not used in progressive tenses, e.g., *contain, consist, hear, know, realize, remember, understand*).
3. As a matter of routine, the teacher should begin collecting various common and frequent errors types from student writing. These can be used as examples for instruction and practice. Identifying and correcting similar errors can become an excellent exercise for pair- and small-group work. Additional analyses and activities for the similar types of errors can be assigned as homework and followed up by discussion.
4. It is important that impersonal error correction and editing of texts be made directly connected and immediately relevant to students' own errors in writing. Most teachers usually note the specific structures or errors that require additional attention when they read, mark, and grade students' written assignments.
5. Students' editing of their own errors can begin simultaneously with text analysis and editing practice. Ideally, the types of errors in the analyses and practice should match those addressed in the teacher's marking and correction of students' work.

At advanced levels of proficiency and closer to the completion of the course, a single and final draft of writing assignments may be evaluated and graded, similar to assignment grading in mainstream courses. While marking student writing, the teacher can gradually increase writers' responsibility for the quality of their writing throughout the course. In many cases, significant instructional and learning benefits can be obtained when students are required to pay close attention to grammatical accuracy in their prose.

Action Point

A sample text for a noticing and analysis activity is presented below. Explain to your colleagues the uses, regularities, and caveats of the underlined constructions as simply and briefly as you can.

> *The Internet is a world-wide system of interconnected computer networks. It carries an a great deal of information and a large number of services, such as those that support email and send files. The Internet continues to grow due to greater amounts of online information and knowledge, commerce, and entertainment. During the late 1990s, it was estimated that traffic on the Internet grew by 100 percent per year, while the mean annual growth in the number of users was thought to be between 20% and 50%.* (Based on http://en.wikipedia.org/wiki/Internet).
>
> Make detailed notes of your explanation of the constructions used in the passage. If you had to do it again, how could you improve your presentation in the future?

Strategy Training for Self-Editing and Building Independence

The following is an example for teaching self-editing and error awareness skills:

1. Initially, the teacher should correct all errors of two or three types after they are analyzed and discussed in class.
2. In subsequent writing, the teacher highlights all remaining errors of these types and corrects many.
3. Then the instructor should correct only some errors of these early types and underline/circle other errors of these same types. Explicit and possibly written instructions need to be provided that the writer needs to correct the underlined structures.
4. Later in the course, the instructor should correct only the most complex occurrences of these types of errors. In this way, the responsibility for the rest—and simpler errors—needs to be shifted to the L2 writer.
5. It is vital, however, that the first two or three error types not be neglected when editing practice on the second set of errors types begins. Rather, students' awareness of and learning to correct errors of the earlier types has to be cumulative, repeated, and persistent.
6. When the analyses and discussion on the second types of errors begin, the teacher should not correct the errors from the first group (except in rare cases of complex constructions) but underline or highlight them in student writing, as they occur. These corrections should be limited to the second group of error types. The responsibility for correcting the first types of errors is now fully shifted to the writer.
7. When correcting earlier types of errors is fully a student's responsibility, the analysis and discussion of errors for self-editing can move on to the next group of two or three error types.

And then the cycle is repeated.

Throughout the course, it is very important that the teacher be consistent in correcting, underlining/highlighting, and shifting the responsibility for editing errors to students. By the end of the course, it is reasonable to expect students to notice and correct 15 to 20 common types of errors in their own writing.

A few examples of work on specific error types can include initially those that are with the easiest to deal with and most accessible.

The Essentials and the Basics

These language elements must be learned and used correctly by the end of the course:

- Common and required academic uncountable nouns, e.g., *advice, education, equipment, information, knowledge*
- Irregular plural forms of a few common academic nouns (focus on academic vocabulary) e.g., *criterion—criteria, phenomenon—phenomena; medium—media; analysis—analyses, basis—bases, hypothesis—hypotheses* (see the University Word List, chapter 7)
- Common and basic quantifiers, e.g., *few/a few, little/a little*; subject noun phrases with quantifiers and verb agreement, e.g., *some/many books* + plural verb or *some/much information* + singular verb
- Subject noun + prepositional phrase and verb agreement, e.g., *The stock market with its aggregation of buyers and sellers fluctuateS daily* vs. *The stock market and prices fluctuate⌀ daily*
- Compound noun phrases, e.g., *(a) five-credit-hour university biology course(s), (a) twenty-five-year old student(s)* vs. *the student is twenty five years old*

Slightly Beyond the Basics

- Word order in noun and adjective clauses, e.g., *The authors state that they know which way the wind is blowing; It is not clear whether the price will rise; The lab where the research takes place is located in Pennsylvania.*
    - Also, word order in *how*-noun clauses, e.g., *The scientists described how they identified the virus; The scale was used to measure how much the minerals weighed.*
- Word order with adverbs of manner, time, and indefinite frequency, e.g., *Stock market buyers need to consider the prices carefully; Typically, large companies (typically) have their stocks listed on many exchanges across the world.*
- The placement of *even* and *also*, e.g., (*Also*—a sentence transition function) *Share prices even/also* (verb modifier) *affect the wealth of households and their consumption;* (*Also/Even*) *The wealth of the households was even/also affected by share prices; Share prices affect the wealth of households and their consumption also in the current market.*

- The placement and uses of *enough*, e.g., *high enough, enough time/funds, enough of that/them, enough to complete the experiment;* optional: the placement and uses of *almost, almost + enough*, e.g., *almost + enough time/funds; almost never, almost the same, almost finished/the tallest, almost + every* (+ noun)
- Quantifiers with prepositional phrases, e.g., *some/many/most managers* vs. *some/many/most <u>of the</u> managers <u>in the accounting department</u>; most* as an adverb, e.g., *the stock price of dot-coms grew <u>the most</u> in 1999.*

The examples of the structures above are very common and highly error-prone (it's not hard to understand why) in student academic writing. Addressing them proactively (and repeatedly) in text analysis and discussion may be highly advisable and relatively easy to do. In addition, L2 writers need to pay close attention to the occurrences of these constructions while writing.

Talking Shop

In your opinion, what does the term "conventionalized uses" mean when it comes to the uses of English tenses in formal academic writing? Can you think of other conventionalized constructions in academic text? Do textual conventions exist in written genres other than the academic? Can you think of a few examples?

Action Point

All sentences below contain at least one error. Please correct the errors and develop specific rules that can be followed to avoid making such errors in the future. What types of errors have you noticed in these sentences? How many?

1. *A few research has showed that there is many difference between younger and older learners.*
2. *The Internet Generation spend much times to surf the web and watching television and play video games.*
3. *The decreased percentage of literary readers felt by 15 points. It is hardly able to say that there is a clear relationship between decreasing readers and Internet.*
4. *Getting educations is a part of growing up in age of informations and many knowledges.*
5. *For our ancestors, distance is the biggest problem for communication, and for us, high-tech has solved the problems of distance.*

6. It is not appropriate for the student just complained about her teacher through email because email cause misunderstanding. I also face miscommunication with my advisor several times.
7. Love is the basic part of the word and humankinds has no exception. Everyone likes to be love and needs love.
8. In eastern world, there are larger portions of people don't know how to express their love by word, though one understands himself that is falling in love.
9. There are many ways provided by the university to help students with financial aids, but sometime the benefit is little.
10. As the society develops, the competitive is getting more fierce, especially the technology is high development, most works can be finished by the machine.

Most L2 writers may not be able to notice, identify, and correct all errors covered in the instruction no matter how much effort and time during one or two L2 writing courses is devoted to the task. Teaching learners to edit their writing independently does not have the goal of making their writing error-free (nor could it). It is crucial that both teachers and students set realistic learning goals and have reasonable expectations of noticeable improvement in students' grammatical accuracy.

> The purpose of self-editing instruction and error correction is not the elimination of errors, but error reduction and improvement.

The goal of error analysis, discussion, and learning practice—and self-editing training—is to provide L2 writers with the skills needed to reduce the number and frequency of the most egregious error types in their academic prose.

> A key to effective and productive teaching of self-editing skills is to hold students responsible for correcting their errors and editing their texts.

Chapter Summary

In the context of applications of construction grammar to teaching L2 academic writing, research has shown that making use of formulaic expressions and memorizing long chunks of text (and making substitutions within them) is far more efficient and effective than learning to assemble new linguistic strings in the process of language production.

Construction grammar is an approach to analyzing and teaching language in which the main unit of language is the grammatical construction, and not incremental grammar and vocabulary elements that require rules to combine them into phrases and sentences. Construction grammar in language teaching and learning presents "a whole unit" approach to all kinds of formulaic and conventionalized form-meaning combinations. The greatest benefit of construction grammar is that it allows language teachers to work with more efficient pathways in practical language teaching.

A grammar curriculum for L2 writing at any proficiency level, beginning with the intermediate, needs to include ongoing and persistent noticing activities. These typically include examinations and analyses of constructions and grammar features in formal written prose (e.g., textbooks and academic readings). Noticing and awareness of collocations and constructions encountered in academic texts play a particularly important role in developing accuracy in uses of structures and noticing errors.

Self-correction and editing are activities that focus on an analysis of errors, and this process begins with noticing how constructions are used accurately in formal texts. Both noticing of accurate constructions in text and self-correction have a place in practically every L2 writing class.

Teaching L2 writers how to pay attention to errors and providing self-editing and self-correction strategies are valuable components of a curriculum that can serve L2 writers well in the long run. Teaching learners to self-edit is a gradual process that proceeds in stages, which build on one another.

While marking student writing, the teacher can gradually increase writers' responsibility for the quality of their writing throughout the course. For many learners, significant instructional and learning benefits can be obtained when students are required to pay close attention to grammatical accuracy in their prose. Expectations of grammatical accuracy in writing represents a critical part of schooling and education at practically all levels, as well as a necessary quality of effective written communication.

Further Reading

Celce-Murcia, M. (1991). Discourse analysis and grammar instruction. *Annual Review of Applied Linguistics, 11,* 135–151.

Celce-Murcia, M. (1991). Grammar pedagogy in second and foreign language teaching. *TESOL Quarterly, 25,* 459–480.

Celce-Murcia, M. (2002). Why it makes sense to teach grammar in context and through discourse. In E. Hinkel & S. Fotos (Eds.), *New perspectives on grammar teaching in second language classrooms* (pp. 119–134). Mahwah, NJ: Lawrence Erlbaum Associates.

Ellis, R. (2002). The place of grammar instruction in the second/foreign language curriculum. In E. Hinkel & S. Fotos (Eds.), *New perspectives on grammar teaching in second language classrooms* (pp. 17–35). Mahwah, NJ: Lawrence Erlbaum Associates.

Ellis, R. (2006). Current issues in the teaching of grammar: An SLA perspective. *TESOL Quarterly, 40*(1), 83–107.
Frodesen, J. (2014). Grammar in second language writing. In M. Celce-Murcia, D. Brinton, & M. Snow (Eds.), *Teaching English as a second or foreign language* (4th ed., pp. 238–255). Boston, MA: National Geographic Learning/Cengage Learning.
Hinkel, E., & Fotos, S. (Eds.). (2002). *New perspectives on grammar teaching in second language classrooms.* Mahwah, NJ: Lawrence Erlbaum Associates.
Larsen-Freeman, D. (2002). The grammar of choice. In E. Hinkel & S. Fotos (Eds.), *New perspectives on grammar teaching in second and foreign language classrooms* (pp. 103–118). Mahwah, NJ: Lawrence Erlbaum Associates.
Weaver, C. (Ed.). (1998). *Lessons to share: On teaching grammar in context.* Portsmouth, NH: Boynton/Cook.
Yule, G. (1998). *Explaining English grammar.* Oxford: Oxford University Press.

References

Biber, D., Johansson, S., Leech, G., Conrad, S., & Finegan, E. (1999). *Longman grammar of spoken and written English.* Harlow, Essex: Pearson.
Cowie, A. P. (1988). Stable and creative aspects of vocabulary use. In R. Carter & M. McCarthy (Eds.), *Vocabulary and language teaching* (pp. 126–137). Harlow: Longman.
Ellis, N. (1997). Vocabulary acquisition: Word structure, collocation, word-class, and meaning. In N. Schmitt & M. McCarthy (Eds.), *Vocabulary: Description, acquisition, and pedagogy* (pp. 122–139). Cambridge: Cambridge University Press.
Ellis, R. (1990). *Instructed second language acquisition.* Cambridge, MA: Blackwell.
Ellis, R. (1997). *SLA research and language teaching.* Oxford, UK: Oxford University Press.
Ferris, D. (2003). *Response to student writing: Implications for second language students.* New York: Routledge.
Ferris, D. (2004). The grammar correction debate in L2 writing: Where are we, and where do we go from here? (and what do we do in the meantime . . .?) *Journal of Second Language Writing, 13*(1), 49–62.
Ferris, D., & Hedgcock, J. (2005). *Teaching ESL composition* (2nd ed.). Mahwah, NJ: Lawrence Erlbaum Associates.
Frodesen, J. (2014). Grammar in second language writing. In M. Celce-Murcia, D. Brinton, & M. Snow (Eds.), *Teaching English as a second or foreign language* (4th ed., pp. 238–255). Boston, MA: National Geographic Learning/Cengage Learning.
Graff, G., & Birkenstein, C. (2014). *They say, I say: Moves that matter in academic writing* (3rd ed.). London: Norton.
Hinkel, E. (2002a). *Second language writers' text.* Mahwah, NJ: Lawrence Erlbaum Associates.
Hinkel, E. (2002b). Teaching grammar in writing classes: Tenses and cohesion. In E. Hinkel & S. Fotos (Eds.), *New perspectives on grammar teaching in second language classrooms* (pp. 181–198). Mahwah, NJ: Lawrence Erlbaum Associates.
Hinkel, E. (2003). Simplicity without elegance: Features of sentences in L2 and L1 academic texts. *TESOL Quarterly, 37,* 275–301.
Hinkel, E. (2004a). *Teaching academic ESL writing: Practical techniques in vocabulary and grammar.* Mahwah, NJ: Lawrence Erlbaum Associates.
Hinkel, E. (2004b). Tense, aspect, and the passive voice in L1 and L2 writing. *Language Teaching Research, 8,* 5–29.

Hinkel, E. (2005). Analyses of L2 text and what can be learned from them. In E. Hinkel (Ed.), *Handbook of research in second language teaching and learning* (pp. 615–628). Mahwah, NJ: Lawrence Erlbaum Associates.

Hinkel, E. (2006). Current perspectives on teaching the four skills. *TESOL Quarterly, 40*(1), 109–131.

Hinkel, E. (2009). The effect of essay prompts and topics on the uses of modal verbs in L1 and L2 academic writing. *Journal of Pragmatics, 41*(4), 667–683.

Hinkel, E. (2011). What research on second language writing tells us and what it doesn't. In E. Hinkel (Ed.), *Handbook of research in second language teaching and learning* (Vol. 2, pp. 523–538). New York: Routledge.

Hinkel, E. (2013). Research findings on teaching grammar for academic writing. *English Teaching, 68*(4), 3–21.

James, C. (1998). *Errors in language learning and use.* London: Longman.

Leki, I., Cumming, A., & Silva, T. (2008). *A synthesis of research on second language writing in English.* New York: Routledge.

Lewis, M. (1993). *The lexical approach.* Hove, UK: LTP.

Lewis, M. (1997). Pedagogical implications of the lexical approach. In J. Coady & T. Huckin (Eds.), *Second language vocabulary acquisition: A rationale for pedagogy* (pp. 255–270). Cambridge: Cambridge University Press.

Liu, D. (2011). The most-frequently used English phrasal verbs in American and British English: A multi-corpus examination. *TESOL Quarterly, 45,* 661–688.

Liu, D. (2012). The most frequently-used multi-word constructions in academic written English: A multi-corpus study. *English for Specific Purposes, 31,* 25–35.

Mankiw, N. G. (2014). *Principles of macroeconomics* (7th ed.). Boston: Cengage Learning.

McCarthy, M., & Carter, R. (1994). *Language as discourse.* London: Longman.

Nation, I. S. P. (1990). *Teaching and learning vocabulary.* New York: Newbury House.

Nation, I. S. P. (2008). *Teaching vocabulary.* Boston: Heinle & Heinle.

Nation, I. S. P. (2009). *Teaching ESL/EFL reading and writing.* New York: Routledge.

Nation, I. S. P. (2013). *Learning vocabulary in another language* (2nd ed.). Cambridge: Cambridge University Press.

Nation, I. S. P., & Webb, S. (2011). Content-based instruction and vocabulary learning. In E. Hinkel (Ed.), *Handbook of research in second language teaching and learning* (Vol. 2, pp. 631–644). New York: Routledge.

Nattinger, J., & DeCarrico, J. (1992). *Lexical phrases and language teaching.* Oxford: Oxford University Press.

Pawley, A., & Syder, F. (1983). Two puzzles for linguistic theory: Nativelike selection and nativelike fluency. In J. Richards & R. Schmidt (Ed.), *Language and Communication* (pp. 191–225). London: Longman.

Peters, A. (1983). *The units of language acquisition.* Cambridge: Cambridge University Press.

Schmidt, R. (2001). Attention. In P. Robinson (Ed.), *Cognition and second language instruction* (pp. 3–32). Cambridge: Cambridge University Press.

Swales, J., & Feak, C. (2012). *Academic writing for graduate students* (3rd ed.). Ann Arbor: The University of Michigan Press.

Widdowson, H. (2003). *Defining issues in English language teaching.* Oxford: Oxford University Press.

Wilkins, D. (1972). *Linguistics in language teaching.* London: Edward Arnold.

Wray, A. (2002). *Formulaic language and the lexicon.* Cambridge: Cambridge University Press.

Wray, A., & Perkins, M. (2000). The functions of formulaic language: An integrated model. *Language and Communication, 20,* 1–28.

APPENDIX A

Sentence Stems for Written Academic Discourse

The teaching of sentence and phrase structure needs to co-occur with instruction on vocabulary and common academic collocations. Using stock sentence stems in actual writing can become probably one of the most efficient ways of expanding L2 writers' vocabulary and grammatical repertoire, particularly when supplemented with substituting their discrete elements. Grammatical constructions, such as commonly occurring sentences, clauses, and phrases, can be "viewed as big words" and memorized as (almost) idiomatic sentence and phrase stems.

All sentence stems presented below can be used in teaching and learning a range of grammar constructions, vocabulary, and discourse patterns prevalent in academic language.

Openings/Introductions

The central issue in xxx is yyy . . .
The development of xxx is a typical/common problem in . . .
Xxx and yyy are of particular interest and complexity . . .
For a long time xxx, it has been the case that yyy
Most accounts/reports/publications claim/state/maintain that xxx
According to Smith/recent (media) articles/reports/studies, xxx is/seems to be yyy.
One of the most controversial/important/interesting issues/problems/xxxS (recently/in recent literature/media reports) is yyy.
In recent discussions/debates/reports of xxx, a controversial/complex/intertwined issue has been whether xxx. On the one hand, some argue that xxx. On the other hand, however, others argue that yyy. (Modified from Graff & Birkenstein, 2014)
It is becoming increasingly difficult/challenging to ignore zzz.
Xxxx plays an important/significant/prominent role in the maintenance/support/dissemination of zzz.

In the new global/changing/evolving aaa, bbb has become a central/most important/
   pivotal/persistent issue for ccc.
Xxx is an increasingly important area/field in ccc.
Xxx and yyy have been an object of research since the 1920s/1960s/1990s.
Bbb is a major/vital/central area of interest within the field of zzz.
The issue of xxx has received notable/considerable critical/favorable attention.
Xxx is a classic problem in zzz.
Yyy has been studied by many researchers using/employing/utilizing vvv.

Negative Openings with Countable Nouns

few reports   have discussed/examined zzz
few discussions   have addressed/noted/examined
few articles   have focused on/noted
few studies   have investigated/dealt with

Thesis/Topic Statements

The purpose of this essay/paper/analysis/overview is to xxx
   (e.g., take a look at/examine/discuss yyy).
The main emphasis/focus/goal/purpose of the/this essay/paper/project is to xxx
   (e.g., is to analyze/provide an overview/discussion of xxx)
This paper describes and analyzes . . . xxx.
This paper discusses/examines/investigates xxx.
This paper claims/shows that xxx is/is not yyy.
This essay/paper addresses/examines/
         is designed to
               analyze/provide an overview of/take a look at xxx.
My aim in this paper is to . . .
In this paper, I/we report on/discuss . . .
I intend/will demonstrate/show/explain/illustrate that xxx
My (basic/main/most important) argument/claim is largely/essentially that xxx . . .
The idea/notion/concept/thought/proposition that xxx is yyy is a
      striking/provocative/thoughtful/promising/thought-provoking one, and this is what
      I support/subscribe to/advocate.

Secondary Purpose

The primary aim/purpose of this paper is xxx. In addition, it examines/discusses . . .
   yyy.
Additionally, yyy is discussed/examined.
A secondary aim of this paper is to yyy.
Another reason/point/issue addressed/discussed in this paper is yyy.

Rhetorical Mode/Discourse Organization Statement

This paper (will) compare(s)/describe/illustrate xxx first
  by analyzing/comparing/demonstrating yyy (that yyy is zzz),
  then by yyying zzz, and finally by yyying aaa).
This paper first analyzes/discusses xxx,
  followed by an examination/illustration/overview of yyy and zzz.
The differences/similarities between xxx and yyy are
  important/pronounced/striking/unmistakable,
    and they merit/warrant/deserve/call for a
      close/careful/thoughtful/thorough/rigorous
        examination/analysis/scrutiny.
While some differences between aaaaa and bbbbb are
  clear/evident/noticeable/pronounced/unmistakable,
  the similarities are (also) evident/striking/prominent/noticeable/relevant.
The main points/questions/issues addressed/discussed in this essay/paper are: aaa, bbb, and ccc.
This paper begins by ddd. It will then/later go on/move on to xxx.
The first/second/third section of this essay/paper will examine/take a look at/discuss vvv.

Introducing Review of Literature and Evidence from Readings

In recent discussions of xxx,
The issue of zzz is important: (stated reasons)
In recent publications, the topic/issue of xxx has received considerable/prominent attention.
Recently researchers/investigators/scholars have examined the effects of ccc on ddd.
In the past two/three/four decades/twenty/thirty years, a number of researchers/authors have sought/attempted to identify/determine . . .
Previous/earlier/studies/investigations have reported/noted/determined that . . .
A considerable/substantial/notable amount of literature has been published on vvv.
These studies/reports/investigations have found that . . .
Surveys/studies/investigations such as that conducted by Smith (2015)
  showed/demonstrated that . . .
Recent evidence/findings suggest(s) that . . .
Several attempts have been made to . . .
A large body of literature on xxx has been published/made public on zzz.
A number of researchers/investigators have reported that . . .
Studies of ccc show/demonstrate/emphasize the importance of bbb in/for xxx.

Other Types of Sentence Stems for Essay Development

(1) Assertion
  It can be claimed/said/assumed that xxx

It seems certain/likely/doubtful that xxx
I/we maintain/claim that xxx

(2) Agreement with the author/source

As XXX perceptively/insightfully states/
    correctly notes/
    rightly observes/
    appropriately points out,   xxx is/seems to be yyy (adjective/noun)
I/we rather/somewhat/strongly agree with/support (the idea that) xxx
XXX provides/lends support to YYY's argument/claim/conclusion that zzz

(3) Disagreement with the author/source

I/we rather/somewhat/strongly disagree with XXX/that yyy.
As XXX states (somewhat) unclearly/erroneously,
XXX does not support YYY's argument/claim/conclusion about zzz/that zzz.
Although XXX contends that yyy, I/we believe that zzz.
However, it remains unclear whether . . .
It would (thus) be of interest to learn more about yyy/how . . .
Xxx is mistaken because he/she overlooks/neglects to account for aaa.
I disagree with XXX's view that aaa because, as recent research has shown that . . .

(4) Comparison

Both xxx and yyy are (quite) similar in that zzz . . .
Xxx is like/resembles yyy
Both xxx and yyy are/see.m to be zzz (adjective/noun).
Xxx and yyy have/share some aspects of zzz.
Xxx is similar to/not unlike yyy (with respect to zzz).

(5) Contrast

Xxx is (quite) different from yyy (in regard to zzz).
Xxx is not the case with yyy/the same as yyy.
Xxx does not resemble yyy (in regard to zzz).
Xxx contrasts with yyy (with regard to zzz).
Xxx is unlike yyy in that/with respect to zzz.

(6) Recommendations

Let me recommend/suggest that xxx be/have/do yyy.
What I want/would like to recommend/suggest is that xxx . . .
One suggestion is/may be that xxx (do yyy).

(7) Citing sources/Supporting arguments, claims, conclusions, and generalizations

As proof/evidence/an example (for this), (let me cite/quote xxx)
According to xxx,
As XXX says/claims,
XXX provides evidence/support for yyy/that yyy . . .
XXX demonstrates that yyy
    shows evidence for yyy/that yyy . . .
Xxx is an illustration/example of yyy.

(8) Citing sources/Referring to external sources of knowledge
   It is/has been (often) asserted/believed/noted that xxx   *(YYY, 2003)*
   It is believed that xxx   *(YYY, 1999)*
   It is often asserted that xxx
   It has been noted that xxx
(9) Classification
   Xxx can/may be divided/classified into yyy (and zzz).
   Xxx and yyy are categories/divisions of zzz.
   There are xxx categories/types/classes of yyy.
(10) Giving examples
   A well-known/prominent/notable/memorable/classic/useful/important
   example of vvv is xxx/can be found in Smith (2015).
(11) Generalization
   Overall,
   In general,
   On the whole,
   Generally speaking,
   In most cases,
   One can generalize that xxx
   For the most part,
   With the exception of xxx,
   With one exception,
(12) Summarizing

   Reporting Verbs and Noun Clause Chunks for Summaries (author first)

   The author goes on to say/state/show that xxx
   The author further argues/explains/shows that
   The article further states that
   (Smith) also states/maintains/argues/asserts that
   (Smith) also believes/concludes/feels that
   In the second half of the article/report, (Johnson) presents xxx to show/explain that

   Sentence Stems and Noun Clause Chunks for Summaries (essay/paper first)

   The article/report concludes that
   This essay/paper has examined/reviews/given an account of vvv/the reasons/ causes for ccc.
   This essay/paper/project has argued/made it clear that vvv is the best/worst bbb to aaa.
   This assignment/essay/paper has explained the central/crucial/vital importance of ddd in aaa.
   This assignment has investigated . . .

The present investigation has compared three different yyys in terms of zzz.
This essay/paper has examined the role of ccc in/for ddd.
(12) Closing statement
In sum/conclusion,
To sum up/conclude,
To tie this (all) together,

(Based on Nattinger and DeCarrico [1992], Swales and Feak [2012], and Graff and Birkenstein [2014])

APPENDIX B

The most common verb/preposition combinations in academic prose (Biber, Johansson, Leech, Conrad, & Finegan, 1999):

The Top Most Common Verb/Preposition Combinations

be applied to
be associated with
be based on
be derived from
be knows as
be used in
deal with
depend on
lead to
refer to
result in

The Second Most Common Verb/Preposition Combinations

account for
add to
be composed of
be divided into
be included in
be involved in
be related to

be required for
belong to
come from
consist of
contribute to
differ from
look at
look for
obtain [noun] from
occur in
think of

APPENDIX C

The Most Frequent Passive Verbs in Academic Writing (in declining order)
For all verbs: *be (is/are/was/were)* + **the Past Participle Form** of the Main Verb (form as listed)

made	given	seen	used
found	done	considered	shown

(Based on Biber et al., 1999; Nation, 1990, 2013)

Other Academic Verbs Predominantly Used in the Passive Voice
For all verbs: *be (is/are/was/were)* + **the Past Participle Form** of the Main Verb (form as listed)

achieved	aligned (with)	applied	approved
asked	associated (with)	attributed (to)	based (on)
born	brought	calculated	called
carried	chosen	classified (as)	compared
composed (of)	coupled (with)	deemed	defined
derived	described	designed	determined
discussed	distributed	documented	drawn
entitled (to)	estimated	examined	expected
explained	expressed	extracted	flattened
formed	given	grouped (with/by)	held
identified	illustrated	inclined	intended
introduced	involved	kept	known
labeled	left	limited (to)	linked (to/with)
located (at/in)	lost	measured	needed
noted	observed	obtained	performed
plotted	positioned	prepared	presented

recognized	regarded	related (to)	replaced
reported	represented	required	said
situated	stored	studied	subjected (to)
thought	told	transferred	treated
understood	viewed		

Verbs That Are Always (or Almost Always) Used in the Active Voice (in declining order)

The verbs in the bold font are *always* used in the active voice.

appear	**die**	**occur**	stay
arrive	**happen**	**resemble**	wait
belong	fall	rest	
consist	lack	**remain**	
come	last	seem	

(Based on Biber et al., 1999)

APPENDIX D

Most Common Noun Phrases Found in Academic Prose

The following lists have been extracted from Biber et al., 1999:

Nouns with Prepositional Phrases

>the relationship between the
>the difference between the
>an important part in
>an important role in
>an increase in the
>the same way as

Prepositional Phrases Followed by the *Of*-phrase

>as a result of the
>as in the case of the
>at the end of the
>at the beginning of the
>at the time of the . . .
>at the time of writing
>from the point of view (of)
>in the context of the
>in the division of labor
>in the course of the
>in the early stages of

APPENDIX E

Evaluative Adjectives and Noun Pre-Fabs Frequent in Academic Writing

Evaluative Adjective	Main (Head) Noun
good	judges, readers, separation, communication, relations, fortune, yields, indication, e.g., good judges, good fortune
important	changes, advances, step, part, consequences, respect, role, point, factor, e.g., important changes, important step(s)
special	cases, process, regulations, class, types, method, e.g., special cases, special process(es)
right	principles, level, relation, direction, answer, criteria, e.g., right principles, right level(s)

(based on Biber et al., 1999)

Contrasting Pairs of Adjectives for Paraphrasing

large—small
low—high
general—particular
primary—secondary
long—short
final—initial
same—different
necessary—possible
young—old
previous—following
simple—complex
positive—negative

APPENDIX F

Most Common Lexical (Word and Phrase) Hedges Found in Academic Prose

The following lists are based on Hinkel, 2004a:

Frequency adverbs as hedges (in declining order):

- *frequently, often*
- *generally/in general, usually, ordinarily*
- *occasionally/on occasion, sometimes, at times, from time to time, every so often*
- *most of the time, on many/numerous occasions*
- *almost never, rarely, seldom, hardly ever (negative meanings)*
- *almost/nearly always, invariably*

Quantifiers as hedges:

- *all, many/much*
- *some, a few/a little*
- *a number of* + *noun/noun phrase*
- *a good/great deal of* + *noun/noun phrase*
- *a bit (of)*

Formal Hedges for Academic Writing

about	*fairly*	*relative(-ly)*
according to (+noun)	*likely*	*relative to*
actually	*merely*	*slightly*
apparent(-ly)	*most* (+ adjective)	*somehow*
approximate(-ly)	*nearly*	*somewhat*
broad(-ly)	*normal(-ly)*	*sufficiently*
clear(-ly)	*partly*	*theoretically*
comparative(-ly)	*partially*	*potential(-ly)*
essential(-ly)	*presumably*	*unlikely*

9
LANGUAGE FOCUS
From Text to Discourse

This chapter discusses:

- Discourse and idea structuring in L2 writing
- Curricular perspectives on teaching academic writing
- Academic discourse conventions and text discourse markers
- Outlines and outlining to construct L2 academic writing
- Evidence (thesis support) and academic register

Discourse and Idea Structuring in L2 Writing

This chapter presents a set of specific teaching techniques that have proven to be highly effective for L2 writing and in some cases even for writing in L1. Teaching learners how to organize discourse and ideas in L2 writing represents one of the major areas that specifically require additional attention throughout the L2 writing curriculum. As was discussed in chapters 2 and 3, a great number of studies have noted that intensive and extensive instruction is required in teaching discourse organization in Anglo-American academic writing.

Since the 1970s, a great deal of research has been conducted to investigate the effects of text on discourse (e.g., introductory or concluding statements). Many studies have determined that the grammar and lexical (vocabulary and meaning) constructions used in writing, and how and when they are used, alter a text's structure, clarity, cohesion, and communicative effectiveness (Christie & Derewianka, 2008; Ferris, 2011; Halliday & Hasan, 1976; Kaplan, 2005). The techniques discussed below seek to capitalize on the effects of text on discourse organization and structuring, which have long been established in research.

It is well known today that English-language academic writing is governed by a number of rigid conventions in its discourse structure (Hinkel, 2011; Swales, 1990, 2004). These conventions are adhered to and marked by certain prescribed uses of language elements, such as grammatical constructions, phrases, and vocabulary.

> What is appropriate and inappropriate in structuring academic written discourse in English is highly formulaic.

Typically, writing instruction focuses on such fundamental features of formal academic discourse as the organization of information (e.g., introduction, body, conclusion, and other discourse moves), the presence and the placement of the thesis statement, the structure of the paragraph (e.g., the topic sentence), the rhetorical support for the thesis included in every paragraph, and an avoidance of needless digressions, repetition, and redundancy, among many other factors (Ferris, 2011; Scollon, Scollon, & Jones, 2012). A curriculum for teaching L2 writing has to focus learners' attention on these throughout the course of instruction.

The reason that the discourse properties of academic writing are difficult for most L2 students to learn is that they represent for the most part culturally bound, conventionalized, and abstract characteristics of academic prose that are frequently absent in written discourse in rhetorical traditions other than the Anglo-American (Hinkel, 1999a, 2014).

> Even educated and proficient L2 learners who are taught to read and write in other rhetorical traditions are rarely aware that a clear thesis statement should be placed close to the beginning of one's essay (Jin & Cortazzi, 2006).

Hinkel's (1994) study demonstrates that the advanced abstract concepts widely prevalent in the teaching of L2 writing can be very difficult even for highly proficient L2 writers to understand and implement in practice. Such abstract constructs as the text's purpose, audience (many students are correct to say that the teacher is their sole audience), support for the main idea, clarity, and information relevance are culturally bound, vague, complex, and subjective. They require a detailed familiarity with the L2 culture, as well as the academic culture to be understood and applied. For example, there can be many interpretations of such concepts as *persuasiveness, precise meaning,* or *rhetorical support.*

According to Hinkel, instructors tend to teach L2 writing by directly or indirectly referring to and exemplifying discourse conventions accepted as the norm in academic writing in English. They bring their students' attention to the fact that a text addresses an audience and has a clear purpose, but for most students, the purpose of an essay may be to complete the assignment. Students are taught that the writer needs to include specific and explicit information to support the main idea, and clearly and convincingly show the author's views on the topic.

> To construct a text that demonstrates L2 writers' familiarity with the Anglo-American discourse norms and conventions, learners need to understand these essential and abstract concepts, interpret them according to L2 discourse conventions, relate them to text, and apply them to their writing.

Many L2 writing teachers know from experience that students frequently have difficulty accomplishing these tasks (Hinkel, 1992).

Academic writing and discourse structuring rules prescribe what can or cannot be included in academic writing or what can or cannot be discussed in an academic essay (Coffin et al., 2003). For example, discussions of family affairs, one's religious beliefs or political views, or certain social attitudes is considered unacceptable in academic writing. The assumed purpose of student writing is to display and present knowledge of a subject matter in accordance with the socio-cultural and discourse expectations prevalent in higher education (Celce-Murcia & Olshtain, 2005; Swales, 2004).

Talking Shop

Most L2 writers are instructed that English academic prose must be clear, convincing, and specific. On the other hand, Matalene (1985) reports, for example, that, in the Chinese rhetorical tradition, the primary function of text is harmony maintenance; the need to be explicit is not self-evident. The purpose of writing to "adjust people to people" (Oliver, 1972, p. 98), rather than explicitly state a point of view. (Doing this could lead to disharmony, just as discussing one's religious beliefs, political views, or various social attitudes is considered to be unacceptable in Anglo-American academic writing).

In your own teaching, how would you explain to L2 writers such concepts as *clear*, *convincing*, and *specific* texts? How would you go about demonstrating to L2 writers that they need to produce explicit texts with clearly and directly stated points of view?

Discuss your thoughts along with possible teaching techniques with your colleagues and see what kind of ideas they might have. What are some possible ways of conveying to L2 writers the need to be clear, convincing, and specific in their writing?

Typically, in L2 writing curricula and the sequencing of instructional units (chapter 5), modules on organizing ideas, consisting largely of analyses of short (or long) excerpts of high quality sample text, precede modules on grammar and vocabulary. However, many elements of grammar and vocabulary serve as markers needed to identify discourse moves, such as introductions, theses, and conclusions.

In this chapter, based on the findings of numerous studies and in simple terms, the teaching of the language elements that function as identifiers of discourse moves precedes detailed instruction in how to organize ideas and structure discourse. The rationale for this instructional order of teaching seeks to maximize learning gains by taking advantage of the rigidity and high degree of conventionalization of academic discourse in English.

Talking Shop

Some researchers, such as Sunderland and Spiegel (2009), report that even learners who can write fluently and accurately in English may have challenges in organizing written discourse. They explain that what would be seen as a "logical" and "clear" piece of writing in one culture may be perceived as "blunt" and "rude" in another when the purpose of writing, for example, is stated at the beginning. They note that occasionally L2 writers may not choose to change their way of writing and adopt the Anglo-American way of structuring their writing.

In your opinion, why might a willingness to follow the norms adopted in Anglo-American academic writing lag behind developing high proficiency in the English language? What are the connections between written discourse conventions and learners' cultural values? Why are such adjectives as *clear, logical, blunt,* or *rude* associated with how text and ideas are organized in writing? What does the term *logical* mean to you?

Curricular Perspectives on Teaching Academic Writing

The curriculum in higher education and the university centers on student reading and writing. University and college writing fulfills a number of learning and assessment goals. As has been mentioned, conventions and rules prescribe what academic writing is, what it can discuss, how it is structured, and how it is evaluated.

Many in the academy assume that how writing should be organized and presented is simply a matter of "common sense" (Coffin et al., 2003, p. 3) or that they are basic prerequisites for participating in the academic community. In addition, many teaching faculty believe that when students are not familiar with these conventions and rules at the outset, the writers are simply able to learn them intuitively and from practice. It is quite possible that such assumptions were true at one time when higher education was intended for the select few, students were less diverse, and schooling more rigorous than it is at present. It seems, however, that those days are long gone.

Students of varied family, economic, and geographic backgrounds, educational preparation, ethnicities, nationalities, cultures, and genders have dramatically changed the face of higher education. Furthermore, in addition to the traditional practices of teaching and learning, the teaching curricula have also undergone profound changes that impact much of what can and cannot be learned in the process of obtaining education and in the opportunities for learning "on the fly."

For example, teaching and the content of teaching can be delivered via distance education, with colleges and universities that exist entirely online, or hybrid courses that combine classroom and online delivery of material. To put it another way, contemporary higher education, curricula, and various types of teaching and learning do not easily lend themselves to learning how to construct written academic discourse without specific, focused, and clear instruction. These undeniable facts apply to both L1 and L2 academic writers and writing.

In the 1950s and 1960s, with the influx of first-generation college and university students in higher education, courses in humanities, and particularly in literature, provided academic writing models that students could imitate. Little teaching of writing, the writing process, or considerations of audience and genre took place during those years. However, the assessment and evaluation focus on writing style, text structure, and vocabulary and grammar quality did result in the improvement of students' writing in the course of their education.

In reaction to rigid and constraining views of stylistic quality and evaluations, the teaching of rhetoric and composition began to move away from a focus on the writing product to focus on the process. "Models of good writing" were widely eliminated because they had little to contribute to curricular approaches for teaching writing as a process.

In the teaching of the writing process, composing came to be seen as a means of learning and personal development. The pedagogical value of instruction in the writing process includes considerations of audience and purpose and the reason for writing, within the format of expressive and expository rhetoric (Hairston, 1982; Reid, 1993, 2000; Zamel, 1996).

However, as was discussed in chapter 3, in higher education outside composition programs, little has changed in terms of expectations and evaluations of student writing. Since time immemorial (and probably going back to the very beginnings of European universities in the 11th century), written work has served as an almost universal measure of students' level of understanding of the course material and facility with language.

The quality of writing and discourse, that is, content organization, academic vocabulary, and grammatical accuracy are almost universally seen as a reflection of students' learning and academic achievement (ACT, 2007, 2010; Applebee, 1982; ICAS, 2002).

Talking Shop

Based on decades of research into various rhetorical traditions, it is well known that culturally driven discourse conventions determine what is considered to be appropriate or inappropriate in various text genres (e.g., formal or informal speaking, or literary fiction). In your experience, do discourse conventions exist in written genres other than the academic? Can you think of a few examples?

For the purposes of teaching and learning, how can one learn to notice and identify written discourse conventions? What is the role of the teacher in this process? Do your colleagues have experience in teaching L2 discourse conventions?

The fact is that most L2 writers have trouble with abstract concepts that dominate in the teaching of writing.

For example, if students are informed that the thesis statement is a sentence or two that represents the main idea of the essay, it can be very hard to determine what the main idea of an essay actually is. From a student's perspective, a piece of academic writing has a number of ideas, and they may be equally or almost equally important.

If a student learned that the thesis tells the reader what the essay is going to be about, as is almost always the case, essays can be about many things at one time. If one thinks about it for a minute, it may well be very difficult to figure out what thesis support is, why a thesis needs to be supported, and what "solid" thesis support consists of. Summarizing an author's main point, for instance, is a vague and abstract concept that requires an accurate identification of the main points, isolating them from the supporting information, and condensing them. It is hard to imagine more mysterious, confusing, and mind-blowing tasks, which are hard to conceptualize, not to mention implement.

Action Point

An extended definition of wheat is provided below. Within this definition, there are a number of discourse moves that follow Anglo-American conventions of discourse structuring for extended definitions. Note and identify these discourse moves.

Wheat is a cereal grain, originally from the Levant region of the Near East but now cultivated worldwide. In 2010, world production of wheat was 651 million tons, making it the third most-produced cereal after corn (844 million tons) and rice (672 million tons).

> This grain is grown on more land area than any other commercial food. World trade in wheat is greater than all other crops combined. Globally, wheat is the leading source of vegetable protein in human food, having a higher protein content than other major cereals, corn, or rice. In terms of total production tonnages used for food, it is currently second to rice as the main human food crop and ahead of maize, after allowing for corn's more extensive use in animal feeds.
>
> Wheat was a key factor enabling the emergence of city-based societies at the start of civilization because it was one of the first crops that could be easily cultivated on a large scale, and had the additional advantage of yielding a harvest that provides long-term storage of food. In commercial use, harvested wheat grain that enters trade is classified according to grain properties for the purposes of the commodity markets. In 2007 there was a dramatic rise in the price of wheat due to freezes and flooding in the northern hemisphere and a drought in Australia.
>
> Retrieved from http://en.wikipedia.org/wiki/Wheat, July 31, 2014.
>
> Compare your findings with those of your colleagues. Why might there be various divergent analyses of the discourse moves?

Academic Discourse Conventions and the Text Discourse Markers

In higher education and various English writing programs, it is fashionable to say that academic writing has a range of purposes typically referred to by means of verbs, such as *to inform, entertain, express, explain, describe, argue, persuade, define, convince, evaluate, mediate,* and *negotiate*. In reality, however, these various lofty and abstract verbs usually refer to student university writing that has the unstated (and hidden) goal of demonstrating knowledge of the content of study and quality of language and writing skills.

To this end, most pieces of academic writing in the humanities actually take the form of an assignment or essay. In the old-fashioned days before the explicit teaching of the writing process, students were taught to begin by making basic essay outlines—introduction, body, and conclusion—at school or in basic academic writing classes. Currently, however, there are probably few L1 students who can ably and efficiently create an essay outline.

> Most L2 writers have probably never heard of making an essay outline or have never been taught how to do it, unless it was incidentally included as a side-note in their writing textbooks without much instruction.

For this reason, the first order of business in writing instruction is to show L2 academic writers that:

1. Most academic essays have a very similar structure, regardless of how their abstract purpose is referred to in teaching.
2. Outlines are instrumental for getting the skeletal structure of the essay in place.
3. Academic essay outlines are relatively easy to make, but may be harder to adhere to in actual writing.

Outline—Step 1

In Anglo-American academic writing, sample outlines might have variations, but these are actually minor. A basic Sample Outline—the essay skeletal structure—is presented in Table 9.1. This is the first step of guiding L2 writers to clearly identify the conventionalized organization of an academic essay and discourse in Anglo-American higher education.

Additional benefits of presenting the basic structure of an academic essay to L2 writers are:

- The bare-bones outline takes the mystery out of written discourse organization.
- The expectations of the essay evaluation criteria become a great deal more transparent and clear.

TABLE 9.1 Outline Basics—Step 1

I. **Opening/Introduction**
   2–5 sentences that describe or explain the topic/issue
   Thesis Statement—1–2 sentences
II. **Background**
   From readings, a summary of a reading, or other types of information—directly connected to the Thesis Statement.
III. **Main Point 1 (Thesis support)**
   Minor Points—Optional
IV. **Main Point 2 (Thesis support)**
   Minor Points—Optional
V. **Major Point 3 (Thesis support) (for long essays: Optional)**
   Minor Points—Optional
VI. **Conclusion**
   Restatement of the Thesis Statement with added information from the Main Points
   Closing statement(s) (and recommendations)

By and large, this outline is not particularly useful to L2 writers until the pedagogical activity of outline-making moves on to Step 2. Experience has shown that at this juncture many advanced L2 writers begin to figure out how they can employ the rigid and conventionalized structure of the academic discourse to their best advantage.

As the next step, the rudimentary outline in Table 9.1 needs to become more useful, practical, and less abstract for L2 writers. In real terms, it should become more material, and this can be accomplished by means of enhancing it with a bit of language.

Speaking generally, all writers of prose in any genre have stock expressions (chapters 7 and 8) that are used repeatedly and that are not their own invention (Graff & Birkenstein, 2014). Many of the formulaic expressions and markers of discourse moves are encountered so frequently that they usually go unnoticed.

However, these formulaic expressions have important functions in discourse organization. One classical analogy is to think of such expressions as road signs. The functions of the stock formulas are essential because they mark and pivot the discourse flow:

- Formulaic expressions mark discourse moves and identify the discourse structure (e.g., the opening/introduction, the thesis statement, or the conclusion).
- Formulaic pre-fabs[1] guide the discourse flow (e.g., from the thesis to the main points, and to the conclusion).
- They mark the order of essay sections and connect them with the discourse structure (e.g., *the next important point, another significant observation,* or *in sum*).
- The writer who produces the text is aware of its structure, but the reader needs to be able to identify the discourse moves. Formulaic pre-fabs signal an occurrence of moves within the flow.

Action Point

Some linguists, including Michael Hoey (2000), call formulaic markers in written discourse "signposts" that alert readers to its moves and elements. Identify these formulaic signposts in the text excerpt below and discuss your findings with your colleagues to see if their findings are similar to yours.

For a long time, it has been an issue that young people dress to keep up with the fashion, and fashionable clothes cost a lot of money, like sneakers and jeans. Most high school students can't afford to buy expensive regular clothes. This essay claims that students in public schools should be required to wear uniforms.

To begin, most sociology studies show that when school uniforms are required, students worry less about their clothes, but spend more time and effort on their

> *homework, like reading a book. Requiring school uniforms could lead to reduced costs and other school problems because students would concentrate on their studies and grades.*
>
> *In addition, when students wear uniforms and don't have to compete for the best-dressed, school discipline and attitude can improve. To make this point, one of the sociology studies interviewed a high school principal in California. He said, "There are several schools here that have uniforms. According to the teachers, in all those schools grades have improved, and students can concentrate on their academics."*
>
> *In conclusion, uniforms can be expensive, but they almost always cost less than fashionable clothes. It costs more than a couple of hundred dollars to buy clothes for an outfit these days, but uniforms are slightly more than a hundred.*

The greatest benefit of Textual Outline—Step 2 is that L2 writers can address their attention to what to do next, after they identify the discourse structure, and how to do it. Learning what discourse move to make and in what order—or even whether to make it—is of crucial importance in instruction.

> Knowing when and how to make a discourse move in constructing academic writing represents an essential skill, without which no passable essay can be produced.

Textual Outline—Step 2

Step 2 entails selecting the formulaic expressions commonly used in academic writing to begin to identify and select suitable formulaic pre-fabs for building the text in the basic Outline (Table 9.1).

A relatively comprehensive list of formulaic expressions written academic discourse is included in chapter 8, Appendix A. These expressions are classified and arranged based on their functions in written discourse structure, and in the order of the essay progression. A few examples are listed below.

For example, the first set of expressions is for Openings/Introductions, such as:

- *The central issue in xxx is yyy ...*
- *The development of xxx is a typical/common problem in ...*
- *Xxx and yyy are of particular interest and complexity ...*
- *For a long time xxx, it has been the case that yyy.*
- *Most accounts/reports/publications claim/state/maintain that xxx.*
- *One of the most controversial/important/interesting issues/problems/xxxS (recently/ in recent literature/media reports) is yyy.*

The second set includes formulaic expressions that are suited for Thesis Statements, such as:

- *The purpose of this essay/paper/analysis/overview is to xxx (e.g., take a look at/ examine/discuss) yyy.*
- *The main emphasis/focus/goal/purpose of the/this essay/paper/project is to xxx (e.g., is to analyze/provide an overview/discussion of) xxx.*
- *This paper describes and analyzes . . . xxx.*
- *This paper discusses/examines/investigates xxx.*
- *This paper claims/shows that xxx is/is not yyy.*

The order and type of the discourse organization structure are also explicitly marked, and the main points are highlighted:

- *This paper (will) compare(s)/describe/illustrate xxx*
  - *first by analyzing/comparing/demonstrating yyy (that yyy is zzz),*
  - *then by yyying zzz, and*
  - *finally by yyying aaa)*
- *This paper first analyzes/discusses xxx,*
  - *followed by an examination/illustration/overview of yyy and zzz.*
- *The main points/questions/issues addressed/discussed in this essay/paper are: aaa, bbb, and ccc.*

Starting off with the formulaic pre-fabs also helps students to begin to think about what they actually want to say, as is shown in Table 9.2.

> In fact, these expressions, as they begin to mark the Outline, serve as prompts for thinking with real words and phrases.

In many cases, the pre-fabs become the very first words in the essay.

> A long-term benefit of learning to write with formulaic pre-fabs is that their uses and functionality enable students to **notice** how these expressions mark and prompt discourse moves in academic writing.

When discourse moves vary in academic writing across disciplines, L2 writers who are prepared to notice them in one type of writing can adjust their discourse organization as appropriate in their subsequent writing.

The purpose of these formulaic expressions is not to provide instruction in how to make or construct persuasive, logical, or brilliant expository prose or sophisticated rhetorical arguments. Although students are typically taught to develop logical argumentation, there is a preponderance of evidence that many L2 writers

TABLE 9.2 Textual Outline Basics—Step 2

I. Opening/Introduction

For a long time xxx, it has been the case that yyy +1–4 sentences about the topic
The development of xxx is a typical/common problem in +1–4 sentences about the topic
The issue of xxx has received notable/considerable critical/favorable attention. + 1–4 sentences about the topic

Thesis Statement

This paper describes and analyzes ... xxx
The main emphasis/focus/goal/purpose of the/this essay/paper/project is to xxx
My aim in this paper is to ...

II. Background

From readings, a summary of a reading, or other types of information—directly connected to the Thesis Statement.

Recently researchers/investigators/scholars have examined the effects of ccc on ddd.
Previous/earlier/studies/investigations have reported/noted/determined that...
Several attempts have been made to ...

III. Main Point 1 (Thesis support)

As XXX perceptively/insightfully states/(agreement)
As XXX states (somewhat) unclearly/erroneously, (disagreement)
Both xxx and yyy are (quite) similar in that zzz (comparison)

IV. Main Point 2 (Thesis support)

<u>*In addition*</u>, *Xxx correctly notes/*(agreement)
<u>*However*</u>, *Xxx is mistaken because he/she overlooks/neglects to account for aaa.* (disagreement)
<u>*Also*</u>, *Xxx and yyy have/share some aspects of zzz.* (continuing)

V. Conclusion

Restatement of the Thesis Statement with added information from the Main Points

Xxxx plays an important/significant/prominent role in the zzz
According to Smith/recent (media) articles/reports/studies, xxx is/seems to be yyy.
Most accounts/reports/publications claim/state/maintain that xxx

Closing statement(s) (and recommendations for the future)

In conclusion, what I want/would like to recommend/suggest is that xxx
One suggestion is/may be that xxx (do yyy)

are not well versed in doing that, and learning how to do it takes a long time and a great deal of practice (Ferris, 2001, 2011; Hinkel, 2005, 2011; Leki, 2007; Leki, Cumming, & Silva, 2008; Silva, 1993).

> Outlines and formulaic expressions that mark discourse moves represent a starting point from which their writing can begin. They provide a great deal of clarity about how the elements of academic discourse come together and how they are marked in text.

At the very least, outlines and pre-fabs make the structure of an academic essay plain to see and easier to understand.

> It is very important that L2 writers have an opportunity and time to work with Textual Outline—Step 2 to expand and think through what they plan to say in their essays. Working to get rough notes in place for Textual Outline—Step 2 can be assigned as homework. Usually, class time is not very well suited for this learning activity.

Action Point

Even advanced L2 writers often have challenges in constructing paragraphs where the ideas are connected to the main point or to one another. Idea connectedness (or text cohesion) is a culturally bound and abstract concept.

In the examples presented, identify the possible disconnections of ideas. How can these be explained to their L2 authors? How can these be addressed in teaching of what represents idea connectedness in Anglo-American academic writing? Discuss your teaching suggestions with your colleagues.

(1) *Advance technology brings us a new world, especially during the recent years, phenomenons progressing in computer science make us humans feeling enormous convenience. We can have a conference without going out of doors and driving for a couple of hours. However, everything is a two-edge sword. Every time when I plan to use a computer, I will open some music website, read some fiction stories or find plenty of other recreations except for my purpose. And after I realize that all the things I've done have no related to my destination, time is spent too much. So, this happened many times before I told myself not to do like that again, and next time, I find something again.*

(2) *Human beings developed many things through our history, like social systems, technology, norms, and so on. To maintain things that were developed*

> in the past, people needed to teach them to their sons and daughters. When the society got complex and specialized, people needed to teach their descendants in specialized and official way. This is why we have schools in our society. Therefore, schools need to deliver all the things that can help to maintain our society, not just academic skills. This is the goal of school and if schools deliver only academic skills to our descendants, they will be doing only a part of their role.

Textual Outline—Step 3

The purpose of Textual Outline—Step 3 is provide L2 writers an opportunity to further focus their thinking, find ideas, formulate views and positions, and organize information in some sort of a logical sequence. Additional formulations of thoughts and ideas take place as learners begin to write the actual text.

Following work on Textual Outline—Step 3, it may be helpful for writers to work in pairs or small groups of 3 or 4 to expand the beginnings of rough ideas, as they are outlined in Table 9.3. Another technique to facilitate the transition from Textual Outline—Step 3 to fuller text is to demonstrate the process (text modeling is discussed in the next section of this chapter) on the blackboard or overhead display.

> **Talking Shop**
>
> In Anglo-American academic writing, it is customary to see formulaic expressions and pre-fabs as stifling and constraining. On the other hand, Europeans have used rhetorical models throughout the history of education, and probably going back to the times of ancient Greece and Rome (Graff & Birkenstein, 2014). In classical rhetoric, Aristotelian argumentation is driven by *topoi*: in Greek, *places*, literary sources—"places to find something"—that are categories to delineate the relationships among ideas.
>
> What do you think the reasons may be that such disparate views of formulaic pre-fabs—*topoi*—exist in Anglo-American and European formal discourse? Can you think of other common uses of conventionalized expressions in daily life? Can you and your colleagues think of a few examples?

Once the writers' rough ideas are formulated, however vaguely, work can begin on ordering and organizing the information flow. Re-ordering and re-organizing ideas in written discourse is part and parcel of all academic writing.

> L2 writers need to be taught explicitly that the order of ideas in discourse is usually arranged and re-arranged—and re-arranged again—as their ideas are formulated more fully and better than in the initial outline.

An example in Textual Outline—Step 3 presents the very beginnings of—rudimentary notes—ideas. There are a number of ubiquitous and time-tested non-fiction writing topics that can be found in most writing prompts (e.g., school and local policies, smoking policies, immigration policies and trends, laws associated with consumption of various substances, gender roles, co-ed education, school and college sports, misbehaving sports figures, the role of technology in society, the impact of medical advancements on longevity, or influential historical personages).

In most cases of non-fiction university writing, the topics are usually based on readings. The example below is based on the topic of benefits of early second or foreign language learning. Presumably, L2 writers can be provided an opportunity to read on the topic and become familiar with it before they begin writing. In Textual Outline—Step 3 (Table 9.3), the pre-fab sentence stems are accompanied by brief starts of ideas (possible "topical fillers"), and these are underlined. It is crucial that L2 writers read about the topic before they begin writing in all cases of academic writing, other than narrating their personal stories.

> In classroom teaching, it is very important that the students' writing topic be different from the one in the actual instructional exemplar.

The reason is that students, like all humans, tend to take the shortest and easiest path possible to achieving their immediate goal. In the case of all written assignments, for students, the goal is to produce and submit a passable quality draft with as little fuss as possible. Since the initial stages of writing are exemplified in Table 9.3, they also represent the beginning of a passable draft.

Talking Shop

Conventionalized discourse markers in academic essays often vary from one discourse move to the next, as is the case with, say, introduction, body, and conclusion. Many, however, are flexible and ambiguous and can be usable in a few or any sections in a piece of academic writing.

In the list of discourse markers below, which ones are section-specific and which ones can be used in any essay section? What are the reasons that some are more flexible than others? In your opinion, does the flexibility of discourse marker functions make them more or less complex for L2 writers to learn to use appropriately?

Discourse Markers:

therefore	for this reason	all in all	regardless of the fact that
thus	on one hand + on	in particular	in spite of the fact that
as a result	the other hand	in sum	consequently furthermore
in addition	for example	moreover	on the contrary first of all

TABLE 9.3 Textual Outline Basics—Step 3

I. **Opening/Introduction**

> (a) For a long time, it has been the case that <u>second/foreign language learning starts in high school</u>. <u>Studies have shown, however, that early second/foreign language learning has (many) important advantages</u>.
> (b) The development of <u>advanced second language fluency</u> is a typical/common problem <u>for students in many countries</u>. <u>Today, second language skills are needed more than ever</u>.
> (c) The issue of <u>developing second or foreign language skills</u> has received considerable attention <u>in many publications</u>.

Thesis Statement

> (a) This paper describes <u>the **educational** and **economic** advantages of beginning second/foreign language learning at an early age</u>.
> (b) The main goal/purpose of the paper is to focus on <u>the **educational** and **economic** advantages of beginning second/foreign language learning at an early age</u>.
> (c) My aim in this paper is to illustrate <u>the **educational**, **economic**, and social</u> (optional) <u>advantages of beginning second/foreign language learning at an early age</u>.

II. **Background**

(From readings, a summary of a reading, or other types of information—directly connected to the Thesis Statement.)

> (a) Recently researchers have examined <u>the effects of age on the development of advanced and fluent second/foreign language skills</u>. <u>They have found that the earlier students start to learn another language, the more advanced their language abilities can become</u>.
> (b) Many studies have reported that <u>second/foreign language skills are required for college and university education</u>.
> (c) Several attempts have been made to <u>determine why children have the most to gain from learning another language</u>. <u>Starting early is an ideal time to learn another language quickly</u>.

III. **Main Point 1 (Thesis support)**

> (a) As Peterson found, <u>most colleges and universities encourage/require knowledge of more than one language</u>. <u>These studies have shown that knowing another language lead to improved overall academic performance and superior problem-solving skills</u>.
> (b) Many studies have shown that <u>early second/foreign language learning affects students' future educational opportunities</u>. <u>Students who begin their study of second/foreign languages early score statistically higher on standardized tests</u>.

IV. **Main Point 2 (Thesis support)**

> (a) In addition, Bobson correctly emphasizes that <u>students who started learning languages in childhood have a greater number of career possibilities and develop an understanding of their own and other cultures that can be useful for employment</u>.
> (b) Also, according to Johnson and Thompson, <u>early learners who have better knowledge of another language have more job opportunities and higher salaries</u>. <u>Those without language skills are likely to be at a disadvantage if they have a job in an international company</u>.

(Continued)

TABLE 9.3 *(Continued)*

V. Conclusion
(Restatement of the Thesis Statement with added information from the Main Points.)

> (a) <u>Early leaning of a second/foreign language</u> plays an important role in <u>the future</u> **academic** <u>and</u> **career** <u>opportunities for individuals.</u> <u>Knowing another language well begins in childhood, and it lead to better</u> **academic** <u>performance and higher</u> **income**.
> (b) <u>The</u> **educational** <u>and</u> **economic** <u>advantages of beginning second/foreign language learning at an early age have been shown in many publications Students who begin their study of second/foreign languages early do better in their</u> **universities**, <u>on their tests, and in their future</u> **job** <u>possibilities.</u>

(Closing statement(s) (and recommendations))

> One suggestion <u>for both parents and schools</u> may be <u>to give children a chance to start learning a second or foreign language at a young age.</u>

Idea and topic expansion, elaboration, and development, based on the initial stages of writing in Textual Outline—Step 3 can take several forms:

- Narrowing down broad generalizations and a wide focus (the most common scenario)
- Expanding a small scope to a broader discussion
- Adding or omitting extraneous information and ideas where needed or preferred

> After L2 writers have a bit of practice and become familiar with the written academic discourse moves and the functions of formulaic expressions in organizing ideas, pre-fabs can be eliminated and abandoned altogether.

Experience has shown, however, that most L2 academic writers recognize the value, functionality, and expediency of using pre-fabs very quickly. Using them as a means of functional outlining can take as long or as short as an individual L2 writer prefers.

Evidence (Thesis Support) and Academic Register

Evidence occupies the pride of place in Anglo-American academic writing. The purpose of using evidence in academic writing is to support—back up—claims, assertions, and views presented in a piece of writing. To achieve this goal, academic writers summarize, synthesize, or analyze the findings of research or views of another writer (e.g., a polemic—a controversial argument—analyzes and often disputes views of another writer or other writers).

Evidence in L2 Academic Writing

Typically, in Anglo-American academic writing, evidence can be quantitative or qualitative, or sometimes both. In student writing in higher education, evidence can be empirical (derived from experience or experiments) or statistical, or merely based on readings, illustrations, examples, descriptions of specific instances (case studies), or generally known facts.

However, what represents evidence or appropriate evidence is a strongly culturally bound and abstract rhetorical concept. In discourse analysis studies carried out since at least the 1960s, a vast body of research has reported that what constitutes appropriate evidence in one rhetorical tradition is probably incongruous with the concept of evidence in another (Cope & Kalantzis, 1993; Kaplan, 1997, 2005; Mauranen, 1993; Swales, 1990, 2004; Ventola & Mauranen, 1996). As has been mentioned, for example, religious sources, ancient philosophical treatises, personal stories, small anecdotes, proverbs, fairy tales, or sayings are not likely to be accepted as valid—or even usable—evidence in Anglo-American higher education.

L2 writers need to be taught explicitly about the conventions of evidence in Anglo-American higher education (Angelova & Riazantseva, 1999; Carlson, 1988; Hinkel, 1995, 1997, 2014; Kamimura & Oi, 1998; Pecorari & Shaw, 2012).

Usually, student writing employs three or four types of evidence that are considered to be appropriate:

- Direct or indirect references to or citations from published sources, including assigned readings (e.g., direct quotes, paraphrases, and, occasionally, summaries of full or partial published materials)
- Illustrative and representative examples of cases from readings or published sources
- Factual data and statistics obtained from sources (e.g., facts, tables, or figures)

It seems clear from the list that instruction in evidential support of the thesis is likely to be intensive and extensive. To be productive, the teaching of Anglo-American rhetorical constructs also has to take into account that various rhetorical traditions have divergent views of evidence, its types, and its purposes in writing. For example, teaching L2 writers how to refer to and cite from published sources, paraphrase, or summarize the author's points is not a trivial task. Similarly, what in fact represents an illustrative or representative example is also not necessarily obvious or clear-cut.

> The teaching of what represents evidence in Anglo-American student writing is a time- and work-intensive process that may take a great deal of instruction and require a substantial cultural adjustments for L2 writers.

Talking Shop

Johanne Myles (2002, p. 5) notes in passing that most of her L2 university students say explicitly that they "hate writing in English" and that they only take the writing courses because they are required in their education or career. However, a vast majority of college and university L1 and L2 writers alike spend much time on writing (e.g., email messages, social media, online posts and comments, and blogs).

Do you think that L1 and L2 students similarly "hate" writing in English? What are the profound differences and similarities between writing in one's L1 or one's L2? What are some of the cultural differences that can have a considerable impact on whether one "hates" or does not hate to write in higher education?

How to integrate evidence into the discourse structure and text is another crucial component of learning to produce formal academic writing. Providing clear and simple illustrations and text analyses (chapter 8) may prove to be an excellent technique for teaching and learning how to structure information from sources, as is demonstrated in Table 9.4.

TABLE 9.4 How to Integrate Supporting Evidence into the Text

Unsupported Facts or Assertions	*Facts or Assertions with Support (Evidence)*
Early second language learning leads to greater levels of fluency that may not be possible when language learning starts late.	References to published sources (1) According the study published by Smith (2015)// Based on Smith's (2015) findings, on the tests of second language fluency, early second language learners achieved the scores that may not be possible for those learners who started late. (2) Smith (2015) reports that on the tests of second language fluency, early second language learners achieved the scores that may not be possible for those learners who started late.
Early second language learning can be beneficial when children study another language several times a week.	Illustrative and representative examples from published sources (1) The American Council on the Teaching of Foreign Languages (2015) recommends that second and foreign language classes for children should be taught three to five times a week for no less than 30-40 minutes per class. (2) Smith (2015) describes a very successful program created by the Language Learning for Children foundation where children are taught a second or foreign language three to five times a week for no less than 30–40 minutes per class.
Early second language learners score higher on academic tests than those who had a late start.	Factual data and statistics (1) Johnson (2016) reports that the academic test scores of 109 early second language learners are higher that the test scores of 120 learners who had a late start in language learning. (2) The College and University Board (2015) claims that early second language learners scored higher than late learners on academic tests in math and reading between 2006 and 2014, with important differences of 20 to 30 points.

In Anglo-American higher education, L2 writers are usually taught that in written discourse, rhetorical evidence must be convincing and well structured. Some L2 writing methodologists claim that presenting evidence logically is the most important part of academic writing in higher education (Dornan & Dees, 2010). The Anglo-American rhetorical tradition is founded on the framework of convincing arguments developed in ancient Greece and later in Rome. However, most rhetorical constructs (concepts) that dominate in the teaching of L2 writing are crucially culturally bound in a great number of ways.

> Learning to produce L2 written academic discourse and text in higher education requires much effort and practice (and practice and practice).

Action Point

In addition to cultural considerations that affect learning to produce written academic discourse in another language, what represents appropriate or inappropriate, or persuasive or not-so-persuasive supporting evidence is also a matter of subjective judgment.

Which of the following statements do you think are more or less supported by evidence? Identify and make a list of the specific text elements in each pair of sentences that makes you assess one as more persuasive than the other. Compare your analyses with those of your colleagues.

1. a. The recent rapid increase in Asian higher education—from 26 million students in 2004 to over 40 million in 2009—has posed a number of challenges in the context of changing teaching and learning.
   b. The past several decades have seen a dramatic growth in international student enrollments in the U.S.: college and university students, short-term language learners, professionals, employees of international companies, scholars, exchange visitors, business leaders, medical residents, or technology specialists, as well as their family members.
2. a. In Asia, English has long been compulsory in the middle schools but it is now being introduced nationally at the upper primary levels and, where schools are able to do so, is increasingly offered to the lower primary grades or in kindergartens.
   b. Major academic essays typically have a specified length of 5–10 pages, or sometimes more than 10 pages, and most are out-of-class assignments in courses in psychology, economics, history, English, sociology, and political science.

3   a. There is common agreement that European values are significant for modern socio-cultural attitudes affecting learning and communication practices (Bond, 1999; Dench & Craig, 2006; James & Peters, 2008; Willis, 2000).
    b. L2 writers are often faced with a complex adaptation to U.S. academic and cultural norms, and particularly those that apply in the Anglo-American culture of academic writing (Dobson, 2005).

Academic Register and Academic Language

To be sure, the term register can be found in much TESOL and applied linguistics literature. To give it a somewhat formal definition, a register is a type of a language used for a particular purpose or in a particular social setting; it may involve different vocabulary, grammar, levels of formality, and social constructions (e.g., forms of address or politeness) are frequently used to speak to a faculty member, a medical doctor, parent, child, or a friend.

However, in simple terms, register refers to the level of formality appropriate for settings and participants in speech and writing. Varied uses of formal and informal language exist in practically all human languages, and this universal characteristic makes the concept of register relatively easy to convey to L2 writers.

> In writing, register, that is, the level of formality, is generally established by means of vocabulary, grammar, and phrasal expressions.

In writing, the uses of formal and informal register are determined by two fundamental factors in communication:

- The audience
- The context: why, where, and when

That is, for example, an email message to a friend or the dean of faculty is likely to contain distinct vocabulary, grammar, and social features of language, which, when taken together, reflect the formality of the text.

> The audience and the context of writing determine the appropriate language formality and its linguistic elements, and as an outcome, the degree of success of the communication.

TABLE 9.5 Register Distinctions in Writing

Informal Register	Formal Academic Register
A note to a friend or a roommate:	A note to a professor:
	Hi Dr. Rogers,
I am off to see my parents, back this evening.	I'd like to let you know that I plan to visit my parents this afternoon. I will return tonight if everything goes as planned.
See ya, Mary	Thank you, Mary
An informal request email* to Dean Powell:	A formal request email to Dean Powell:
Hi there,	Dear Dean Powell,
I took Algebra 1 in high school, and now they are making me take it again. Could you waive that? Thanks, Brian (*This is an actual message sent to a university dean; the names have been changed.)	I would like to request a waiver of Algebra 1 that is required for my degree. The reason is that I already took Algebra 1 in high school. It seems that repeating the same course would not be very useful for me. Instead, I could take a course that has new material for me and learn from it, such as Algebra 2 or Algebra 3. Thank you for considering my request. I hope that my Algebra 1 requirement can be waived. With best regards, Brian

A highly productive technique for teaching register distinctions in informal and formal writing may be to simply contrast various types of language features found in the two varieties (Coffin et al., 2003). Two parallel and illustrative examples of informal and formal written registers are presented in Table 9.5.

> **Talking Shop**
>
> Two variants of Brian's request for a course waiver can be found in Table 9.5. Which of the two is more likely to be granted? Why do you think that this might be?

As a follow-up to noticing instruction (chapter 8), a classroom activity that centers on the analyses of differences and similarities between informal and formal writing can be illustrative for L2 writers.

Action Point

In the examples of different texts below, identify the specific language features that enable the reader to recognize that the texts are written for distinct audiences and purposes.

1. A beef hamburger sandwich with a white bun has a nutritional value of 1,326 calories, total fat 87 grams, saturated fat 23 grams, total sodium 2146 milligrams, carbohydrates 51 grams, protein 55 grams, dietary fiber 0, and sugars 0; iron content 14%. Condiments: lettuce, tomato, pickles, ketchup, and mustard.
2. A hamburger is a blend of ground beef and ground chuck with rib meat. The irregular patties are shaped loosely by hand, with a firm bite due to the medium-coarse grind in creating those loosely formed patties. The burger was cooked to well-done on the small, crazy-hot griddle, to preserve the moisture. It has a bit of a meatloafy, damp chewiness to it, seasoned both inside and out with a proprietary blend of spices, all of which come together to highlight the beefy and aged notes of the quality blend.
3. The hamburger buns are big, fresh, moist, floppy, seeded, airy, oiled (not buttered), and grilled brown and crispy. The crunch of the bun ties into the satisfying crispness of the sear and the creaminess of the dough. The bottom bun is beautifully toasted, to catch any drippings from the burger patty, surprisingly firm and chewy.
4. Hamburger buns are soft rolls, usually split horizontally to accommodate a burger patty, 3½ to 4 inches in diameter, and made to fit the size of a hamburger. They may be made with regular or whole-wheat flour and variously topped with flavorings, such as sesame seed, poppy seed or toasted chopped onion.
5. A pickle in the United States and Canada, also known generically as a gherkin in the United Kingdom, is a cucumber that has been pickled in a brine, vinegar, or other solution and left to ferment for a period of time, by either immersing the cucumbers in an acidic solution or through souring by lacto-fermentation.
6. Cut pickling cucumbers into discs, spears, or sandwich slices and add to the jar together with dill, sugar, vinegar, and salt. Fill the jar to the very top with distilled or filtered water and screw lid on very tightly. Shake the jar up to distribute flavors and leave for 12 hours. Shake again and turn upside down for another 12 hours, making sure the lid is screwed on tightly to avoid leakage. After a total of 24 hours, the pickles are ready. Store in refrigerator and enjoy within a month for maximum freshness.

In general terms, formal and academic written register is characterized by specific vocabulary and grammar constructions (Biber, 1995; Biber, Johansson, Leech, Conrad, & Finegan, 1999; Hinkel, 1996, 1999b, 2003, 2012; Hyland, 1994, 1997, 1998; Ventola, 1996; Ventola & Mauranen, 1996):

- High frequency of abstract nouns, noun phrases, and noun + *of* constructions (nouns and noun phrases are underlined), e.g., *The <u>result of the experiment</u> encourages further <u>development of the law enforcement tracking systems</u>*. Sometimes, this type of writing is called *nominal style*.
- Low frequency of verbs per unit of text and a high rate of passive verb constructions, e.g., *Outside of multiple choice tests, a great deal of writing <u>is expected</u> in most undergraduate courses.*
- A high rate of hedging and hedges, words and phrases that reduce the writer's commitment to the truthfulness of a statement, or to show hesitation or uncertainty, or display politeness and indirectness. That is, hedging means being cautious and tentative in making assertions and claims, e.g., *Informal attire is <u>often</u> <u>considered</u> to be <u>somewhat</u> unsuitable in job interviews for executive or managerial positions.*
- Impersonal (and detached) constructions, e.g., *<u>It</u> is important to note that; <u>It</u> seems that; <u>It</u> is reasonable to suppose; <u>There</u> might be a few additional possibilities.*

It may be ambitious to expect that many L2 writers can become proficient users of formal academic register. However, discussing, illustrating, exemplifying, and practicing it has the goal of reducing the degree of informality that typically characterizes L2 written prose (Hinkel, 2002, 2003; Shaw and Liu, 1998). (A few tips for teaching basic punctuation rules adopted in academic English are presented in Appendix B.)

> Correct spelling and punctuation are prominent attributes of formal academic written register. The basics are and have always been important to remember.

Speaking generally, using and analyzing purposeful professional and student model texts is indispensable in teaching L2 writing. Model texts play a central role as clear and explicit illustrations and demonstrations of academic writing components, discourse structuring, organization of ideas, and language elements. Noticing discourse moves (introduction, thesis, body, and conclusion) and the required language constructions (register) is a foundational beginning of learning to write in Anglo-American higher education. Demonstrating what evidence is and how it is integrated into discourse and text is probably far more useful than describing them.

> Show such components of academic writing as discourse moves, evidence integration, and academic register, rather than tell.

Chapter Summary

What is appropriate and inappropriate in structuring academic written discourse in English is highly conventionalized. Among many other factors, it includes such fundamental features of formal academic discourse as:

- The organization of information (e.g., introduction, body, conclusion, and other discourse moves)
- The presence and the placement of the thesis statement
- The structure of paragraphs (e.g., the topic sentence)
- The rhetorical support for the thesis included in every paragraph
- An avoidance of needless digressions, repetition, and redundancy

A curriculum for teaching L2 writing has to focus learners' attention on these throughout the course of instruction.

Many elements of grammar and vocabulary serve as markers needed to identify discourse moves, such as introductions, theses, and conclusions. For this reason, the recommended order of instruction is to teach the language elements that function as identifiers of discourse moves **prior** to detailed instruction in how to organize ideas and discourse. That is, first the structure and discourse markers; then, the production of ideas and text.

The teaching of what represents evidence in Anglo-American student writing is a time- and work-intensive process that may take a great deal of instruction and require a substantial cultural adjustments for L2 writers.

Using and analyzing professional and student model texts is indispensable in teaching L2 writing. These play a central role as clear and explicit illustrations and demonstrations of academic writing components, discourse structuring, organization of ideas, academic register, and language elements.

Notes

1 Pre-fab is short for prefabrication, a building process wherein large constructions are built from pre-assembled components (see chapter 8 for an extended discussion).
2 Some grammar reference books suggest that the comma after a short introductory expression is optional. However, other reference books indicate the comma is required, and it is easier to explain to L2 writers that the comma is required so that they do not need to deliberate at what length of the introductory phrase the comma does become necessary.

Further Reading

Celce-Murcia, M., & Olshtain, E. (2005). Discourse-based approaches: A new framework for second language teaching and learning. In E. Hinkel (Ed.), *Handbook of research in*

second language teaching and learning (pp. 729–742). Mahwah, NJ: Lawrence Erlbaum Associates.
Hinds, J. (1975). Korean discourse types. In H. Sohn (Ed.), *Korean language* (pp. 81–90). Honolulu: University of Hawaii Press.
Hinds, J. (1976). *Aspects of Japanese discourse structure.* Tokyo: Kaitakusha.
Hinds, J. (1983). Linguistics and written discourse in English and Japanese: A contrastive study (1978–1982). *Annual Review of Applied Linguistics, 3,* 78–84.
Hinkel, E. (2014). Culture and pragmatics in language teaching and learning. In M. Celce-Murcia, D. Brinton, & M. Snow (Eds.), *Teaching English as a second or foreign language* (4th ed., pp. 394–408). Boston: Heinle & Heinle.
Hinkel, E. (1999). *Culture in second language teaching and learning.* Cambridge: Cambridge University Press.
Hoey, M. (2000). *Textual interaction: An introduction to written discourse analysis.* London: Routledge.
Shen, F. (1989). The classroom and the wider culture: Identity as a key to learning English composition. *College Composition and Communication, 40,* 459–466.
Swales, J. (1988). Discourse communities, genres, and English as an international language. *World Englishes, 4,* 211–220.

References

ACT. (2007). *Writing framework for the 2011 National Assessment of Educational Progress: Pre-publication edition* [Prepared for the National Assessment Governing Board in support of Contract No. ED-05-R-0022]. Iowa City, IA: Author.
ACT. (2010). *A first look at the Common Core and college and career readiness.* Iowa City, IA: Author.
Angelova, M., & Riazantseva, A. (1999). "If you don't tell me, how can I know?": A case study of four international students learning to write in the U.S. way. *Written Communication, 16,* 491–525.
Applebee, A. (1982). Writing and learning in school settings. In M. Nystrand (Ed.), *What writers know* (pp. 365–381). New York, NY: Academic Press.
Biber, D. (1995). *Dimensions of register variation.* Cambridge: Cambridge University Press.
Biber, D., Johansson, S., Leech, G., Conrad, S., & Finegan, E. (1999). *Longman grammar of spoken and written English.* Harlow, Essex: Pearson.
Carlson, S. (1988). Cultural differences in writing and reasoning skills. In A. Purves (Ed.), *Writing across languages and cultures: Issues in contrastive rhetoric* (pp. 109–137). Newbury Park, CA: Sage.
Celce-Murcia, M., & Olshtain, E. (2005). Discourse-based approaches: A new framework for second language teaching and learning. In E. Hinkel (Ed.), *Handbook of research in second language teaching and learning* (pp. 729–742). Mahwah, NJ: Lawrence Erlbaum Associates.
Christie, F. & Derewianka, B. (2008). *School discourse: Learning to write across the years of schooling.* London: Continuum.
Coffin, C., Curry, M., Goodman, S., Hewings, A., Lillis, T., & Swann, J. (2003). *Teaching academic writing: A toolkit for higher education.* London: Routledge.
Cope, B., & Kalantzis, M. (Eds.). (1993). *The powers of literacy: A genre approach to teaching writing.* Pittsburgh: University of Pittsburgh Press.
Dornan, A., & Dees, R. (2010). *The brief English handbook: A guide to writing, thinking, grammar, and research* (9th ed.). New York: Pearson Education.

Ferris, D. (2001). Teaching writing for academic purposes. In J. Flowerdew & M. Peacock (Eds.), *Research perspectives on English for academic purposes* (pp. 298–314). Cambridge: Cambridge University Press.

Ferris, D. (2011). Written discourse analysis and second language teaching. In E. Hinkel (Ed.), *Handbook of research in second language teaching and learning* (Vol. 2, pp. 645–662). New York: Routledge.

Graff, G., & Birkenstein, C. (2014). *They say, I say: Moves that matter in academic writing* (3rd ed.). London: Norton.

Hairston, M. (1982). The winds of change: Thomas Kuhn and the revolution in the teaching of writing. *College Composition and Communication, 33*, 76–88.

Halliday, M. A. K. & Hasan, R. (1976). *Cohesion in English.* London: Longman.

Hinkel, E. (1992). L2 tense and time reference. *TESOL Quarterly, 26*, 556–572.

Hinkel, E. (1994). Native and nonnative speakers' pragmatic interpretation of English text. *TESOL Quarterly, 28*, 353–376.

Hinkel, E. (1995, April). *Projecting credibility in academic writing: L1 and L2 discourse paradigms.* Paper presented at the Ninth International Conference on Pragmatics & Language Learning, University of Illinois, Urbana, IL.

Hinkel, E. (1996, March). *Audience and the writer's stance in L2 writing.* Paper presented at TESOL, Chicago, IL.

Hinkel, E. (1997). Indirectness in L1 and L2 academic writing. *Journal of Pragmatics, 27*, 360–386.

Hinkel, E. (1999a). *Culture in second language teaching and learning.* Cambridge: Cambridge University Press.

Hinkel, E. (1999b). Objectivity and credibility in L1 and L2 academic writing. In E. Hinkel (Ed.), *Culture in second language teaching and learning* (pp. 90–108). Cambridge: Cambridge University Press.

Hinkel, E. (2002). *Second language writers' text.* Mahwah, NJ: Lawrence Erlbaum Associates.

Hinkel, E. (2003). Simplicity without elegance: Features of sentences in L2 and L1 academic texts. *TESOL Quarterly, 37*, 275–301.

Hinkel, E. (2005). Analyses of L2 text and what can be learned from them. In E. Hinkel (Ed.), *Handbook of research in second language teaching and learning* (pp. 615–628). Mahwah, NJ: Lawrence Erlbaum Associates.

Hinkel, E. (2011). What research on second language writing tells us and what it doesn't. In E. Hinkel (Ed.), *Handbook of research in second language teaching and learning* (Vol. 2, pp. 523–538). New York: Routledge.

Hinkel, E. (2012). Cultures of learning in the U.S.A. In M. Cortazzi & J. Cortazzi (Eds.), *Cultures of learning* (pp. 31–35). London: Palgrave-McMillan.

Hinkel, E. (2014). Culture and pragmatics in second language teaching and learning. In M. Celce-Murcia, D. Brinton, & M. Snow (Eds.), *Teaching English as a second or foreign language* (4th ed., pp. 394–408). Boston, MA: National Geographic Learning.

Hyland, K. (1994). Hedging in academic writing and EAP textbooks. *English for Specific Purposes, 13*(3), 239–256.

Hyland, K. (1997). Scientific claims and community values: Articulating in academic culture. *Language and Communication, 17*(1), 19–31.

Hyland, K. (1998). *Hedging in scientific research articles.* Amsterdam: John Benjamin Publishing Company.

ICAS. (2002). *Academic literacy: A statement of competencies expected of students entering California's public colleges and universities.* Sacramento, CA: Intersegmental Committee of the Academic Senates of California Colleges and Universities.

Jin, L., & Cortazzi, M. (2006). Changing practices in Chinese cultures of learning. *Language, Culture and Curriculum, 19*(1), 5–20.

Kamimura, T., & Oi, K. (1998). Argumentative strategies in American and Japanese English. *World Englishes, 17*(3), 307–323.

Kaplan, R. B. (1997). Is there a problem in writing and reading texts across languages? In M. Pütz (Ed.), *The cultural context in foreign language teaching* (pp. 19–34). Frankfurt: Peter Lang.

Kaplan, R. B. (2005). Contrastive rhetoric. In E. Hinkel (Ed.), *Handbook of research on second language teaching and learning* (pp. 375–391). Mahwah, NJ: Lawrence Erlbaum Associates.

Leki, I. (2007). *Undergraduates in a second language: Challenges and complexities of academic literacy development*. New York: Lawrence Erlbaum Associates.

Leki, I., Cumming, A., & Silva, T. (2008). *A synthesis of research on second language writing in English*. New York: Routledge.

Matalene, C. (1985). Contrastive rhetoric: An American writing teacher in China. *College English, 47,* 789–807.

Mauranen, A. (1993). *Cultural differences in academic rhetoric*. Frankfurt: Peter Lang.

Myles, J. (2002). Second language writing and research: The writing process and error analysis in student texts. *TESL-EJ, 6*(2), 1–20.

Oliver, R. (1972). *Communication and culture in ancient India and China*. Syracuse, NY: Syracuse University Press.

Pecorari, D., & Shaw, P. (2012). Faculty attitudes toward source use strategies and their implications for second-language academic writers. *Journal of Second Language Writing, 21*(2), 149–164.

Reid, J. (1993). *Teaching ESL writing*. Englewood Cliffs, NJ: Prentice Hall.

Reid, J. (2000). *The process of composition* (3rd ed.). New York: Longman.

Scollon, R., Scollon, S., & Jones, R. (2012). *Intercultural communication* (3rd ed.). London: Blackwell.

Shaw, P., & Liu, E. (1998). What develops in the development of second language writing. *Applied Linguistics, 19,* 225–254.

Silva, T. (1993). Toward an understanding of the distinct nature of L2 writing: The ESL research and its implications. *TESOL Quarterly, 27,* 657–677.

Sunderland, H., & Spiegel, M. (2009). The written word. In A. Paton & M. Wilkins (Ed.), *Teaching adult ESOL: Principles and practice* (pp. 103–130). Maidenhead: Open University Press.

Swales, J. (1990). *Genre analysis*. Cambridge: Cambridge University Press.

Swales, J. (2004). *Research genres: Explorations and applications*. Cambridge: Cambridge University Press.

Ventola, E. (1996). Packing and unpacking of information in academic texts. In E. Ventola & A. Mauranen (Eds.), *Academic writing: Intercultural and textual issues* (pp. 153–194). Amsterdam/Philadelphia: John Benjamins.

Ventola, E., & Mauranen, A. (1996). *Academic writing: Intercultural and textual issues*. Amsterdam: John Benjamins.

Zamel, V. (1996). Transcending boundaries: Complicating the scene of language teaching. *College ESL, 6,* 1–11.

APPENDIX A

The diagram below, *The Structure of an Academic Essay*, is intended to illustrate the fundamental structure of the classical, traditional, and sometimes deprecated academic essay. An advantage of a clear and not-too-complex diagram is that it is easy to present on a chalkboard, a white board, or a display screen.

Academic essays usually include an **Introduction** that names and briefly describes the topic. The essay must include a **Thesis Statement** that specifies how the writer will approach the topic and what supporting **Main Points** (1, 2, 3, or more) are needed for the thesis. The thesis statement serves as discourse marker—a highly condensed version—for the rest of the essay:

- The **order of the Main Points** made in the thesis statement always determines the **order of Thesis Supports** (1, 2, 3, or more) and information flow in the piece of writing.
- A useful analogy is that a Thesis Statement is the miniature synopsis of the entire essay.

Thesis Support

Each **Main Point** made in the **Thesis** has to be **supported**. The information to support the Thesis should be divided into **Paragraphs** (Minor Points), with one expanded and developed idea per paragraph (a.k.a "one thought at a time").

Each paragraph should include a **Topic Sentence** that **supports the Thesis Statement** and is directly connected to a particular **Point in the Thesis Statement**, according to a given order of the Points.

Similarly, each **Topic Sentence** also has to be supported by **Topic Supports** (A, B, C, or D, E, F) that are directly connected to the Topic Sentence. If more than one paragraph is used to support a **Main Point** (1, 2, 3, +), other **Topic Sentences** in each paragraph also need to be directly relevant to the **Main Point**.

All **Topic Supports** (A, B, C, and D, E, F) have to be directly, clearly, and explicitly connected to their own **Topic Sentence**, and all **Topic Sentences** have to support the **Thesis** (every Topic Sentence wants to be the Big Kahuna—the Thesis).

The Structure of an Academic Essay

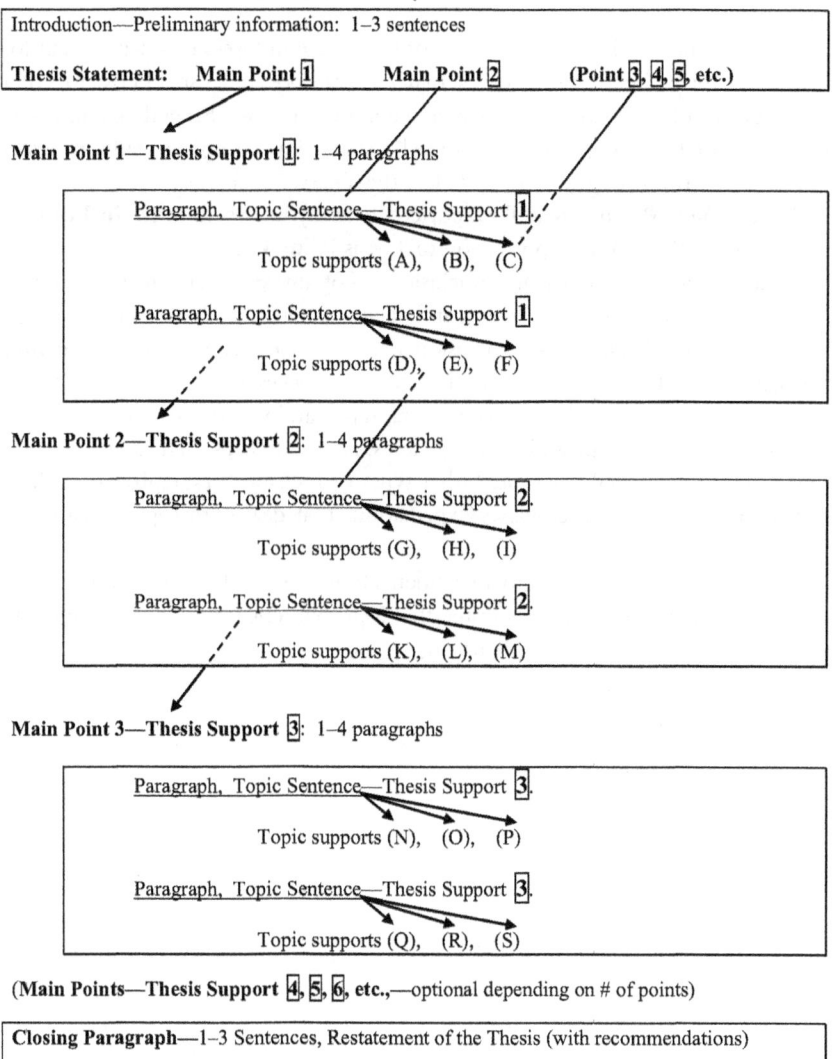

FIGURE 9.1 The Structure of an Academic Essay

When **Thesis Point 1** is well supported, the essay moves on to **Thesis Point 2**.

Main Point 2—Thesis Support

Main Point—Thesis Support 2 can consist of a number of paragraphs (1–4). Each paragraph includes a **Topic Sentence** that is directly connected to **Main Point 2** in the **Thesis**. Topic Sentences are supported by **Topic Supports** (G, H, I) and (K, L, M). All **Topic Supports** are directly connected to their own **Topic Sentences**, which are directly connected to the **Main Point 2—Thesis Support**.

A useful analogy: in an organization or business, employees in a department (or unit) have their direct boss, who is actually a small boss. The small boss, together with several other small bosses, has a medium-size boss. Several medium-size bosses report to an upper-medium-size boss, and several upper-medium bosses report to the Big Boss, the Kahuna (a.k.a. the Thesis Statement).

When **Main Point 2** is well supported, the essay moves on to **Main Point 3**. When Thesis Point 3 is supported, on to Thesis Point 4 . . .

In academic essays, a proper Conclusion is not always possible to make simply because many academic assignments and papers are written about issues that have not been resolved. However, conclusion-making is not required, but a **Closing Paragraph** is. To "close" an essay, it is also not necessary to repeat the Thesis Points (as students often do). A closing paragraph can look forward into the future and, for example, note possible developments, events, or steps than can be taken in regard to the essay topic or issue. Other types of Closing Paragraphs can include the writer's personal hopes/views/expectations that deal with topic or simply a couple of summative sentences.

A practical exercise can be to ask students to underline the Thesis Statement in their assignment/essay, then underline the Topic Sentence in each paragraph and connect it to a specific Thesis Point, <u>one at a time</u>.

APPENDIX B

In English academic writing, about a dozen punctuation rules make up the relatively rigid basics. An academic text written without using them can appear ungrammatical, no matter how well it adheres to the rules of the English sentence structure.

In all languages, punctuation rules are largely based on convention, and for this reason, they may seem somewhat random and haphazard to L2 writers who were not exposed to them from the time when they began reading. One of the outcomes of this view can be the L2 writers' tendency to ignore punctuation rules altogether, with the exception of capitalization and periods, on which most writing teachers insist.

> In English, the fundamental purpose of punctuation marks is to divide sentences into their component parts. Therefore, to a great extent, the rules of punctuation follow those developed for sentence and phrase structures.

It is possible to think of punctuation marks as sentence and phrase dividers or partitions that most often adhere to boundaries of sentence and phrase slots. A small number of punctuation rules depend on the meaning of sentence elements (e.g., restrictive and non-restrictive clauses), and the semantic purposes of punctuation are usually the hardest for L2 writers to use correctly.

> In teaching, it is important to emphasize that the purpose of punctuation (and the punctuation rules) is to make the sentence easy to read by visually dividing it into component parts.

The basic punctuation rules outlined below represent the bare bones of the punctuation system in English. These rules must be learned and used in the production of academic writing.

The Basic and Most Important Punctuation Rules
Sentence Transitions and Prepositional Phrases

- All sentence transitions at the beginnings of sentences have to be "separated" by a comma, e.g., *However, . . . For this reason, . . . In addition, . . .*

    | Transition | , | the rest of the sentence | . |

- Sentence transitions in the middle of a sentence are separated by commas on both sides, e.g., *Thompson's research , however , emphasizes the importance of . . .; The American democracy, on the other hand, . . .*

    | The beginning of the sentence | , | transition | , | the rest of the sentence | . |

- In compound sentences, two **short** simple sentences can be separated by a semicolon (see chapter 4 for a detailed discussion).

    | Sentence #1 | ; | sentence #2 | . |

- If the short sentences in a compound construction are also conjoined by a transition, the transition has to be separated by a comma in all cases, as in:
    - *Crops, such as potatoes and soybeans, require a microclimate ; however, their cultivation has been expanded in North America and further south.*
    - *Factories concentrate in cities ; additionally, distribution networks center around major water ways.*

    | Sentence #1 | ; | transition | , | sentence #2 | . |

Example and Other Markers

- Example markers (e.g., *for example, for instance, namely*), information sequencers/discourse organizers (e.g., *in the first place, second, finally, also, then*), as well as adverbial emphasizers (e.g., *indeed, above all, most important*), play the role of connectives/transitions and follow the same punctuation rules.

Prepositional Phrases and Other Preliminary Information

- Prepositional phrases [preposition + phrase], adverbials of all types (time, place, and evaluation), and infinitives at the beginnings of sentences often play the role of sentence connectives and transitions (e.g., *In 2015*, . . . *In the state capital*, . . . *At the start of the 21st century*, . . . *In the view of the author*, . . . *In light of the study findings*, . . . *In spite of the rain*, . . . *Usually*, . . . *Perhaps*, . . . *Fortunately*, . . . *To begin/conclude/summarize*).
- When they are placed at the beginnings of sentences, **all** elements that supply **preliminary information** and/or that have **connective functions** have to be separated by commas.[2]

| Prepositional phrase/connective/adverbial | , | the rest of the sentence |

- **Prepositional phrases** in the **middle** or at the **end** of sentences are not separated out, and **commas are not used** (e.g., *Corn and wheat are the main crops cultivated <u>in relatively mild climatic conditions</u>. Mass production techniques emerged <u>after World War I</u> and formed the basis of advanced industrial societies.*).

Parallel Structure

- In parallel structures, punctuation depends on the number of elements in the string.
- **Two** elements take **no commas** (e.g., <u>rain</u> or <u>snow</u>; <u>advertising</u> and <u>marketing</u>; <u>cities</u> and <u>suburbs</u>).

| xxx | and | yyy |

- **Three or more** elements: **comma after each element**; a phrase conjunction (e.g., **and/but/or**) is required **before the last element**. In fact, the conjunction **and** marks the last element in the parallel structure, as in:
  - *corn, wheat, and soybeans*
  - *water, soil, and climatic conditions*
  - *manufacture, transportation, or sale of goods*

| xxx | , | yyy | , | **and zzz**   OR | aaa | , | bbb | , | ccc | , | **or ddd** |

Various punctuation marks have different "power," with the period being the most powerful sentence divider, followed by the semicolon, and the comma. In some contexts, the semicolon and <u>a conjunction + a comma</u> can have the same power, e.g.,

The United States is inhabited by 5% of the world population [, but] / [;] *it uses roughly 25% of the world's commercial energy.*

The comma, possibly because of its relatively small dividing power, has a large number of uses. It can set off prepositional phrases; sentence transitions; elements of parallel structures (words or phrases alike); subordinate clauses; or short simple sentences, when boosted by a conjunction. It is in part due to the comma's flexibility that L2 writers find the punctuation rules dealing with commas confusing.

APPENDIX

Curriculum-Development Checklists

This is a master checklist. Not all portions of it are necessary for each type of curriculum, course, or unit design. Parts of this list can work as independent stand-alone checklists for any instructional planning. Mostly, the points on this list serve as prompts for doing or remembering something, similar to to-do lists or notes-to-self.

Course Design

Analyses of the Learning Context

- ☐ **Who are the learners?**
    - ☐ What are their ages? Genders? What are their L1s? Are their L1s helpful for L2 learning?
    - ☐ What are learners' levels of schooling/education?
    - ☐ What are their personal, professional, and educational goals for learning another language?
    - ☐ What are the students' main and stated learning goals?
    - ☐ What are the students' previous education and experience?
- ☐ **Instructional Time?**
    - ☐ How much is available for the entire course? Per class meeting?
    - ☐ How many contact hours overall?
    - ☐ How much out-of-class work can be reasonably expected?
    - ☐ What additional demands exist on learners' time?

Establishing Learners' Skills and Abilities

- ☐ **What are learners' initial language proficiency levels?**
  - ☐ Language test scores (e.g., TOEFL, TOIEC, or IELTS)? Standardized test scores other than language (e.g., SAT, ACT, or GRE)? Diagnostic/placement writing? Proficiency interviews?
  - ☐ What additional sources of establishing learners' proficiencies are available?
    School transcripts? Recommendations of previous teachers? Earlier work?
  - ☐ What are learners' experiences in language learning and motivation?
  - ☐ What emphases do learners place on developing their language skills? Primarily conversation and communication? Primarily reading and writing? Primarily listening and aural comprehension?

Needs Analysis

(These may change throughout instructional time/course.)

- ☐ What are learners' real-life goals for learning and using the language (e.g., finding employment, obtaining education or a job promotion, or taking tests and exams)?
- ☐ What skills do learners already have and what do they need to improve to achieve their goals?
- ☐ What are the skills (or language attributes) that learners state they would like to learn? Stated language learning goals are not necessarily the same as learning objectives and outcomes (e.g., if learners state that they would like to correspond with pen-pals—a stated real-life learning goal—learning objectives are to compose relatively fluent and suitable letters or email messages).

Learning Objectives and Outcomes

(These may need to be modified and refined throughout instructional time/course.)

- ☐ Establish **overall learning objectives**.
  - ☐ List and quantify the language skills, and language attributes and features that learners are expected to learn.
  - ☐ Determine how well these should be learned and how these are quantified and measured.
  - ☐ Learning objectives must be **specific**, **realistic**, and **measurable**.

  Ideally, learning objectives should be the same as learning outcomes.

- Describe in **specific and quantifiable terms** what students should be able to do and how well they should be able to do it.

Evidence and Assessments

- What is the purpose of incremental (short-term) assessments of learning progression and achievement? What types of information to collect and at what times? Who gets the assessments and evidence of learning progression?
- What are the types of incremental assessments of learning progression and achievement available? What are their quantifiable components? What are their structures and designs?
- How frequently and systematically are learning progress and achievement assessed?
- Are the assessment instruments relatively reliable? Are they tried-and-true? Are they newly created? What are the planned instrument reviews, modifications, and refinements? How frequently?
- How is the overall achievement of the learning objectives assessed and quantified at the end of the instructional course?
- **Ongoing and systematic evaluation of curriculum design**: What are the extent and types of modifications and refinements required?
- **Ongoing and systematic evaluation of learning objectives**: What are the extent and types of modifications and refinements required?

Resources to Help Learners Achieve Learning Objectives

- Chose appropriate textbook(s) and materials for the course. Can materials be photocopied/are permissions available?
- Modify the materials as necessary to adapt to learners' proficiencies and learning objectives. Are supplementary materials available?
- Organize and sequence the material into instructional units and learning progressions.
- **Ongoing and systematic evaluation of textbook(s) and materials**: Are they suitable? What are the extent and types of modification and adaption required?

Unit and Material Sequencing

- **Organize material, activities, and task sequencing:**
    - From simpler to more complex
    - From less demanding to more demanding
    - From more controlled/teacher-guided to less controlled/teacher-guided
    - From more familiar and practiced to less familiar and practiced

- ☐ Make sure that **the order of the incremental learning objectives** corresponds to **the order of material in the instructional sequence**.
- ☐ Incorporate regularly timed and systematic reviews and assessments of learning in the instructional sequence.
- ☐ **Ongoing and systematic evaluation of unit and material sequencing**: What is the extent and types of modifications and refinements required?

Syllabus

Make the course syllabus. It should include:

- ☐ Basic information, including the name of the course; the particular term and year (e.g., Fall 2018); meeting times; the instructor's name, email address, office location, and office hours.
- ☐ Course description and objectives.
- ☐ Course progression, topics, and schedule.
- ☐ Assessment and evaluation specifics, including the types and format of major assignments (e.g., papers and drafts, projects, presentations), tests, quizzes, and exams.
- ☐ Grading scales, rubrics, and policies, together with their weights in the course grade, including homework and participation.
- ☐ Additional course policies, including attendance, late submissions, deadline extensions, missed tests and exams and rescheduling, academic integrity and plagiarism.
- ☐ An obligatory note that the instructor reserves the right to make changes and adjustments throughout the term.
- ☐ **Ongoing and systematic evaluation of the syllabus**: What is the extent and types of modifications and refinements required?

Lesson Plan(s)

Make several lesson plans in advance to see a bigger picture. These can be always adjusted as needed.

- ☐ Figure out—even if approximately—the amount of time needed for each incremental portion of the lesson.
- ☐ Take notes about the reasons for making decisions associated with textbook modifications, supplementary materials, or sequence changes.
- ☐ Write down what sections or pages of the textbook material are covered in class and/or assigned as homework.
- ☐ List the language components, such as grammar structures or vocabulary to be covered.

- ☐ Write out detailed instructions to students and directions for the practice activities.
- ☐ If you plan to ask students comprehension questions on readings, or questions to elicit the uses of particular grammar constructions, write down the questions.
- ☐ In group activities, decide ahead of time how many students each learner group should include.
- ☐ If your lesson plan entails using teaching materials that are not in the textbook, prepare these ahead of time.
- ☐ Make sure that the lesson plan
    - ☐ is visible at a glance to keep track of material progression and timing of activities (it should fit on one sheet of paper).
    - ☐ is clear and easy to read and follow on one's feet and while teaching.
    - ☐ establishes direct and clear connections between the lesson in progress and earlier lesson(s).
    - ☐ has clear and direct applications to students' current work and projects.
    - ☐ accounts for time and timing of activities.
    - ☐ provides for contingencies (overplan, overplan, and overplan).

INDEX

academic community 260
academic discourse 105, 106, 224, 245, 257–8, 260–8, 269, 273, 276, 280
academic language 32, 33, 34, 35, 38, 40–5, 73, 79, 80, 162, 165, 185, 186, 192, 199, 205, 210, 216, 224, 245, 277
Academic Word List 197
accuracy 25, 31, 52, 58, 62, 64, 66, 68, 83, 93, 105, 153, 217, 222, 233, 235, 237, 241–2, 261
ACT 19, 22, 45, 46, 51
active voice 253,
adjective 23, 84, 88, 90, 95, 157, 159, 199, 220, 227, 229, 255
affix 35, 36, 37, 100, 195, 198, 205
antonym 36, 172, 208,
Applebee, A. 30, 31, 50, 261
assessment 22, 60, 70, 92, 98, 117, 125, 132, 134–9, 142, 148, 149, 150, 161, 189, 192, 260–2, 295, 296
audience 24, 25, 27, 29, 51, 59, 64, 65, 66, 92, 94, 120, 134, 143, 153, 223, 258, 261, 277, 278

behaviorism 10
Bloom, A. 9, 119

capitalization 34, 35, 36, 37, 39, 51, 101, 138, 153, 288
case study 78, 218, 224, 230, 273
causative constructions 90, 91

chunk 179, 217, 219, 221, 222, 225, 241, 249
clause 27, 29, 86, 88
coherence 29, 57, 63, 64, 65, 68, 72, 87, 95, 99, 100, 105, 134, 153, 186
cohesion 27, 29, 87, 95, 100, 102, 105, 132, 134, 153, 156, 158, 203, 230–2, 257, 269
cohesive chain 210, 231
collaboration 25, 45, 135
collocate (n) 200, 201, 202
collocation 85, 88, 89, 95, 105, 144, 157, 159, 166, 175, 185, 190, 199, 200, 202
Common Core (CCSS) 18–30, 33–45, 61 ; Writing Standards 25, 26, 27
complex sentence 59, 74, 79, 86, 88, 105, 121, 125, 157, 159, 169
complex text 19, 40, 41
composition 77, 78, 79, 80, 98, 102, 104
compound sentence 85, 101, 125, 144, 157, 159, 227, 289
comprehension 163, 167, 175, 177, 178, 188, 191, 193, 194, 196, 294, 297
conjunction 35, 36, 87, 88
constructivism 10–3, 15
content word 81, 82, 83, 86, 95, 105
conversational vocabulary 86, 87, 89, 90, 94, 107, 185
course design 14, 194, 293
course policy 132, 135, 296
cultural value 6, 8, 9, 260
culture 40, 164, 175, 228, 258, 260, 261, 276

curricular objectives 5, 117, 226, 236
curricular thinking 4, 9, 11, 13, 38,
curriculum organization 3, 6–15, 80, 103, 115
curriculum sequencing 117, 124, 129, 131, 137, 138, 142, 143, 144
curriculum, definition of 4–5, 9–13

diagnostic essays 118, 154, 294
dictionary 82–9
digression 64, 69, 72, 105, 258, 281
disciplines 11, 29, 34, 52–4, 57–9, 73, 77, 78, 79, 98, 103, 119, 186, 224, 228, 267
discourse flow 265
discourse markers 87, 92, 257, 263, 271, 281, 285
discourse moves 94, 224, 258, 260, 262, 263, 265, 266, 267, 269, 271, 273, 280, 281
discourse norms 259, 260
discourse, conversational 73, 81, 89, 91, 185
draft 24, 70, 77, 237, 271, 296,
educational objective 4, 7–10, 62, 119–21, 186

ELA 20–7, 78, 94
ELL 21–7, 30–40
error analysis 87, 98, 101, 156, 158, 241
error awareness 98, 107, 237
error correction 97, 216, 234–7, 241
error gravity 77, 98, 99, 101, 107
error types 100, 102, 238–9, 241

figurative language 34, 35, 38–9
flash cards 197, 198, 205, 209, 210
fluency 24, 44, 59, 74, 86, 93, 105, 156, 190, 218, 222, 272, 275
formulaic expression 102, 187, 202, 203, 217, 218, 222, 224, 241, 242, 258, 265, 266, 267, 269, 270, 273
frequency adverb 88, 157, 159, 256
frequent word 38, 81, 86, 107, 185, 191, 197

genre 56, 59, 143, 172, 220, 224, 240, 261–2, 265
gloss 169, 174, 179, 200
grading 132, 135, 136, 137, 138, 155, 237, 296
grammar 20, 28–9, 31, 32, 34, 35–7, 44–5, 62–73, 80, 86–8

grammar teaching 130 216, 218, 220, 229
Greek and Latin affixes 35–7

hedges/hedging 81, 87, 88, 89, 95, 105, 157, 159, 224, 229, 234, 235, 256, 258, 280
high frequency words 81–2, 95, 128, 209
history (as subject) 19, 38, 52, 93, 102, 175, 229, 269, 276
homework 85, 132, 144, 145, 147, 197, 231, 237, 266, 269, 296

idiom 36, 63, 64, 69, 72, 85, 88, 89, 99, 166, 168, 169, 175, 176, 177, 179, 199, 202, 204, 209, 211, 220, 223, 229, 245
IELTS 118, 294
immigrant 135, 136
incidental learning 37, 38
instructional time 28, 117, 118, 123, 124, 126, 128, 141, 142, 148, 293, 294
intensifiers 90, 95
interjection 35
irregular verb 140, 153, 156, 158

language skill 5–6, 14–5, 18, 20–2, 31–45, 50–8, 69–74, 78–9, 83–7, 96, 117–29, 133–9, 162–3, 187–93, 209–11, 294
learning goal 7, 9, 18–9, 22–5, 31–3, 44–5, 118, 120, 135, 142–3, 148–9, 161–6, 293, 294
learning needs 13, 77, 92, 104, 124, 135, 154, 155
learning outcome 5, 6, 10, 15, 119, 121, 122, 123, 170, 295
lesson plan 115, 141–8
lesson preview 143, 149
lexical repetition 87, 93, 95, 105
lexical tie 156, 158, 231
listening 5, 6, 20, 32, 33, 34, 36, 37, 40, 42, 61, 71, 81, 91, 117, 120, 125, 126, 129, 139, 144, 160, 162, 163, 167, 169, 171, 178, 179, 190, 191, 194, 195, 209, 224, 294
literacy 8, 12, 22, 26–7, 29, 35, 44–5, 52, 93, 149

materials, authentic 163, 164, 166, 175, 176, 194, 206, 227
medium of instruction 83
memorization 197, 217, 221, 222, 241, 245, 261
metaphor 29, 33–7, 39, 40, 42, 45, 46, 104
modal verbs 87–8, 95, 99, 100, 157, 159, 229

modeling 270
model texts 280, 281
morphology 87, 92, 99, 100, 153, 235
multi-word unit 218, 219

NAEP 19, 22–3, 61, 69
narrative 24, 27–8, 30, 45, 52, 90, 91, 95, 174, 195
natural science 50, 58
nominalization 88, 95, 157, 159
note-taking 5, 96, 117,
noticing 216, 217, 226, 227, 228, 229, 230, 231, 232, 233, 237, 242, 278, 280
nouns, abstract 87, 89, 95, 279
numeracy 12, 14

orthography 191, 195, 210
outline 5, 263, 264, 265, 266, 267, 268, 269, 270, 271, 272, 273

paragraphing 102, 105, 138
paraphrase 28, 52, 74, 95, 134, 226, 255, 274
passive voice 87, 95, 99, 145, 172, 229, 231, 252, 279
past tense 140, 224, 229, 230, 237
personal pronouns 95, 229, 231, 293
phrasal verb 121, 144, 210, 218
pivot word 201, 202
plagiarism 25, 28, 132, 135, 236, 296
polysemy 197, 210
predicate adjectives 88
preposition 12, 35, 36, 81, 84, 87, 94, 95, 99, 100, 109, 153, 156, 158, 174, 195, 199, 200, 210, 218, 220, 223, 239, 240, 250, 254, 289, 290
present tense 218, 224, 229, 230
pre-teaching 166, 169, 173, 178, 179, 196, 209
proficiency 5, 13, 19, 34, 42, 59, 60, 61, 68, 70, 74, 83, 91, 136, 139, 140, 142, 149, 160, 161, 162, 164, 165, 167, 168, 170, 171, 174, 175, 178, 179, 180, 189, 197, 216, 219, 221, 225, 227, 229, 236, 242, 260, 294
pronunciation 40, 44, 206
punctuation 20, 34, 35–7, 45, 51, 58, 59, 66–9, 73

quantifier 99, 153, 157, 159, 227, 229, 239, 240, 256

reading 5, 20, 22, 31, 34, 42–5, 55, 73, 80, 81–8, 96, 106, 115, 116, 120, 126, 129, 136, 139, 140, 144, 162, 164, 166, 167, 169, 171, 172, 174, 175, 176, 177, 178, 180, 185, 186, 190, 191, 194, 200, 206, 209, 217
reading strategies 82, 176, 178
recycling 128, 148, 161, 162, 186, 204, 209
register 35, 36, 89, 99, 153, 157, 159, 220, 224, 225, 257, 273, 277, 278, 279, 280; academic 89, 224, 257, 273, 277–80
relative clauses 99, 101
reporting verb 203, 226, 249
restatement 52, 73
retention 126, 128, 185, 190, 191, 197, 211
revision 25, 28, 29, 61, 93, 146, 155, 164
rhetorical question 90, 91, 94
rhetorical tradition 258, 259, 262, 273, 274, 275
role-play 156
root, word 35, 36, 37, 204
rubric 49, 61, 62, 63, 64, 68, 69, 70, 71, 72, 132, 136, 152, 168, 296
run-on 99, 100, 153, 156, 158

scanning 83, 174
schooling 6–9, 13, 18–21, 27, 31, 32, 38–9, 41, 42, 44–5, 51, 73, 79, 90, 93, 102, 105, 186, 194, 221, 226, 235, 242, 260, 293
school subject 19, 20, 22, 30, 43
self-correction 59, 74, 217, 233, 235, 242
self-editing 236, 237, 238, 241, 242
sentence fragment 95, 99, 100, 153, 223
sentence stem 224, 229, 245–9, 271
sentence structure 36, 43, 45, 51, 52, 57, 59, 60, 67, 68, 72, 74, 87, 92, 95, 97, 99, 100, 102, 125, 153, 156, 158, 224, 288
sentence transition 27, 77, 87, 90, 95, 99, 153, 231, 239, 289, 291
simplified text 82, 162, 175, 176, 177, 228
social class 166
social studies 19
social values 6, 106, 115, 204
spaced repetition 123, 140, 197, 198, 202, 211
speaking 4, 5, 6, 16, 20, 32, 33, 34, 35, 36, 37, 39, 42, 44, 49, 77, 80, 81, 88, 96, 117, 120, 122, 123, 129, 136, 139, 144, 163, 169, 173, 179, 190, 191, 193, 195, 196, 206, 218, 262
spelling 20, 34, 36, 37, 39, 51, 57, 58, 66, 67, 69, 73, 92, 97, 99, 100, 101, 153, 191, 195, 198, 280

spoken discourse 105, 122, 129
spoken English 8, 32–4, 38, 40–5
spoken text 121, 167
standard English 20, 21, 32, 33, 34, 35, 36, 37, 39, 43, 45, 51, 58, 74
standardized test 49, 50, 60, 62, 70, 74, 164, 192, 294
subordinate clause 86, 87, 88, 95, 100, 105, 157, 159, 174, 224, 227, 291
summarizing 29, 30 52
summary 52, 53, 59, 143, 249, 274
syllabus 4, 5, 15, 80, 95, 115, 117, 128, 131, 132, 133, 135, 149, 180, 220, 296
synonym 36, 87, 95, 105, 156, 158, 172, 197, 204, 207, 211, 233; cluster 157, 159
synthesis 10, 25, 28, 29, 41, 50, 52, 53, 54, 92, 134, 273

teacher effectiveness 11, 14, 15
teacher quality 35
teaching effectiveness 3, 9, 10, 11
teaching method 4–5, 8, 93, 165, 166, 204, 219
technology 13, 24–8, 39, 44–5, 61, 100, 174, 228, 236, 241, 271, 276
text analysis 227, 228, 229, 231, 232, 233, 237, 240
text coverage 83, 84, 85,
text modification 160, 174, 229
thesis 54, 55, 56, 58, 63, 64, 65, 69, 73, 94, 102, 105, 106, 121, 134, 138, 144, 152, 156, 158, 186, 203, 246, 257, 258, 262, 264, 265, 267, 268, 272, 273, 280, 281, 285, 286, 287,
TOEFL 49, 50, 60, 61, 62, 63, 64, 65, 66, 68, 69, 70, 72, 73, 74, 118, 136, 164, 193, 294
topic sentence 147, 152, 156, 158, 177, 258, 281, 285

TWE 49, 50, 61, 62, 63, 64, 65, 66, 68, 70, 71, 72, 73, 74
Tyler, R. 6–7, 9, 12, 15

undergraduates 51, 53, 59, 74, 78, 80, 96, 101, 104, 134
unit sequence 115, 124, 148
University Word List 197, 201, 207, 239
unsimplified texts 82, 163, 176, 193

verb tense 35, 36, 79, 80, 87, 92, 95, 99, 125, 155, 218, 224, 230, 235
vocabulary 20, 27–9, 31, 32–7, 38, 40–4, 51, 58, 59, 62–73, 74, 79, 81–8
vocabulary base 38, 42, 185, 186, 187, 190, 193, 197–9
vocabulary range 8, 41, 43, 82, 83, 84, 92, 93, 106, 186–9, 190–4, 203, 204, 210, 225
vocabulary review 197
vocabulary size 82, 83, 84, 85, 86, 188, 189, 194, 196
vocation 12, 103, 116, 176

word family 41, 81–6, 106, 188, 191, 194, 197
word form 40, 64, 65, 66, 67, 72, 87, 94, 99, 100, 105, 153, 195, 207, 220, 235
word order 92, 99, 153, 156, 158, 235, 239
writing practice 145, 171, 191, 196, 209, 211
writing style 85, 261
writing tasks 30, 52, 53–5, 61, 70, 71, 73, 271, 293
writing, clarity 25, 27, 31, 95, 105, 138, 153, 257, 269
writing, expository 261, 267; informative 23, 25, 27, 29